D1460498

EACH IN HIS PRISON

By the Same Author
LOVE IS MY MEANING (Darton, Longman & Todd)

'*We think of the key, each in his prison*
Thinking of the key'   T. S. ELIOT

Each in His Prison

AN ANTHOLOGY

EDITED BY
Elizabeth Basset

FOREWORD BY
Richard Hauser & Hephzibah Menuhin Hauser
CO-DIRECTORS OF THE CENTRE FOR
HUMAN RIGHTS AND RESPONSIBILITIES

SPCK
LONDON

First published 1978
SPCK
Holy Trinity Church
Marylebone Road
London NW1 4DU

Selection © Elizabeth Basset 1978
For copyright reasons, this edition is not for sale in the U.S.A.

All royalties earned by the sale of this book are being given to
the Centre for Human Rights and Responsibilities
Nansen House, 64 Millbank, London SW1

Printed in Great Britain by
Fletcher & Son Ltd, Norwich

ISBN 0 281 03600 4

Dedicated to those
'Which have no Memorial'

And some there be, which have no memorial; who are perished, as though they had never been; and are become as though they had never been born; and their children after them.

But these were merciful men, whose righteousness hath not been forgotten.

. . . Their seed shall remain for ever, and their glory shall not be blotted out.

Their bodies are buried in peace; but their name liveth for ever more.

The people will tell of their wisdom, and the congregation will shew forth their praise.

Ecclesiasticus, 44.9–10, 13–14, 15 AV

FOR THE FORGOTTEN

Let us never forget, O Lord, the innocent victims of man's inhumanity to man: the millions who were destroyed in the gas chambers and in the holocaust of Hiroshima and Nagasaki, and the few who survived, scarred in mind or body; the uncounted numbers all over the earth who will never have enough to eat, and who, through poverty or ignorance, must watch their children die of hunger; the lepers and the cripples, and the countless others who will live out their lives in illness or disease for which they are given no relief; all who suffer because of their race or their creed or the colour of their skins; and all the children who in their weakness, are torn from their parents and robbed of the loving care which is their birth-right. Help us, as we go unheedingly about our daily lives, to remember those who silently call to us; and to remember also that, though the need of those in distress is so vast and of such an infinite complexity, it is by the steadfast effort of individuals that it must be conquered.

Anonymous

CONTENTS

EDITOR'S NOTE

The material in this book has been drawn from a great variety of sources, from the Old Testament to *The Times*. Where I feel it is helpful, I have supplied a short prefatory note or heading to put the extract in context. In some cases (Frankl's *Man's Search for Meaning* is an example) I have included a number of extracts from the same book which I feel can usefully be seen as part of a sequence as well as in relation to the surrounding material. I have headed such passages with the title of the book, followed by a number in brackets indicating their place in the sequence. By referring to the index of authors and sources on p. 331, the reader can easily trace all the extracts from one book, and can also ascertain the bibliographical details of each source.

E.B.

FOREWORD

But for the witness of those men and women who throughout history reaffirm the loving purpose of life, even at times of overwhelming crises and cruel suffering, the Dark Ages would still be upon us.

The stories which move us most and which eventually shape human destiny are those which record *a will to live*—socially, caringly, intensely—helping others who cannot yet help themselves to know the joy of life or else, if that is not to be, to attain *a willingness to die*, greater than the fear of death. Thus the deepest value of life can be transmitted and its message proclaimed at the moment of truth. This moral quality at the core of conscious life illuminates the thoughts that Elizabeth Basset has collected. Though they spring out of torment and torture, they reveal the spiritual fulfilment experienced by sensitive individuals, some very young indeed to be confronting death. Thanks to the faithful concern she has served in sharing with us these revelations of great souls, we are able to gain glimpses of the infinite life which speaks to the eternal in us beyond our senses and sometimes even beyond our reason.

In the lonely hours of the night we may wonder in awe and gratitude at the maturity of these human beings who, at their loneliest and most helpless, conveyed messages of love and courage to the survivors. But in the working hours of the day we must heed the messages within these messages: You who are alive, you who are free, fight for those who are not free. Think, however repellent the thought, that half a century after the Second World War, which cost fifty million lives ostensibly to end dictatorships, people are being tortured in over sixty countries: they are being beaten, roasted alive on racks, treated in psychiatric hospitals with drugs which drive them insane, made to watch their loved ones beaten, raped, and tortured, thrown out of windows, buried alive. Their message to us is: 'We who died in times of dramatic violence without hating our killers, like Socrates and Jesus, beg you, many of whom live in comfort and forgetfulness, to carry out your task, which is different from ours. You are to engage yourselves in a worldwide fight against social ignorance, employing every means that human imagination and good will can invent, and you are to make these available at every level so that they may be used by everyone: by children, by youth, by women, by the old.'

Remember the words oft quoted by Martin Luther King to the effect that what enables tyranny to triumph is not the power of evil but the silence of 'good' people. Elizabeth Basset has helped to break the shamed silence that hangs over the horror of violent death imposed on innocents and idealists, so often in the name of political and religious dogma. It was usual in traditional communities for death to bring families together to experience in great intensity one of life's deepest mysteries. We might now, upon reading her book, gather together in tenderness as a human family, focused on the good thoughts of so many known and unknown spirits at their time of greatest suffering, and will our lives to relay to future generations the essence of their message.

Resisting injustice brings out the best in people at very great cost. What democracy still has to teach is true responsibility, so that human greatness is translated from outstandingly tragic witness into an everyday struggle *against* the social ignorance which produces evil and *for* the maturity in each of us which allows for justice and joy.

RICHARD HAUSER
HEPHZIBAH MENUHIN HAUSER

PREFACE

There are so many kinds of captivity. I suppose most of us have experienced a captivity, an imprisonment of one kind or another. There is the captivity caused by an illness or a handicap of our own or of someone we love and are caring for. There is that of the young mother in a new town, that of the old person confined to one room, lonely and unable to communicate with anyone. Then there is the captivity which has been described as 'the nailed situation', when one is tied for every minute of the twenty-four hours, unable to escape into the fresh air, to read, or even to think or to pray. Unable ever to be alone. Unable to do any of the things that one had always thought were essential for one's health and happiness. Then sometimes, paradoxically, there comes a feeling of freedom, so fleeting that one fears it could be imagined, but so real that it makes something that has seemed unbearable able to be borne.

There are endless other kinds of captivity, such as enslavement to one thing or another: smoking, drinking, sex, drugs. Carried to excess, all these can be very real captivities and one could go on listing them indefinitely. However, almost all the writings in this collection come from people who have literally been behind bars: prisoners of war, political prisoners, the kidnapped, or those serving prison sentences.

There are, I think, three things which have particularly impressed themselves upon my mind as I have done my research. Firstly, that while the body is imprisoned the spirit can remain free. It seems that in the deepest centre of our being there is an inviolable area which nothing can harm or destroy. Secondly, the awe-inspiring fact that it is those who have suffered most who are most able to forgive—and to understand. This fills one with amazement and admiration and surely also with hope. Of course there is the other side of the coin. Of course there must be countless instances of the brutalizing and coarsening effect of imprisonment and torture on those who have endured it. But nothing can alter the fact that there are those shining examples, not just one or two but legion, proof of the victory, the triumph, the transcendence of the spirit in these men and women. Thirdly, the evidence of the strength which comes from belief in a loving God in spite of the cruelty of men, and also the signs of faith being born anew in the hearts of those who had been unable to believe before.

I do not know how to begin to express my gratitude for all the help I have been given in collecting these writings on captivity. Almost everyone I have spoken to on the subject has contributed some relevant anecdote, gleaned either from their own experience or from something they have read or heard. All have seemed to wish to add something to this tribute to the courage, faith, and endurance of the countless heroes and heroines whose lives and deeds are here recorded.

I am most grateful to Richard and Hephzibah Hauser for their moving foreword, which serves to remind us so vividly that the 'torture' and 'torment' are sadly not horrors of the past but are practised widely and diabolically in the world today.

A fitting epilogue for these sagas of courage could be the words bequeathed to us by a German Jewish prisoner, which were found written on the walls of his cell in Cologne:

I believe in the Sun even when it is not shining.
I believe in love even when I cannot feel it.
I believe in God even when he is silent.

April 1978   ELIZABETH BASSET

PART I

CAPTIVITY

The spirit cannot die—in no circumstances, under
no torment, despite whatever calumnies, in no bleak
places.

Franz Marc

DYING WE LIVE

'I trust and I pray. I have learned much in this rigorous year. God has become more real and more immediate to me.' So wrote one who was to die within a month of having written these words; and who knew what lay ahead of him. . . . Nothing, I suppose, in the long story of human cruelty, has exceeded the Nazi concentration camps and the vile philosophy of life which produced them.

It is natural for us today to wish to close the door for ever upon those dark and terrible days, when the full horror of Belsen and Buchenwald and Dachau was revealed. It is natural because—after all—this horror was perpetrated by civilized, cultured, Christianized, Western man. It is not easy to escape the horrid fear that *perhaps* it could have happened here. It is natural, too, because we are only too well aware of the fact that the world is still haunted by the fear of another war, and one which would inevitably be more ghastly and more totally destructive than the mind can envisage. And so it is easier to shut the door of memory altogether.

To adopt such an attitude is, I believe, a kind of treason to those who died. But it is also to miss a glorious opportunity of learning what Faith can do. And, I would suggest, there never was a time when Faith was more needed than the days through which we are presently living. We are confronted not so much with a conflict between Faith and Fear. Whatever view we may have of the dilemma in which nuclear power and its misuse has placed us, one thing is sure: to live under the shadow of fear alone is to create a spiritual paralysis which must be deadly . . .

To a generation such as ours, and especially to the young whose eyes are turned to the future, nothing is more absolutely essential than to grasp the meaning of Faith. It is so easy, and so deadly, to write and talk as if Faith were a soft option: to be enjoyed, if you have it; to be regretted if you have not. Whereas, in fact, Faith demands what Love demands: an act of the will; a hold, firm and forceful, upon reality. It is a positive and glorious and flaming thing, which only glows more splendid in the darkness.

Trevor Huddleston

From the Introduction to Man's Search for Meaning *by Viktor Frankl*

From this autobiographical fragment the reader learns much. He learns what a human being does when he suddenly realizes he has 'nothing to lose except his so ridiculously naked life'. Frankl's description of the mixed flow of emotion and apathy is arresting. First to the rescue comes a cold detached curiosity concerning one's fate. Swiftly, too, come strategies to preserve the remnants of one's life, though the chances of surviving are slight. Hunger, humiliation, fear and deep anger at injustice are rendered tolerable by closely guarded images of beloved persons, by religion, by a grim sense of humor, and even by glimpses of the healing beauties of nature—a tree or a sunset.

But these moments of comfort do not establish the will to live unless they help the prisoner make larger sense out of his apparently senseless suffering. It is here that we encounter the central theme of existentialism: to live is to suffer, to survive is to find meaning in the suffering. If there is a purpose in life at all, there must be a purpose in suffering and in dying. But no man can tell another what this purpose is. Each must find out for himself, and must accept the responsibility that his answer prescribes. If he succeeds he will continue to grow in spite of all indignities. Frankl is fond of quoting Nietzsche, 'He who has a *why* to live can bear with almost any *how*.'

Gordon W. Allport

MAN'S SEARCH FOR MEANING (2)

The religious interest of the prisoners, as far and as soon as it developed, was the most sincere imaginable. The depth and vigor of religious belief often surprised and moved a new arrival. Most impressive in this connection were improvised prayers or services in the corner of a hut, or in the darkness of the locked cattle truck in which we were brought back from a distant work site, tired, hungry and frozen in our ragged clothing. . . .

It had been a bad day. On parade, an announcement had been made about the many actions that would, from then on, be regarded as sabotage and therefore punishable by immediate death by hanging. Among these were crimes such as cutting small strips from our old blankets (in order to improvise ankle supports) and very minor 'thefts'. A few days previously a semi-starved prisoner had broken into the potato store to steal a few pounds of potatoes. The theft had been discovered and some prisoners had recognized the 'burglar'. When the camp authorities heard about it they ordered that the guilty man be given up to them or the whole camp would starve for a day. Naturally the 2,500 men preferred to fast.

On the evening of this day of fasting we lay in our earthen huts—in a very low mood. Very little was said and every word sounded irritable. Then to make matters even worse, the light went out. Tempers reached their lowest ebb. But our senior block warden was a wise man. He improvised a little talk about all that was on our minds at that moment. He talked about the many comrades who had died in the last few days, either of sickness or of suicide. But he also mentioned what may have been the real reason for their deaths: giving up hope. He maintained that there should be some way of preventing possible future victims from reaching this extreme state. And it was to me that the warden pointed to give this advice.

God knows, I was not in the mood to give psychological explanations or to preach any sermons—to offer my comrades a kind of medical care of their souls. I was cold and hungry, irritable and tired, but I had to make the effort and use this unique opportunity. Encouragement was now more necessary than ever.

So I began by mentioning the most trivial of comforts first. I said that even in this Europe in the sixth winter of the Second World War, our situation was not the most terrible we could think of. I said that each of us had to ask himself what irreplaceable losses he had suffered up to then. I speculated that for most of them these losses had really been few. Whoever was still alive had reason for hope. Health, family, happiness, professional abilities, fortune, position in society—all these were things that could be achieved again or restored. After all, we still had all our bones intact. Whatever we had gone through could still be an asset to us in the future. And I quoted from Nietzsche. 'That which does not kill me, makes me stronger.'

Then I spoke about the future. I said that to the impartial the future must seem hopeless. I agreed that each of us could guess for himself how small were his chances of survival. I told them that although there was still no typhus epidemic in the camp, I estimated my own chances at about one in twenty. But I also told them that, in spite of this, I had no intention of losing hope and giving up. For no man knew what the future would bring, much less the next hour. Even if we could not expect any sensational military events in the next few days, who knew better than we, with our experience of camps, how great chances sometimes opened up, quite suddenly, at least for the individual. For instance, one might be attached unexpectedly to a special group with exceptionally good working conditions—for this was the kind of thing which constituted the 'luck' of the prisoner.

But I did not only talk of the future and the veil which was drawn over it. I also mentioned the past; all its joys, and how its light shone even in the present darkness. Again I quoted a poet—to avoid sounding like a preacher myself—who had written, 'What you have experienced, no power on earth can take from you.' Not only our experiences, but all we have done, whatever great thoughts we may have had, and all we have suffered, all this is not lost, though it is past; we have brought it into being. Having been is also a kind of being, and perhaps the surest kind.

Then I spoke of the many opportunities of giving life a meaning. I told my comrades (who lay motionless, although occasionally a sigh could be heard) that human life, under any circumstances, never ceases to have a meaning, and that this infinite meaning of life includes suffering and dying, privation and death. ... They must not lose hope but should keep their courage in the certainty that the hopelessness of our struggle did not detract from its dignity and its meaning. I said that someone looks down on each of us in difficult hours—a friend, a wife, somebody alive or dead, or a God—and he would not expect us to disappoint him. He would hope to find us suffering proudly—not miserably—knowing how to die.

And finally I spoke of our sacrifice, which had meaning in every case. It was in the nature of this sacrifice that it should appear to be pointless in the normal world, the world of material success. But in reality our sacrifice did have a meaning. Those of us who had any religious faith, I said frankly, could understand without difficulty. I told them of a comrade who on his arrival in camp had tried to make a pact with Heaven that his suffering and death should save the human being he loved from a painful end. For this man, suffering and death were meaningful; his was a sacrifice of the deepest significance. He did not want to die for nothing. None of us wanted that.

The purpose of my words was to find a full meaning in our life, then and there, in that hut and in that practically hopeless situation. I saw that my efforts had been successful. When the electric bulb flared up again, I saw the miserable figures of my friends limping toward me to thank me with tears in their eyes. But I have to confess here that only too rarely had I the inner strength to make contact with my companions in suffering and that I must have missed many opportunities for doing so.

Viktor Frankl

PRAYER

Help me, O Lord, so to strive and so to act, that those things which cloud my own way may not darken the path which others have to tread. Give me unselfish courage so that I am ready always to share my bread and wine yet able to hide my hunger and my thirst.

Leslie Weatherhead

Roused from my idle dream,
Freed from all my fetters,
Anointed, accoutred,
I stand ready.

Asked if I have courage
To go on to the end,
I answer Yes without
A second thought.

The gate opens: dazzled,
I see the arena,
Then I walk out naked
To meet my death.

The combat begins: calm,
Yet exultant, I fight,
Until they cast the net
And I am caught.

I have watched the others:
Now I am the victim,
Strapped fast to the altar
For sacrifice.

Dumb, my naked body
Endures the stoning, dumb
When slit up and the live
Heart is plucked out.

Dag Hammarskjöld

O Jesu, into your keeping
My love and my loneliness,
The dearest of my possessions
As well as the bitterest,
I'm giving you them forever,
I bow my head in pray'r;
You see they are both beyond me,
My hope and my despair.

Each feeling I have, each longing
Are driftwood upon the sea;
Oh cup them within your hands, Lord
Consoling them with your love,
Which passes all understanding
And given will never cease,
And fills to the brim my nothing
With your eternal peace.   *Viola Renvall*

MAN'S SEARCH FOR MEANING (3)

In spite of all the enforced physical and mental primitiveness
of the life in a concentration camp, it was possible for spiritual
life to deepen. Sensitive people who were used to a rich intellectual life may have suffered much pain (they were often of
delicate constitution), but the damage to their inner selves was
less. They were able to retreat from their terrible surroundings
to a life of inner riches and spiritual freedom. Only in this way
can one explain the apparent paradox that some prisoners of a
less hardy make-up often seemed to survive camp life better
than those of a robust nature.

In order to make myself clear, I am forced to fall back on
personal experience. Let me tell what happened on those early
mornings when we had to march to our work site.

There were shouted commands: 'Detachment, forward
march! Left 2–3–4! Left 2–3–4! Left 2–3–4! First man about left
and left and left! Caps off!' These words sound in my ears even
now. At the order 'Caps off!' we passed the gate of the camp,
and searchlights were trained upon us. Whoever did not march
smartly got a kick. And worse off was the man who, because of
the cold, had pulled his cap back over his ears before permission was given.

We stumbled on in the darkness, over big stones and through
large puddles, along the one road leading from the camp. The
accompanying guards kept shouting at us and driving us with
the butts of their rifles. Anyone with very sore feet supported
himself on his neighbour's arm. Hardly a word was spoken; the
icy wind did not encourage talk. Hiding his mouth behind his
upturned collar, the man marching next to me whispered sud-

denly: 'If our wives could see us now! I do hope they are better
off in their camps and don't know what is happening to us.'

That brought thoughts of my own wife to mind. And as we
stumbled on for miles, slipping on icy spots, supporting each
other time and again, dragging one another up and onward,
nothing was said, but we both knew: each of us was thinking of
his wife. Occasionally I looked at the sky, where the stars were
fading and the pink light of the morning was beginning to
spread behind a dark bank of clouds. But my mind clung to my
wife's image, imagining it with an uncanny acuteness. I heard
her answering me, saw her smile, her frank and encouraging
look. Real or not, her look was then more luminous than the
sun which was beginning to rise.

A thought transfixed me: for the first time in my life I saw
the truth as it is set into song by so many poets, proclaimed as
the final wisdom by so many thinkers. The truth—that love is
the ultimate and the highest goal to which man can aspire.
Then I grasped the meaning of the greatest secret that human
poetry and human thought and belief have to impart: The
salvation of man is through love and in love. I understood how
a man who has nothing left in this world still may know bliss,
be it only for a brief moment, in the contemplation of his
beloved. In a position of utter desolation, when man cannot
express himself in positive action, when his only achievement
may consist in enduring his sufferings in the right way—an
honorable way—in such a position man can, through loving
contemplation of the image he carries of his beloved, achieve
fulfillment. For the first time in my life I was able to understand the meaning of the words, 'The angels are lost in perpetual contemplation of an infinite glory.'

. . . My mind still clung to the image of my wife. A thought
crossed my mind: I didn't even know if she were still alive. I
knew only one thing—which I have learned well by now: Love
goes very far beyond the physical person of the beloved. It finds
its deepest meaning in his spiritual being, his inner self.
Whether or not he is actually present, whether or not he is still
alive at all, ceases somehow to be of importance.

I did not know whether my wife was alive, and I had no
means of finding out (during all my prison life there was no

outgoing or incoming mail); but at that moment it ceased to matter. There was no need for me to know; nothing could touch the strength of my love, my thoughts, and the image of my beloved. Had I known then that my wife was dead, I think that I would still have given myself, undisturbed by that knowledge, to the contemplation of her image, and that my mental conversation with her would have been just as vivid and just as satisfying. ... 'Set me like a seal upon thy heart, love is as strong as death.'

... As the inner life of the prisoner tended to become more intense, he also experienced the beauty of art and nature as never before.

Under the influence he sometimes even forgot his own frightful circumstances. If someone had seen our faces on the journey from Auschwitz to a Bavarian camp as we beheld the mountains of Salzburg with their summits glowing in the sunset, through the little barred windows of the prison carriage, he would never have believed that those were the faces of men who had given up all hope of life and liberty. Despite that factor—or maybe because of it—we were carried away by nature's beauty, which we had missed for so long.

Viktor Frankl

ON THE EXTERMINATION OF JEWS UNDER HITLER

Cain rose up against his brother Abel
   A silence lay upon the world
   As horror's tentacles unfurled.
   Bloodied truth, honor, compassion,
   Dripping on ears that would not hear,
   On eyes unseeing in the light.
   Expediency won the day.
   Ask why six million died that way—
   (Were they all expendable?)
   In universal guilt, man knows,
   All humanity is diminished.

Mary Ascher

While women weep as they do now, I'll fight; while little children go hungry as they do now, I'll fight; while men go to prison, in and out, in and out, I'll fight; while there is a poor lost girl upon the street, I'll fight; while there yet remains one dark soul without the light of God, I'll fight—I'll fight to the very end.

William Booth

MAN'S SEARCH FOR MEANING (4)

When a man finds that it is his destiny to suffer, he will have to accept his suffering as his task; his single and unique task. He will have to acknowledge the fact that even in suffering he is unique and alone in the universe. No one can relieve him of his suffering or suffer in his place. His unique opportunity lies in the way in which he bears his burden.

For us, as prisoners, these thoughts were not speculations far removed from reality. They were the only thoughts that could be of help to us. They kept us from despair, even when there seemed to be no chance of coming out of it alive. Long ago we had passed the stage of asking what was the meaning of life, a naïve query which understands life as the attaining of some aim through the active creation of something of value. For us, the meaning of life embraced the wider cycles of life and death, of suffering and of dying.

Once the meaning of suffering had been revealed to us, we refused to minimize or alleviate the camp's tortures by ignoring them or harbouring false illusions and entertaining artificial optimism. Suffering had become a task on which we did not want to turn our backs. We had realized its hidden opportunities for achievement, the opportunities which caused the poet Rilke to write, 'How much suffering there is to get through!' Rilke spoke of 'getting through suffering' as others talk of 'getting through work'. There was plenty of suffering for us to get through. Therefore, it was necessary to face up to the full amount of suffering, trying to keep moments of weakness and furtive tears to a minimum. But there was no need to be ashamed of tears, for tears bore witness that a man had the greatest of courage, the courage to suffer. Only very few realized that. Shamefacedly some confessed occasionally that they had wept, like the comrade who answered my question of how he had gotten over his edema, by confessing, 'I have wept it out of my system'.

. . . I remember two cases of would-be suicide, which bore a striking similarity to each other. Both men had talked of their intentions to commit suicide. Both used the typical argument— they had nothing more to expect from life. In both cases it was a question of getting them to realize that life was still expecting something from them; something in the future was expected of them. We found, in fact, that for the one it was his child whom he adored and who was waiting for him in a foreign country. For the other it was a thing, not a person. This man was a scientist and had written a series of books which still needed to be finished. His work could not be done by anyone else, any more than another person could ever take the place of the father in his child's affections.

This uniqueness and singleness which distinguishes each individual and gives a meaning to his existence has a bearing on creative work as much as it does on human love. When the impossibility of replacing a person is realized, it allows the responsibility which a man has for his existence and its contin-uance to appear in all its magnitude. A man who becomes conscious of the responsibility he bears towards a human being who affectionately waits for him, or to an unfinished work, will never be able to throw away his life. He knows the 'why' for his existence, and will be able to bear almost any 'how'.

Viktor Frankl

We come to the moment, Lord, when we say, 'We cannot go on, we have reached the end, we cannot face another day, another hour.' And then the will returns, just a little, 'One more try' we say, 'One more day.' And we know that you have met us and taken some of the burden on to yourself.

Anonymous

THE REAL ENEMY (1)

In its way solitude is an enriching experience, and it was as
well that I was able to find it so, for I was to be in solitary
confinement for two and a half years. The first effect it is likely
to produce on one is an examination of the conscience. Every
now and again it is necessary to take stock of oneself, but in
normal circumstances few of us give ourselves the time to do so.
. . . For many of us in Fresnes this was the first time we had
really been alone with ourselves. Millions of industrialists,
tradesmen, householders make an exact balance sheet for their
activities. The solitude of prison is an excellent climate for
establishing one's interior balance sheet and for that internal
dialogue which is a necessary function of spiritual life. Indeed
there is a real advantage of being brutally detached from
nature and the outside world. For the world which surrounds
us and which makes such calls upon us, is a mixed blessing, an
obstacle to the life of the spirit, as well as a support. It is not
necessarily true that permanent contact with humanity brings
us nearer to man. The fact of being alone makes us aware of the
problem of our relationship with others. In my case it was
necessary for me to be a long time alone to become conscious of
my human responsibilities. Solitude develops in one the sense of
that responsibility. It was in prison that I came to develop a
sense of life as a series of connections with other men, the sense
of human solidarity, which is one of the essential components of
our life-consciousness in society.
. . . My solitude at Fresnes gave me the desire, the need to
communicate spiritually with all the other lonely people who
surrounded me. This seemed to me then, as it does now, to be
what solidarity really means. The solitude which men rightly
seek to avoid because it is sterile and paralyses is that which
consists essentially in the feeling that we are chained in an
ineluctable way to other people and cannot escape. To remake
true life-giving contact with mankind it is necessary that our
being, at its deepest level, should feel the necessity of this
intimate, interior link, which is hidden beneath the rubbish of
conventions, and of exterior necessities.
In prison I discovered this necessary link, this intimate and

profound link, and saw what many have discovered: that it is from there one must start in order to arrive at that love of one's neighbour which Jesus Christ teaches us, and on which is based all morality that merits the name. I saw so clearly in prison how the *conventional* necessities which bind us to each other so often engender only indifference, indeed hatred. With an act of will flowing out of love we can, on the contrary, reach through the solitude of another being and make contact. So long as we do *not* assimilate the pains and the joys of our neighbours, we shall not be able to achieve the profound meaning of the word 'solidarity'. It seemed to me, thinking laboriously through these elementary thoughts, that there will be no true democracy unless it is based on a true solidarity; a solidarity based on love, on a will to understand, on a readiness to be in contact with one another, disengaged from all material contingencies. . . .

There is, and this must sound paradoxical in view of what I have said about the linking power of solitude, a curious dehumanization of experience arising from it which allows a man who can rise above it to feel beyond the capacity of his ordinary powers and to think himself superior to ordinary human beings. In solitude man is conscious of a real power, in the detachment—the contempt even—which he can feel for the human state which threatens normally to invade him, and above which he has now managed to rise. This is perhaps a rather Nietzschean idea, but it is only part of the paradox, compensated for by this search of which I have spoken, of a more perfect love for one's neighbour.

These were the kind of thoughts I had as I walked round and round my cell, carrying out my daily programme of physical activity. I used to walk as far as my strength would allow me, at least a thousand times the length of the cell. It was the equivalent of four kilometres, enough to keep me fit for any eventuality.

Pierre d'Harcourt

Masters have wrought in prison
At peace in cells of stone:
From their thick walls I fashion
Windows to light my own.

Kark Wilson

THE REAL ENEMY (2)

The police know what they are about when they condemn a
man to solitary confinement. Nothing is more demoralizing or
more wearing than that anxiety without an end or focusing
point. Anxiety and waiting became in the end a real suffering.
I think there is no man who would not prefer pain to that kind
of suffering. On the few occasions when I had a bad physical
pain in prison I almost welcomed it as an alleviation of my
suffering. I remember bad attacks of toothache, that continual
gnawing pain which completely holds one's attention. One's
whole self and consciousness is concentrated on the pain. Perhaps when a pain is permanent, it becomes a suffering. But the
quality of pain is to bind one to the instant, while suffering
binds one to time. Pain is a wound, a blow, a toothache. It
touches only the periphery of one's being, but suffering pene-
trates all the defences and takes its seat in one's heart. Against
pain man finds himself defenceless, there is nothing he can do
but bear it, he submits passively, but meanwhile, in this very
passivity, he finds a relief, for pain distracts him from everything which surrounds him, so that he concentrates his entire
attention on the part of his body affected by it. Pain is a severe
trial of character. With strength of will one can limit it, keep it
within the bounds of its own domain. But suffering shrouds the
whole of one's being, it is a burden on one's whole self. There is
no question of rejecting it. One must analyse it, penetrate it, be
penetrated by it. That, it seemed to me, was where the nobility
of suffering was to be found. It obliged us to examine ourselves
thoroughly.

Pierre d'Harcourt

What makes loneliness an anguish
Is not that I have no one to share my burden,
But this:
I have only my own burden to bear.

Pray that your loneliness may spur you into finding something
to live for, great enough to die for.

Dag Hammarskjöld

THE DIARY OF ANNE FRANK

This is Amsterdam in June 1942, and her parents are
German Jews who emigrated from Germany in 1933. Anne
wears a yellow star, cannot enter a tram, a cinema, ride a
bicycle, sit in the garden after eight—a web of harassing restric-
tions. It does not press on her; she accepts it with a child's
involuntary patience, and the vivacity which tried her teachers.
She is attractive, and cannot help knowing it—and is pleased
by it very much as by a fine day. Even in danger she is almost
wholly a child: when, less than a month after her birthday, the
always threatening stroke falls, and the family is forced to
choose between obeying the Gestapo summons or going into
hiding, the first thing Anne packs to take with her is her journal—then her hair-curlers and her school books.

Her father had been preparing for months a place to hide—
in the two upper back floors of an old building, the office of his
firm, now run by two Dutchmen whose courage and loyal
friendship for the Franks made the attempt to escape possible.
In some of these old Dutch houses the rooms at the back,
looking on to a garden or a courtyard, can be shut off. Here
Anne, her sixteen-year-old sister Margot, and her parents now
took refuge, hunted animals burrowing out of sight; they were
joined in a few days by another family, the Van Daans with
their son Peter, not sixteen, and later by a dentist called Dussel.
They had to take endless care, all day, not to be seen or heard,
and for an energetic, spirited little girl the life must often have
been as maddening as the punishment of being sent to bed on a
fine afternoon. Nothing was made easier by the forced intimacy
of the two families in conditions which rasped tempers and
strained nerves.

What did she do in the long hours of silence and inactivity?
She read—books brought by endlessly kind and thoughtful
Dutch friends; and she kept her journal, telling it everything
she might have told an intimate friend, if she had had one.
Hope was an instinct in her. When she admires an author
immensely she decides to give her children his books; she
finishes her prayers with a movement of joy and gratitude for
her safety and her good health, and the beauty of the world:

she is sure that God will never abandon her. And if sometimes, like a cold breath, the thought crosses her mind that some day she may be terribly alone, she believes still that what the future promises her is love and happiness. Then comes D-day, and she thinks that in the autumn, perhaps, she will have left this prison of safety and hunger, and be back at school.

She does indeed, leave it before the autumn, but for a concentration camp. On 4th of August, 1944, the Gestapo put its hand on them. Found later in the disorder left by the Gestapo, Anne's dear journal was given to her Dutch friends.

Exactly four months before this, she had written: 'I want to go on living, even after my death.' She was not counting on her journal to lend her small shade a modest longer existence in men's minds. As it turned out, she had no time to make any other sign before disappearing. But, fortunately for us, it is a marvellously clear image which comes towards us, smiling, from these pages which clumsy murderous hands did not take the trouble to destroy. The door of her hiding-place had closed on a little girl whose irrepressible gaiety seduces the old teacher who punishes her for talking in class by setting her to write an essay on 'A Chatterbox'. As the months pass, this instinctive gaiety, the liveliness and energy of a child, deepens: she stares from an attic window at a blue sky, bare trees, and the dazzling flash of a seagull, and thinks of that moment of supreme happiness when, as she is sure God meant men to do, she will look in freedom at these things; she refuses to despair, and by a sort of grace succeeds again and again in believing that what is approaching her is goodness, joy, and the chance to grow and learn. The current of fear, of tension, is always there in her mind, but her imagination, what she calls her illogical gaiety, springs above it. I should like to help you, she says to Peter. But you do that all the time, he tells her, 'with your gaiety'.

. . . With an astounding lucidity, and without vanity, she tries to analyse her own and her companions' natures. She is growing up quickly in this forcing atmosphere, too quickly, so that she feels absence and silence deepening round her, and even comes to realize that to use a little hypocrisy would make her life easier—but does not come to using it. Instead she breaks a way through herself to something like calm, and to a half-tender, half-indifferent, and wholly unchildlike patience. Already she is learning the hardest of all lessons—detachment. She is convinced that, young as she is, she will not be tempted to compromise with her life. And, in the same moment when in some recess of her being a voice warns her that she is going to die, she knows what life demands is a joyous courage, she knows what she wants to do, she has her religion, she has love. Not yet fifteen she can write: 'I feel that I am a woman, a woman who has both moral energy and courage.'

... It is a strengthening, a humbling experience to watch this child, this young girl, come so far, unfold so richly, in a little more than two years. And as the last entry in the journal shows plainly, she even knew how far she still needed to go to possess herself.

How much further did she go? She died in the concentration camp of Bergen-Belsen, in March 1945, two months before Holland was freed, and three months before what would have been her sixteenth birthday.

Dying, of hunger and misery, in Bergen-Belsen, Anne Frank took with her, into a mass grave, every exquisite intellectual structure which allows its servants to torture, to work to death, to kill, for an idea.

For a little over two years this child worked on herself, with tears, patience, gaiety, with all the energy of a quick mind and a will turned towards goodness. She taught herself a smile of happiness and faith. In all humility, we can—surely—believe that this smile, this profound smile, was not lost, even in Belsen, even when she could no longer hold out against the arrogance of men without God.

Storm Jameson

THE BIRD OF HEAVEN

Catch the bird of heaven,
Lock him in a cage of gold;
Look again tomorrow,
And he will be gone.

Ah! the bird of heaven!
Follow where the bird has gone;
Ah! the bird of heaven!
Keep on travelling on.

Lock him in religion,
Gold and frankincense and myrrh
Carry to his prison,
But he will be gone.

Ah! the bird of heaven! etc.

Temple made of marble,
Beak and feather made of gold.
All the bells are ringing,
But the bird has gone.

Ah! the bird of heaven! etc.

Bell and book and candle
Cannot hold him any more,
For the bird is flying
As he did before.

Ah! the bird of heaven! etc.

Sidney Carter

Nearly twenty years have passed since I was flown home to
England to drive from Croydon to London through streets
hung with the flags of military victory. . . .

Now I continue to ask myself the extent of that victory. With
great sadness, I believe that, for mankind, the choice between
liberty and slavery has still to be made. In the camps, we used
to believe that those of us who might survive would enter a
more tolerant and tranquil world where the ancient virtues of
truth, honour and gentleness would surely prevail. In the war,
we fought a human enemy, one who had been infected with the
germ of inhumanity. Though we defeated the host, we failed to
defeat the parasite. Rendered the more virulent by its recent
frolic, that same parasite is about the world today and, unless it

is utterly destroyed, the Camp of Ravensbrück will merely be
the shadow and the symbol of a greater darkness to come.

Odette

Man's estate is as a citadel: he may throw down the walls to
gain what he calls freedom, but then nothing of him remains
save a dismantled fortress, open to the stars. And then begins
the anguish of not-being.

Antoine de Saint-Exupéry

Saturday, 12th February, 1944

Dear Kitty,

The sun is shining, the sky is a deep blue, there is a lovely
breeze and I'm longing—so longing—for everything. To talk,
for freedom, for friends, to be alone. And I do so long . . . to
cry! I feel as if I'm going to burst, and I know that it would get
better with crying; but I can't, I'm restless, I go from one room
to the other, breathe through the crack of a closed window, feel
my heart beating, as if it is saying, 'Can't you satisfy my
longings at last?'

I believe that it's Spring within me, . . . I feel it in my whole
body and soul. It is an effort to behave normally, I feel utterly
confused, don't know what to read, what to write, what to do, I
only know that I am longing . . . !

Yours, Anne
Anne Frank

One should never a strike a woman
—Not even with a flower.

Seventeenth-century English proverb

THE INTERROGATION OF ODETTE

'Well, Lise, I would now like the answers to my questions.'
'I have nothing to say.'
'It is very foolish of you. We have means of making you talk.'

'I am aware of your methods. Do you think we come to France from England without knowledge of the sort of thing you can do to us? You must give us credit for something, Monsieur.'

There was another man in the room now. He had come in silently and he was standing immediately behind her chair. He caught her arms and held them behind the back of the chair. The fair man who smelt of cold water and eau-de-cologne stood up and walked over to her and began leisurely to unbutton her blouse. She said:

'I resent your hands on me or on my clothes. If you tell me what you want me to do and release one hand, I will do it.'

'As you wish. Unbutton your blouse.'

She undid the top two buttons. The man behind her drew her blouse back so that the corrugations of her spine were bare. On the third vertebra he laid a red-hot poker. Odette lurched forward. The fair young man's mouth moved and his voice came from a long way away.

'Where is Arnaud?'

'I have nothing to say.'

'You are more than foolish.' He opened his cigarette case, offered it to her and snapped a lighter. From it sprang a small sedate flame, like an altar candle. Dumbly Odette shook her head.

. . . 'I have nothing to say.'

He came over to her and stood there, half smiling. The cold bath and eau-de-cologne smell was apparent. He said to her: 'Perhaps you would prefer to take off your shoes and stockings yourself. If not, I can assure you that I am well experienced in the mechanism of feminine suspenders.'

'I will do it myself.'

To be tortured by this clean, soap-smelling, scented Nordic was one thing. To be touched by his hands was another. She slid her feet out of her shoes and unrolled her stockings. The wooden floor was warm and rough to her naked feet. She automatically adjusted her skirt over her knees.

'My colleague here, Lise, is going to pull out your toenails one by one, starting at the little toe of your left foot. In between each evulsion—to use the correct medical term—I propose to repeat my questions. You can bring the ceremony to an end at any moment by answering these questions. There are those who faint after the third or fourth toenail, but I don't think you are of the fainting kind. If you do faint we can always revive you with brandy and the ceremony will continue. Now before we begin, where is Arnaud?'

. . . *Clamor meus ad te veniat* . . .

A man knelt at her feet. He was a young man, under thirty, very good looking in a dark, Mediterranean handsomeness, and he glanced up at her with blind, brown eyes. He did not see her as a woman but only as a living, sensitive adjunct to a naked foot. His impersonality was terrifying. He took her left foot in his left hand and settled the steel jaws of the pincers tightly round the top of her nail. Then with a slow, muscular drag, he began to pull. A semi-circle of blood started to the quick, oozed over the skin, flooded after the retreating nail. . . . He shook the pincers and her nail fell on the floor.

'Now would you care to tell me Arnaud's address?'

She tried to say the word 'no' but no sound came from her mouth. She shook her head. *Clamor meus ad te veniat* . . .

The Commissar nodded to the kneeling man and sat on the edge of the table, swinging his legs. The pincers clasped the next nail, gripped hard, were slowly drawn back. The enclosing flesh ripped and and yielded in agonizing pain as the nail was dragged out. . . . The reiterated questions flew round her head like wasps as the agony leapt from toe to toe, from foot to foot. She gave no cry. After an eternity, her torturer stood up, his pincers in his hands. He looked at the Commissar, waiting obsequiously for more orders. Odette gazed incredulously at the bloody furnace of her feet and at the red litter on the floor, litter of diabolical chiropody. The sound of motor horns below sounded thin in the sunny air and she was aware of a subsidiary ache in the palms of her hands.

'Well, Lise, I think you will find it convenient to walk on your heels for some time. Now I would like to offer you a drink. A glass of wine, a little brandy—or better still, a cup of tea.' He smiled. 'In England, the country of your adoption, a cup of tea is the cure for all evils. I will order you some tea. You are a woman of surprising endurance.'

Sitting on a wooden chair, her body quivering, she drank her tea. He talked to her easily and she hardly heard a word he was saying. She felt as if she were drowning in recurring waves of nausea and she tried desperately to reach the shore. The nausea passed and the walls of the room took shape again and became solid. She leaned back in her chair and shut her eyes. Though her lacerated toes were ten separate hubs of pain, she was conscious of a sudden stab of elation. She was Odette and she had kept silence. Now she had an almost irresistible urge to talk freely and to laugh and to gabble with her mouth, anything to make sounds with her tongue. And then she recognized this sense of triumph for the danger that it was. This was how the Gestapo wanted her to feel. Her sense of relief and of triumph could easily be a better weapon to their hands than a pair of pincers. . . . The Commissar watched like a cat, as if aware of every thought process of her mind. She opened her eyes and looked at him. Just as he saw her as a mere nervous system, she now saw him not as a Commissar of the Gestapo nor even as a man. She saw him for what he was, a creature from whom human pity and human understanding had been deliberately drained and the hollow filled with blasphemy. He half-smiled.

'Well,' he said, 'how do you feel?'

'I have nothing to say.'

Jerrard Tickell

PRAYER FOR THE SORROWING

Almighty and everlasting God, the comfort of the sad, the strength of Sufferers, let the prayers of them that cry out of any tribulation come unto thee. That all may rejoice to find that thy mercy is present with them in their affliction through Jesus Christ our Lord.

The Gelasian Sacramentary

THE SPIRITUAL CHALLENGE OF AUSCHWITZ

No doubt such despair prevailed among many. No doubt a burning hatred to the last remained the legacy of many. Others knew, however inarticulately, in the many languages assembled there, that they were witnesses to God, that they died for God, his law, the prophetic message, the wisdom from of old. They drowned their resentment in holding on to a transcendental cause. They could commit themselves to truth with a 'It is finished' which espied the dawn, the beginning of a better age. The walk through gas and fire became in their intention the release not only from the body and its conditions, but from the murderous ruin. Even Auschwitz held and holds the secret of redemption. The final Credo bursts here all denominational ties and distortions. Man appears before God.

The vindication cannot take the usual forms. Like the victim of Golgotha these dead leave for the most part no children, no report, no property. Few of them leave even a name. Obscurity is the only memorial. Yet the transformation starts here also with the fulfilment of the Scriptures. In as much as they died innocently they became one with the suffering servant, the Israel of God. The Spirit seals their transitory lot with the stamp of eternal purpose.

Seen in this light Auschwitz becomes a spiritual challenge in which the visible phenomenon must be re-interpreted according to the great tradition of prophetic expectation and priestly ritual. Thus we escape from the purely tragic evaluation and negative despair. This holocaust is no less a sacrifice than that prefigured in the Scriptures. Here again the circle closes and the lives of the many are given for the sins of the world.

This acceptance of death as sacrifice was particularly experienced by those trained in the spiritual tradition of Judaism and Christianity. They never doubted the providential nature of their course. This heroic vision was brought to a fine point by a few martyrs who substituted themselves for others in going to death. In the terms of the Bible they regarded their lives as a ransom, their bodies as sin offerings, their death as redemptive.

By seeing their death within the cultic pattern they were transforming death itself. The mechanics of murder were

turned into a Godward oblation. This spiritual achievement
enabled them to 'die unto God', not as animals, caught up in
the mechanics of slaughter, but with a freedom of self-giving.
This power of transformation is itself a token of the divine
Presence in death. The act of transformation shows the
intimate connection between the work of the spirit and the
human will.

The basis of this transformation is God's love for man, given
by the eternal promise in creation and redemption. It is not
merely an ecstatic self-assertion of the higher self, or a feverish
fantasy to meet a desperate situation, but the objectively
grounded union with God which death cannot interrupt. It is
not man at Auschwitz, but God who incorporates the terror
into the pattern of meaningful sacrifice.

Ulrich Simon

TO DEATH

How will you treat me, Death, when I am dying?
    You who touch flowers so tenderly,
Whose hand the birds lean and drop to, fearlessly flying,
Oh, take my breath gently, when I face you dying.

Let me reach to you, Death, tranquilly, slowly,
    As a bloom from the darkness moving,
Rising and lifting to light until I am wholly
Myself, yet immersed—let me reach to you slowly.

Dorothea Eastwood

THE REAL ENEMY (3)

In my own experience our morale and will to live were never
undermined by what the S.S. or the criminal and degenerate
elements in the camp did. It was when we saw our own kind
and our own friends behaving badly that the will to live sank
lowest. When we let each other down all kinds of disruptive

emotions were released, which added to our exhaustion and diminished the will to live.

At these moments the beast in us had its opportunity. Despair produced anger; anger led to aggression, and aggression to guilt; and guilt took us down to yet a lower rung of the ladder of desperation.

Pierre d'Harcourt

ON THE ANNIVERSARY OF AN EXECUTION

In the thought and experience of Mother Maria Skobtsova (1891–1945), martyrdom was not an isolated and exceptional event. It was the culmination of a process, it was itself a process. Her chosen task, 'to quench the suffering of the world with my own self', was part and parcel of it. This suffering could not be quenched by administrative means alone (although she proceeded with a wide-ranging and effective programme to combat it). Ultimately it demanded the unconditional expenditure of love.

To such an expenditure she had committed herself some years before her monastic profession in 1932. Her profession (made at the Russian Orthodox Theological Academy in Paris) set a seal upon it. Yet formal though it was, it was her conviction that it involved the rejection of all formalism and superficial piety. Her anarchic ways were to distress many an Orthodox traditionalist, and she never fitted comfortably into the Russian émigré community at large, however devotedly she served it. Fortunately, comfort of any kind was inimical to her. At all times she insisted on the need 'truly and absolutely to accept the vow of poverty, to seek no Rule, but rather anarchy, the anarchic life of Fools for Christ's sake, to seek no monastic enclosure, but the complete absence of even the subtlest barrier which separates the heart from the world and its wounds'.

The occupation of France in the summer of 1940 found her with such barriers long since removed, a readiness to serve and, if need be, to perish: with her immediate associates she shared the firm intention 'lovingly to lay down our lives for our friends and to follow in Christ's footsteps to the Golgotha appointed for us'.

The Nazi persecution of the Jews directed her towards this Golgotha. Her house and its associated foundations provided refuge for the persecuted. Her chaplain, Father Dimitri Klepinin (1904–44), took it upon himself to issue spurious, backdated certificates of Baptism or parish membership in an attempt to safeguard them ('If Christ had met them and known that this would save their lives he would have done what they ask me to do').

But such activities were to be curtailed in February 1943. The Gestapo arrested Father Dimitri, Mother Maria and several other members of her circle. When Father Dimitri was offered his freedom on condition that he helped Jews no more, he showed his interrogators the figure on his pectoral cross with the comment, 'And do you know *this* Jew?'. The blow which he received in answer to his question was the prelude to a year of imprisonment and degradation—degradation quietly accepted. He died in February 1944 as a slave labourer in the subterranean concentration camp at Dora.

Mother Maria was deported to Ravensbrück concentration camp, where she was to spend the last two years of her life. Earlier she had written:

> We believe. And according to the strength of our belief we feel that death ceases to be death, that it becomes birth into eternity, that our sufferings on earth become our birth pangs. Sometimes we become so much aware of the approach of the hour of our birth into grace that we are prepared to say even to our sufferings, 'Grow stronger, burn me up, be unbearable, quick, merciless, because the spiritual body wants to rise, because I want to be born into eternity ... because I want to fulfil that which has been preordained.'

And in the camp, she composed a comparable (in the event, valedictory) message to those whom she had left behind in Paris: 'My state is such that I completely accept suffering, knowing that this is how things ought to be for me. If I die I see in this a blessing from on high.'

Her faith and vitality were the source of strength for all who came into contact with her. But the validity was gradually eroded by the camp routine and, most of all, by some weeks spent in the camp's extermination annexe, the so-called Youth Camp. Even though she returned from it to the main camp early in 1945 it was to be faced with endless 'selections' for the return journey to the Youth Camp and to the gas chambers adjacent to it.

One of the last selections took place on the Good Friday of 1945. Mother Maria was apparently not selected for extermination. But she perceived the panic on the faces of those who were. Though she knew that a return to the rigours of the Youth Camp could only mean death for her, even if she never reached the gas chambers, she appears to have stepped into the group of those selected and so taken the place of one of them. Thus (as two eye witnesses put it) she proceeded 'voluntarily to her martyrdom in order to help her companions to die'.

Sergei Hackel

'DO NOT HOLD ME' (John 20:17)

Don't hold me to the past;
a new era has dawned,
a new dimension added
　　to life itself.

Between now and then
there stands a cross,
for six long hours
a cross of pain
but now an empty cross
and an empty tomb.

Obedience unto death
is release from death,
not the end of the
　　obeying spirit
but its universal presence.

No longer nailed to a cross,
confined to one fixed place,
limited to the moment
　　of time,

But omnipresent
and immediate,
quick to move
with the speed of light,
with the speed of thought
and swifter still
with the speed of love
and the power of God.

George Appleton

FAITHFUL WITNESSES

Just opposite the window of the factory there is a high hill,
thickly covered with leafy trees. In summer it has often drawn
my eyes up to its rich green colour and refreshed them. So even
now from habit, I am always turning my weary gaze towards
it. Yet when I turn and face it suddenly it fills me with a thrill
of pleasure. For in between the bare branches of the trees I can
catch a clear view of a large Cross with a figure of the Crucified
on it. From its lofty position it dominates the whole region. A
symbol of the peace that is gone from the world.

Quickly, as if it were being drawn by a magnet, my spirit
leaps with joy the distance that separates me from Him and
kneels at his feet with their stains of blood.

Where, O Lord, is the peace on earth which the angels
proclaimed to us at Thy holy Nativity? What has happened to
the peace Thou didst bring to the world? Where is that peace
hallowed by righteousness and true godliness?

It is missing from the world now, and has been for many
years. It has been gone since we rejected Thee. From the time
when we broke the bonds that linked us with Thee, the King of
Peace, and refused Thy friendship. We murmured against
Thee, and left Thee, and moved on for the sake of a new
destiny, for a 'paradise on earth'. And the result? We are living
through that result now and seeing it: smoke, ruins, bloodshed,
famine and pain, deep, keen, prolonged.

Bishop Dionysius Charalambos

See what days are coming—it is the Lord Yahweh who
    speaks—
days when I will bring famine on the country,
a famine not of bread, a drought not of water,
but of hearing the word of Yahweh.
They will stagger from sea to sea,
wander from north to east,
seeking the word of Yahweh
and failing to find it.

Amos 8 : 11–12 JB

EASTER

This one night He is alone;
Adorers, mockers, mourners, all are gone;
Even the angels are not yet come.
He lies so quiet, so deep
In the cool dark of the tomb
He moves no more than corn new sown in ground,
Or than embryo not yet five months in the womb.

Earth is tonight His mother;
Only through her He Is,
Finding the child's womb-walled, profound
Oblivion and bliss.
Tonight Earth holds the Immortal sleeping within her;
So Mithra slept, and Osiris,
And the beautiful, dead Baldur.

So sleeps Christ this night: until at dawn
Earth must release the Immortal from her womb,
From this His waiting place that holds Him tombed.
For though she clothes Him, broken bone and body,
With her own dark flesh, He cannot stay;
The God must rise, the Light to Light return,
The white blade-body break the hold of clay.

O white blade-body no man's hand may touch;
O spirit's Corn;
Food of the Worlds;
Conqueror of Death;
Thou God of Godhead born;
Come forth between the pillars of the Sun!

Dorothea Eastwood

AND THE MORROW IS THEIRS (I)

Of the many individuals with whom I have worked, it is
almost impossible to single out anybody, but I will mention
here very briefly Zofia Chlewicka. The Germans murdered her
husband in October 1939, and she herself worked in the Polish

Resistance until she was arrested on 15th December 1942 and
taken during the night to the infamous prison at Pawiak in
Warsaw. She was eventually transported to the extermination
camp at Majdanek (400,000 victims) right on the main road
leading out of the city of Lublin. This is how she described to
me one of her experiences:— 'Amongst the constant transports
(prisoners in cattle trucks) arriving in Majdanek from different
parts of Europe there were those bearing survivors of the
Warsaw Ghetto Uprising in April 1943. . . . On 3rd November,
after the early morning roll-call the blocks were locked
(Blocksperre). Double lines of S.S. men and women encircled
the camp and reinforcements stood in the watchtowers. From
the top bunks we looked out of the very narrow high windows
and saw double lines, column after column of Jews who were
being marched along the long road outside Majdanek and on
the perimeter to beyond the crematorium. No less than 18,000
people were shot during the course of that day. We all lived
from hand to mouth, day to day, never knowing when the next
batch of us might not be selected for the gas chambers. This
was true even of the prisoners allowed to work as doctors and
nurses in the Revier (hospital), though without any of the
drugs and proper facilities. And indeed, at 4 P.M. on that day of
massacre some S.S. men came to the Revier to seize our Jewish
physicians and nurses. An appalling scene followed as we made
pathetic attempts to protect them by giving them our own
ragged white coats in the vain hope that they might be spared
as essential medical staff. One of the nurses, Helena (widow of
a doctor), a very fair-haired young woman, came up to me and
shook my hand. In the tumult she said quietly: "Before I die, I
want, as one human being to another amongst thousands, to
thank you and to say how I valued our working together as
friends to comfort the sick and each other regardless of our
nationalities or religious beliefs."

'During the second swoop the same afternoon the S.S.
returned drunk and roared about, wrenching an odd thin
blanket away from the sick and dying, and the night was bitterly cold. I asked one of the S.S. men when our doctors and
nurses would return. He shouted at me: "Never." At the height
of this uproar I saw a young 14-year-old girl silhouetted in the

wide doorway of the block. She was slim and beautiful in spite of having suffered from spotted fever: she had been alone ever since her family died. Turning to me she asked in a calm voice, "Do I look very pale?" Trying to comfort her, I said, "No, but why do you ask?" "I am glad," she replied, "because I do not want them to see that I am frightened." Then she was taken away by the S.S. and the alsatian dogs.'

*   *   *

Of the children in just one of the thousands of camps was written:

One of us
Will teach these children how to sing again,
To write on paper with a pencil,
To do sums and multiply:
One of us
Is sure to survive.

These words were written by Dr Karel Fleischmann in Terezin (Theresienstadt), an old fortified town in Czechoslovakia which was in part a 'transit-ghetto' for Jews awaiting extermination and in part a terrible concentration camp for 77,297 known victims.

Sue Ryder

Watch Thou, dear Lord, with those who wake, or watch, or weep tonight, and give Thine Angels charge over those who sleep. Tend Thy sick ones, O Lord Christ. Rest Thy weary ones. Bless Thy dying ones. Soothe Thy suffering ones. Pity Thy afflicted ones. Shield Thy joyous ones. And all for Thy Love's sake.

St Augustine

How falsely doth the world accuse!
How ready justice to refuse!
How eager to condemn me!
In danger's hour,
Lord, show thy power,
From every ill defend me.

St Matthew Passion

AND THE MORROW IS THEIRS (2)

Father Wnuk, a priest from Poland, who had been a prisoner in Dachau for many years, was appointed Chaplain at Werl. Once he said to me, 'I am almost at breaking point, having prepared thirty young non-German prisoners and given them the Last Sacrament before the death sentences are carried out.' In the presence of Boys who were under sentence of death and to whom I knew that faith meant a lot, the prayer by Cardinal Newman called 'A Meditation' was handed out. I had learned from both Survivors and the sick that God gives people special grace and strength to forgive, to overcome adversity and to win confidence.

The Meditation

God has created me to do Him some definite service; He has committed some work to me which He has not committed to another. I have my mission—I may never know it in this life, but I shall be told it in the next.

I am a link in a chain, a bond of connection between persons. He has not created me for nought. I shall do good, I shall do His work. I shall be an angel of peace, a preacher of truth in my own place *while not intending it*—if I do but keep His Commandments.

There I will trust Him. Whatever, wherever, I am, I can never be thrown away. If I am in sickness, my sickness may serve Him; if I am in sorrow my sorrow may serve Him. He does nothing in vain. He knows what He is about. He may take away my friends. He may throw me among strangers. He may make me feel desolate, make my spirit sink, hide my future from me—still He knows what He is about.

An eighteen-year-old boy left the following letter for me:

I am leaving this letter with my companion, for you to remember us. Please if you get the chance have the courage to read this letter to our friends. May I ask you to try and find my father who, as you know, has been missing since the

Gestapo took him, and give him a copy too. I beg you not to let this letter out of your hands, and to say goodbye to everyone. Much as I would like to do so myself, it isn't possible, and I hope to be forgiven.

We are taking leave of you for ever and of our beloved country. In a few short hours we shall be taken to the place of execution. Let us hope that somewhere there will be understanding for what we have done at this early age and in exile. We must die at the hands of our Allies for shooting the S.S. who killed all our families. We fought in the same cause, but this and the things which followed are all forgotten. We are leaving this world after receiving Extreme Unction from Father C.

Four Boys signed the declaration before being taken out to face a British firing squad.

Sue Ryder

LETTER IN ENGLISH FROM HELMUTH VON MOLTKE TO A FRIEND IN ENGLAND IN 1942

I will try to get this letter through to you, giving you a picture of the state of affairs on our side.

Things are worse and better than anybody outside Germany can believe them to be. They are worse, because the tyranny, the terror, the loss of values of all kinds, is greater than I could have believed a short time ago. The number of Germans killed by legal process in November was 25 a day through judgements of the courts and at least 75 a day by judgements of the courts martial, numbers running into hundreds are killed daily in concentration camps and by simple shooting without any pretence of trial. The constant danger in which we live is formidable. At the same time the greater part of the population has been uprooted and has been conscribed to forced labour of some kind and has been spread all over the continent untying all bonds of nature and surroundings and thereby loosening the beast in man, which is reigning. The few really good people who try to stem the tide are isolated as far as they have to work

in these unnatural surroundings, because they cannot trust
their comrades, and they are in danger from the hatred of the
oppressed people even when they succeed in saving some from
the worst. Thousands of Germans who will survive will be dead
mentally, will be useless for normal work.

But things are also better than you can believe, and that in
many ways. The most important is the spiritual awakening,
which is starting up, coupled as it is with the preparedness to be
killed, if need be. The backbone of this movement is to be
found in both the christian confessions, protestant as well as
catholic. The catholic churches are crowded every Sunday, the
protestant churches not yet, but the movement is discernible.
We are trying to build on this foundation, and I hope that in a
few months more tangible proof of this will be apparent outside. Many hundreds of our people will have to die before this
will be strong enough, but today they are prepared to do so.
This is true also of the young generation. I know of two cases
where a whole class of schoolboys, the one in a protestant part
of the country, the other in a catholic part, decided to follow
the calling of priests, something which would have been quite
impossible 6 months ago. But today it is beginning to dawn on
a not too numerous but active part of the population not that
they have been misled, not that they are in for a hard time, not
that they might lose the war, but that what is done is sinful,
and that they are personally responsible for every savage act
that has been done, not of course in a moral way, but as
Christians. Perhaps you will remember that, in discussions
before the war, I maintained that belief in God was not essential for coming to the results you arrive at. Today I know I was
wrong, completely wrong. You know that I have fought the
Nazis from the first day, but the amount of risk and readiness
for sacrifice which is asked from us now, and that which may be
asked from us tomorrow require more than right ethical principles, especially as we know that the success of our fight will
probably mean a total collapse as a national unit. But we are
ready to face this.

The second great asset which we are slowly but steadily
acquiring is this: the great dangers which confront us as soon as
we get rid of the NS force us to visualize Europe after the war.

We can only expect to get our people to overthrow this reign of terror and horror if we are able to show a picture beyond the terrifying and hopeless immediate future. A picture which will make it worth-while for the disillusioned people to strive for, to work for, to start again and to believe in. For us Europe after the war is less a problem of frontiers and soldiers, of top-heavy organizations or grand plans, but Europe after the war is a question of how the picture of man can be re-established in the breasts of our fellow citizens. This is a question of religion and education, of ties to work and family, of the proper relation of responsibility and rights. I must say, that under the incredible pressure under which we have to labour we have made progress, which will be visible one day. Can you imagine what it means to work as a group when you cannot use the telephone, when you are unable to post letters, when you cannot tell the names of your closest friends to your other friends for fear that one of them might be caught and might divulge the names under pressure?

We are, after considerable difficulties, in communication with the christian groups in the various occupied territories with the exception of France, where, as far as we can find out, there is no really effective opposition on a fundamental basis, but only the basis of casual activity. These people are simply splendid and are a great accession of strength to us giving trust to many others. Of course their position is easier than ours: moral and national duties are congruous even to the simple-minded, while with us there is an apparent clash of duties.

Happily I have been able to follow the activities of my English friends, and I hope they will all keep their spirits up. The hardest bit of the way is still to come, but nothing is worse than to slack on the way. Please do not forget, that we trust that you will stand it through without flinching as we are prepared to do our bit, and don't forget that for us a very bitter end is in sight when you have seen matters through. We hope that you will realize that we are ready to help you win war and peace.

Yours ever, James

Helmuth von Moltke

NEAR AS NEAR

Sentenced to death for the mere act of breathing:
To find adjacent cells, what luck that is,
For strangers, if with marked affinities!
Each to the other all he owns bequeathing.
These two, and in the dark hours best of all,
Would lie and have their hearts knock messages,
Near as they could be through the bone-hard wall.

Laurence Whistler

THOUGHTS ON THE DAY OF THE BAPTISM OF
DIETRICH WILHELM RUDIGER BETHGE

Today you will be baptized a Christian. All those great
ancient words of the Christian proclamation will be spoken
over you, and the command of Jesus Christ to baptize will be
carried out on you, without your knowing anything about it.
But we are once again being driven right back to the beginning
of our understanding. Reconciliation and redemption, regener-
ation and the Holy Spirit, love of our enemies, cross and resurrection, life in Christ and Christian discipleship—all these
things are so difficult and so remote that we hardly venture any
more to speak of them. In the traditional words and acts we
suspect that there may be something quite new and revolutionary, though we cannot as yet grasp or express it. That is our
own fault. Our church, which has been fighting in these years
only for its self-preservation, as though that were an end in
itself, is incapable of taking the word of reconciliation and
redemption to mankind and the world. Our earlier words are
therefore bound to lose their force and cease, and our being
Christians today will be limited to two things: prayer and righteous action among men. All Christian thinking, speaking, and
organizing must be born anew out of this prayer and action. By
the time you have grown up, the church's form will have
changed greatly. We are not yet out of the melting-pot, and
any attempt to help the church prematurely to a new expansion of its organization will merely delay its conversion and

purification. It is not for us to prophesy the day (though the day will come) when men will once more be called so to utter the word of God that the world will be changed and renewed by it. It will be a new language, perhaps quite non-religious, but liberating and redeeming—as was Jesus' language; it will shock people and yet overcome them by its power; it will be a language of a new righteousness and truth, proclaiming God's peace with men and the coming of his kingdom. 'They shall fear and tremble because of all the good and all the prosperity I provide for it' (Jer. 33:9). Till then the Christian cause will be a silent and hidden affair, but there will be those who pray and do right and wait for God's own time. May you be one of them, and may it be said of you one day, 'The path of the righteous is like the light of dawn, which shines brighter and brighter till full day' (Prov. 4:18).

Dietrich Bonhoeffer

TO MY SON

Son, I am powerless to protect you though
My heart for yours beats ever anxiously,
Blind through piteous darkness you must go,
And find with a new vision lights I see.
If it might ease you I would bear again
All the old suffering that I too have known,
All sickness, terror, and the spirit's pain,
But you, alas, must make those three your own.
Yes, though I beat away a thousand fears
And forge your armour without flaw or chink,
And though I batter Heaven with my prayers,
Yet from a self-filled cup of grief you drink.
Oh, son of woman, since I gave you breath
You walk alone through life to face your death.

Dorothea Eastwood

THE REAL ENEMY (4)

The French detachment, after all, was not composed entirely of ex-officers of the French Army who had fought with the Resistance. It was indeed a kind of microcosm of Buchenwald as a whole. It included regular soldiers, communists, parliamentary politicians of right, left and centre. Paris crooks, pimps and black marketeers, men of honour, desperadoes and riff-raff. It was a collection of French men, who had nothing in common except nationality. It occurred to me, especially since I seemed to be on good terms with the German prisoners, that my danger might be coming from the French.

Later on another leading member of the French group came to see me. This was C., an influential communist. He told me that as the chances of survival in the camp became more and more slender, as it became more and more necessary for a man to know who his real friends and his enemies were, it was essential for us all to know what we stood for. He said that the French in the camp were now rallying together on the platform of political commitment to action in the post-war world on the basis of three principles. These were complete loyalty to de Gaulle; total acceptance of the Atlantic Charter; and liquidation of the huge industrial and financial monopolies which in France had formed a state within a state. If I would promise to support this programme now and after the war, in return the French in Buchenwald would do their best to secure my survival in face of everything. We talked for some time. I told him that I did not think in terms of political programmes, but in terms of the two things that really mattered to me, my country and my religion. For them I would spend my last drop of blood and it was for them that I had done what I had in the past. It was no use pretending to anything more.

He seemed to find this entirely satisfactory, and said so. But I was now seriously worried. After all, though we were all in daily danger of death from disease or liquidation, the Allies were gaining ground in Europe and the end of the war in the Allies' favour was thinkable, if not in sight. Just as there would be a struggle for power in France and Germany between left, right and centre when the war ended, so there would be a struggle for power in between the elements of each national contingent *now*. Certainly the French communists, if they had any say in the matter, would prefer to see a French Roman Catholic aristocrat on the Dora list rather than one of their own members or sympathizers. T., the German communist, might think more of me than of some French black-marketeer. But if the leading French communists went to him and said that in post-war France the black-marketeer had promised to help them, whereas I was inevitably their enemy, would he, in the interests of the international communist brotherhood, have to comply?

I began to hate my fellow-countrymen as a group almost more than I hated the S.S. In a sense more, because, as I have said, we saw so little of the S.S. anyway. There were a few noble and generous souls among the French, who were at Buchenwald for having served their country and fought for liberty, but the rest were swine. It so often happened that the swindlers, thieves and traitors were on top, and spoke and acted for all the French in camp. They managed everything from the distribution of Red Cross parcels and mail to the rigging of transport rolls, and did so only out of self-interest. How many of the fine workers for the Resistance movement were sent off to be trodden to death in a cattle truck, so that some pimp from a Paris night-club might live? At this time I wrote in my diary:

What an infamous régime. This shameful dictatorship! The dictatorship of all that is most sordid. What happens here is beyond imagination. Stupidity and savagery have attained undreamed of limits. There is nothing to be done but submit, and to continue to bear the weight of captivity. But what is the point of it all? When I look at those who surround me (happily I do not see them the greater part of the time), I am filled with shame and disgust, not only for them but for the Resistance to which these men profess to belong! If this is the Resistance, then I don't want it. At no price do I wish for a Resistance of blackguards, bullies and convicts.

Pierre d'Harcourt

Count Schwerin was executed on September 8, 1944, because of his connection with the abortive plot against Hitler, of July 20, 1944.
The wife of a political prisoner reports:

I was standing at the heavy iron inside door of the prison, trying to talk an S.S. man into taking in a parcel for me. Suddenly the prison door opened, and through it strode calmly and erectly a man with his hands bound behind his back, followed by a little Gestapo man who looked to me like a reptile. The S.S. man whispered to me: 'That is Count Schwerin—Plötzensee.' I knew what Plötzensee meant, and through my mind there flashed the realization, 'This is a man who knows how to die.'

From his will
Further it is my desire that in the part of the gravel bed in my forest of Sartowitz where the victims of the massacres of the late autumn of 1939 are laid to rest, a very high oaken cross be erected as soon as the conditions of the time permit, with the following inscription:

Here lie from 1,400 to 1,500 Christians and Jews
May God have mercy on their souls and on their murderers.
Count Schwerin von Schwanenfeld

Summoned   For one moment
To carry it,   The sail
Alone   In the sun-storm,
To assay it,   Far off
Chosen   On a wave-crest,
To suffer it,   Alone,
And free   Bearing from land.
To deny it,
I saw   For one moment
                                  I saw.

Dag Hammarskjöld

Alexis, Baron von Roenne, born on February 12, 1902, was a colonel of the
German Army. From the moment of the establishment of the régime, he
regarded National Socialism as a disaster for Germany. Considerations of
conscience prevented him from taking part in the preparation of the attempted
coup of July 20, 1944. But the ties of friendship that linked him with the
leaders of the resistance served as sufficient ground for his condemnation. He
died on October 12, 1944 in Berlin-Plötzensee at the hands of the hangman.

Farewell letter to his mother

My only beloved Mama: Today for a very special reason the
notion came to me to write you once again, although a short
letter to you is enclosed with my previous letters of farewell. I
know that in spite of your great longing and joy at the prospect
of going to the Saviour, mortal fear at the thought of just the
physical process of death torments you. And because of that I
have wanted so very much to say to you that our Lord can
completely erase this too, if we ask him to do so. So have no fear at
all.

. . . For a week now I have been awaiting death from day to
day; at this moment, for example, I expect it tomorrow, and
the Saviour in his boundless mercy has freed me of all terror.
All day I pray and think in *perfect calm* and almost exclusively
about Him and at the same time of course about those dearest
to me. I have a good appetite, I take pleasure in the sunshine,
and I have tried to free myself from the world only in so far as I
have given up reading and, as much as possible keep my
thoughts away from all military and political matters and at
the disposition only of the Saviour. I go to bed early with
prayer, I sleep very peacefully and soundly like a child the
whole night through, and immediately upon awakening I turn
to Him; spiritually, with all this I am completely free, and
moreover, apart from thoughts about my little brood (his wife
and two small children), I am a completely happy man—a
phenomenon that has often been found astonishing here and
been explained by reference to Him.

At first I cast about by myself to find avenues of thought that
would give me strength and a joyous mood for dying; then

suddenly God showed me two means of help. First of all, I was to picture my death to myself in its full reality, and then to compare it with His death. That has helped me immeasurably: on the one hand the innocent victim, voluntarily suffering a death of many hours of martyrdom at the hands of those He had saved; on the other, an event of a moment's duration that in any case was bound to confront me at some time, perhaps in much more painful form, as in a long illness. I got this suggestion from two beautiful verses, 'When strength one day shall fail me', and especially, 'And let me see Thine image, crowned in Thine agony'. Thereupon I was ashamed of all my inhibitions and became free of fear. And then he pointed out to me that the moment of death is at the same time of course the first moment of life in his blessed rest and in the peace of God. Keeping these thoughts firmly in my mind, I have for days been looking forward hourly, in *complete calm and detachment*, with perfectly peaceful thoughts and quiet pulse, to my departure on the swift journey home, and I am fully confident that the brief final occurrence will be similarly irradiated by his indescribable grace.

I am writing this to you in such exact detail, my beloved Mama, because perhaps thereby I can, acting in his service, give you a bit of help. Ever since the beginning of this last exceptional period of grace (two and a half months) there has been no doubt in my mind that I owe all this undeserved mercy in very large part to your prayers of a decade, and words are not sufficient to express my thanks to you. I consider this intercession of yours as the greatest gift by far of your unending love for me, and in the life to come we shall be speaking of it often. But I beg you with all my heart for the rest of your time on earth to transfer these prayers to Ursula and my two little ones. Do it, I beg you fervently, with the same love and loyalty. It is an indescribable treasure that you will be giving to my beloved little brood that needs it so desperately. I am certain that you will fulfil my wish.

Alexis, Baron von Roenne

NIGHT VOICES IN TEGEL (I)

Stretched out on my cot
I stare at the grey wall.
Outside, a summer evening
That does not know me
Goes singing into the countryside.
Slowly and softly
The tides of the day ebb
On the eternal shore.
Sleep a little,
Strengthen body and soul, head and hand,
For peoples, houses, spirits and hearts
Are aflame.
Till your day breaks
After blood-red night—
Stand fast!

Night and silence.
I listen.
Only the steps and cries of the guards,
The distant, hidden laughter of two lovers.
Do you hear nothing else, lazy sleeper?

I hear my own soul tremble and heave.
Nothing else?
I hear, I hear
The silent night thoughts
Of my fellow sufferers asleep or awake,
As if voices, cries,
As if shouts for planks to save them.
I hear the uneasy creak of the beds,
I hear chains.

I hear how sleepless men toss and turn,
Who long for freedom and deeds of wrath.
When at grey dawn sleep finds them
They murmur in dreams of their wives and children.

I hear the happy lisp of half-grown boys,
Delighting in childhood dreams;
I hear them tug at their blankets
And hide from hideous nightmares.

I hear the sighs and weak breath of the old,
Who in silence prepare for the last journey.
They have seen justice and injustice come and go;
Now they wish to see the imperishable, the eternal.

Night and silence.
Only the steps and cries of the guards.
Do you hear how in the silent house
It quakes, cracks, roars
When hundreds kindle the stirred-up flame of their hearts?

Their choir is silent,
But my ear is open wide:
'We the old, the young,
The sons of all tongues,
We the strong, the weak,
The sleepers, the wakeful,
We the poor, the rich,
Alike in misfortune,
The good, the bad,
Whatever we have been,
We men of many scars,
We the witnesses of those who died,
We the defiant, we the despondent,
The innocent, and the much accused,
Deeply tormented by long isolation,
Brother, we are searching, we are calling you!
Brother, do you hear me?'

Dietrich Bonhoeffer

THE NIGHT OF THE NEW MOON (1)

They were among the longest days I have ever known,
because everything in the atmosphere around us told me that

the climax was near. .... I was particularly aware at night of
how time dragged on at this moment, and how great was the
strain. I always went at night before lights-out to one or two of
the sections of the prison in which our men were housed. The
Japanese still insisted on keeping officers and men on the whole
in separate quarters. I did this nightly round, not out of a sense
of duty nor just out of the affection I felt for the men who had
shared the long years of captivity with us, but also for the
purely selfish motive that I had never yet gone among them
without being revived and strengthened by my contact with
them.

Great as was my admiration for the British officers in prison
with us, it could not be compared with the respect I had for the
ordinary soldiers, sailors and airmen who formed the majority
of British prisoners. They seemed to me, even in the categories
from which one might have least expected them, to possess
qualities of the highest order as, for instance, men from the
slums of the great cities of Britain . . . whose physical appearance
often showed the consequences of severe malnutrition during the
years of their neglect by the ruling classes before the war, like the
rickets of childhood which gave them bowed legs and Rowlandson
bodies and faces.

Yet their spirit was always high, cheerful and invincible. I
had never yet known a crisis, however brutal, in which they
had lost their nerve. Appeals to their pride and honour had
never been in vain. Always they had responded instinctively in
a measure as great if not greater than officers born, bred, well-
nourished from childhood, schooled and trained for precisely
this sort of trial. Their need of honour, of a life of self-respect
too, was as important as their need for food. They were, as I
said, in the beginning, slowly dying from lack of food at the
time, but there was no hint of impending death in their conversation or sign of defeat in their emaciated faces. Instead there
was only an extraordinary and intense kind of gaiety that to me
was far more moving than any signs of depression, melancholy
or defeat could possibly have been.

Talking to them I would find myself assailed by a fierce kind
of tenderness for them, that was like fire. I wonder if anyone,
except perhaps Wilfred Owen, has ever paid enough attention

to this kind of male tenderness that men feel for flesh and blood
in war, not even exclusively flesh and blood of their own kin
but also of their enemy. It is so perhaps, because the British
have this ridiculous feeling of embarrassment when faced with
emotion and feeling, of which they have such great and sensitive reserves themselves. Any open acceptance of either, however, tended to be discouraged as if it were a kind of unma-
sculine weakness. Yet it is a unique reality of war, and not
being British I was open to it—much to the embarrassment of
my more conventional fellow officers at times. I had no inhibitions in encouraging and welcoming it, but felt immeasurably
strengthened by it always to do what I felt I had to do.
    . . . That night the New Zealand Officer got through not
only to Delhi but to Perth and San Francisco, and listened
exclusively in to news and world comment and reactions which
gave us a clear picture of what had happened at Hiroshima.
Even now after all these years I, who know little about
astrology, am not a follower of astrologers and who have no
wish to make an astrological point of any kind at all, feel
compelled to say that it looked at the very least most strange to
me that the first atom bomb dropped by man should have been
dropped on so moon-swung a people as the Japanese, during
the phase of nothingness between the death of the oldest and
the birth of the newest of new moons.
    It is to me almost as if, out of the depths of life and time from
the far fast expanding perimeter of our universe and its galaxies
of star-foam, some cosmic impulse had come to extinguish the
moon on this occasion so that its extinction and imminent
rebirth could act on the limited awareness of man as an unmistakable symbol of annunciation that the past was dead and a
new, greater phase of meaning about to begin on earth, however catastrophic the introduction.

                                            Laurens Van Der Post

    I do not suppose that at any moment in history has the
agony of the world been so great or widespread. Tonight the
sun goes down on more suffering than ever before in the world.

                                            Winston Churchill

A BAR OF SHADOW (I)

It was he, Hara, who decided how much or rather how little we had to eat. He ordained when we were driven to bed, when we got up, where and how we paraded, what we read. It was he who ordered that every book among the few we possessed wherein the word 'kiss' or mention of 'kissing' appeared, should be censored by having the offending pages torn out and publicly burned as an offence against 'Japanese morality'. It was he who tried to 'purify' our thinking by making us in our desperately under-nourished condition go without food for two days at a time, confined in cramped and overcrowded cells, forbidden even to talk so that we could contemplate all the better our perverse and impure European navels. It was he who beat me because a row of beans that he had made my men plant had not come up and he put the failure down to my 'wrong thinking'. . . . He mounted and controlled our brutal Korean guards, gave them their orders and made them fanatical converts, more zealous than their only prophet, to his outlook and mood. He made our laws, judged us for offences against them, punished us and even killed some of us for breaking them.

. . . It was John Lawrence, who suffered more at Hara's hands than any of us except those whom he killed, who first drew attention to his eyes. I remember so clearly his words one day after a terrible beating in prison. 'The thing you mustn't forget about Hara,' he had said, 'is that he is not an individual or for that matter even really a man.' He had gone on to say that Hara was the living myth, the expression in human form, the personification of the intense, inner vision which, far down in their unconscious, keeps the Japanese people together and shapes and compels their thinking and behaviour. . . .

'But just look in his eyes,' Lawrence had said: 'there is nothing ignoble or insincere there: only an ancient light, refuelled, quickened and brightly burning. . . . He can't help himself,' John Lawrence had said. 'It is not he but an act of Japanese gods in him, don't you see? You remember what the moon does to him!'

And indeed I remembered. . . . If ever there was a moon-swung, moon-haunted, moon-drawn soul it was he. As the moon waxed—and how it waxed in the soft, velvet sky of Insulinda, how it grew and seemed to swell to double its normal gold and mystically burning proportions in that soft, elastic air; how it swung calmly over the great volcanic valleys like a sacred lamp, while the ground mist, mingling with the smell of cloves, cinnamon and all the fragrant spices of Insulinda drifted among the soaring tree trunks like incense round the lacquered columns of a sequined temple—Yes! as this unbelievable moon expanded and spread its gold among the blackness of our jungle night, we saw it draw a far tide of mythological frenzy to the full in Hara's blood. Seven days, three days before and three days after and on the day of the full moon itself, were always our days of greatest danger with Hara. Most of his worst beatings and killings took place then. But once the beating was over and the moon waning he would be, for him, extraordinarily generous to us. It was as if the beating and killing had purged him of impurities of spirit, of madness and evil in some strange way and had made him grateful to them. In fact, the morning after he had cut off the head of one of us, I remember seeing him talking to Lawrence and being struck by the fact that he had an expression of purified, of youthful and almost springlike innocence on his face, as if the sacrifice of the life of an innocent British aircraftman the night before, had redeemed him from all original as well as private and personal sin, and appeased for the time the hungry batlike gods of his race.

. . . 'I shall never forget one night in prison,' Lawrence continued . . . 'Hara sent for me. He had been drinking and greeted me uproariously but I knew his merriment was faked. . . . He wanted someone to talk to about his country and for some hours I walked Japan from end to end with him through all four of its unique and dramatic seasons. The mask of cheerfulness got more and more threadbare as the evening wore on and at last Hara tore it from his face.

' "Why, Rorensu," he exclaimed fiercely at last. "Why are you alive? I would like you better if you were dead. How could an officer of your rank ever have allowed himself to fall alive in our hands? How can you bear the disgrace? Why don't you kill yourself?" '

'I admitted the disgrace, if he wished to call it that,' Lawrence replied. 'But said that in our view disgrace, like danger, was something which also had to be bravely borne and lived through, and not run away from by a cowardly taking of one's own life. This was so novel and unexpected a point of view to him that he was tempted to dismiss it as false and made himself say: "No! no! no! it is fear of dying that stops you all." He spat disdainfully on the floor and then tapping on his chest with great emphasis added: "I am already dead. I, Hara, died many years ago."

'And then it came out, of course. The night before he left home to join the army at the age of seventeen . . . he had gone to a little shrine in the hills nearby to say goodbye to life, to tell the spirits of his ancestors that he was dying that day in his heart and spirit for his country so that when death came to claim him in battle it would be a mere technicality, so that far from being surprised he would greet it either like a bosom friend, long expected and overdue, or merely accept it as a formal confirmation of a state which had long existed.'

. . . Looking back now, he found it most significant, that towards the end of the evening, Hara began to try his hand at composing verses in that tight, brief and extremely formal convention in which the popular hero of the past in Japan inevitably said farewell to the world before taking his own life. He remembered Hara's final effort well: roughly translated it ran:

When I was seventeen looking over the pines at Kurashiyama, I saw on the full yellow moon, the shadow of wild-geese flying South. There is no shadow of wild-geese returning on the moon rising over Kurashiyama to-night.

'Poor devil: as I watched and listened to him trying to break into verse, suddenly I saw our roles reversed. I saw by a flash of lightning in the darkness of my own mind that I was really the free man and Hara, my gaoler, the prisoner. I had once in my youth in the ample, unexacting days before the war when the coining of an epigram had looked so convincingly like a discovery of wisdom, defined individual freedom to myself as freedom to choose one's own cage in life. Hara had never known even that limited freedom. He was born in a cage, a prisoner in an oubliette of mythology, chained to bars welded by a great blacksmith of the ancient gods themselves. And I felt an immense pity for him. And now four years later, Hara was our kind of prisoner as well and in the dock for the last time, with sentence of death irrevocably pronounced.

Laurens Van Der Post

TERROR IS BORN OUT OF TERROR

Terror is born out of terror,
Knows not whence it is come.
Lord, give us faith,
Safety with you in each other.

Fear goes astray for the fearful,
Frightened of its own face.
Lord give us . . . etc.

Frightened, disfigured our world is,
Does what it would not do.
Lord give us . . . etc.

You who in Christ on the cross, Lord
Shattered the evil law.
Lord give us . . . etc.

You who are close in the Spirit,
Still the creator, Lord;
Lord give us . . . etc.

That love which drives out all terror
Always it comes from God.
Lord give us . . . etc.

Anders Frostenson

A BAR OF SHADOW (2)

Hara was sought out and brought to trial before one of our War Crimes Tribunals ... The night before he was hanged, Hara got a message through begging Lawrence to come and see him ... the request did not reach Lawrence until ten o'clock on the night before the morning set for the execution ... Hara's prison was on the far side of the island and he could not, with the best of luck, get there before midnight.

The evening was very still and quiet, rather as if it had caught its own breath at the beauty and brilliance of the night that was marching down on it out of the East like a goddess with jewels of fire. An immense full moon had swung itself clear over the dark fringe of the jungle bound, like a ceremonial fringe of ostrich plumes designed for an ancient barbaric ritual, to the dark brow of the land ahead. ... To the north of the jungle and all along its heavy feathered fringes the sea rolled and unrolled its silver and gold cloak onto the white and sparkling sand, as lightly and deftly as a fine old far-eastern merchant unrolling bales of his choicest silk. The ancient, patient swish of it all was constantly in Lawrence's ears.

... It was the sort of night and the kind of setting in a halfway moment between the end of one day and the beginning of the other. ... All that we had been through, the war, the torture, the long hunger, all the grim and tranced years in our sordid prison, he found light and insignificant weighed in the golden scales of that moment. The thought that yet another life should be sacrificed to our discredited and insufficient past, seemed particularly pointless and repugnant and filled him with a sense of angry rebellion. In this mood and manner he arrived at the prison just before midnight. He found he was expected and was taken at once to Hara's cell ...

'I'm very sorry I am so late. But I only got your message at nine o'clock. I expect you gave me up as a bad job long ago and thought I'd refused to come.'

'No, Rorensu-san,' Hara answered. 'No, not that. I never thought you would refuse to come, but I was afraid my message, for many reasons might not be delivered to you. I am very

grateful to you for coming and I apologize for troubling you. I
would not have done so if it hadn't been so important. Forgive
me please, but there is something wrong in my thinking and I
knew you would understand how hard it would be for me to die
with wrong thoughts in my head.'

Hara spoke slowly and deliberately in a polite, even voice,
but Lawrence could tell from its very evenness that his thought
was flowing in a deep fast stream out to sea, flowing in a deeper
chasm of himself than it had ever flowed before.

'Poor, poor devil, bloody poor devil,' he thought, 'even now
the problem is "thinking", always his own or other people's
"thinking" at fault.'

'There is nothing to forgive, Hara-san,' he said aloud. 'I
came at once when I got your message and I came gladly.
Please tell me what it is and I'll try and help you.'

From the way Hara's dark, slanted, child-of-a-sun-goddess'
eyes lit up at the use of the polite 'san' to his name, Lawrence
knew that Hara had not been spoken to in that manner for
many months.

'Rorensu-san,' he answered eagerly, pleading more like a
boy with his teacher than a war-scarred sergeant-major with an
enemy and an officer, 'it is only this: you have always, I felt,
always understood us Japanese. Even when I have had to punish you, I felt you understood it was not I, Hara, who wanted
it, but that it had to be, and you never hated me for it. Please
tell me now: you English I have always been told are fair and
just people: whatever other faults we all think you have; we
have always looked upon you as a just people. You know I am
not afraid to die. You know that after what has happened to
my country I shall be glad to die tomorrow. Look, I have
shaved the hair off my head, I have taken a bath of purification, rinsed my mouth and throat, washed my hands and drunk
the last cupful of water for the long journey. I have emptied the
world from my head, washed it off my body, and I am ready
for my body to die, as I have died in my mind long since. Truly
you must know, I do not mind dying, only, only, only, why
must I die for the reason you give? I don't know what I have
done wrong that other soldiers who are not to die have not
done. We have all killed one another and I know it is not good,

but it is war. I have punished you and killed your people, but I punished you no more and killed no more than I would have done if you were Japanese in my charge who had behaved in the same way. I was kinder to you, in fact, than I would have been to my own people, kinder to you all than many others. I was more lenient, believe it or not, than army rules and rulers demanded. If I had not been so severe and strict you would all have collapsed in your spirit and died because your way of thinking was so wrong and your disgrace so great. If it were not for me Hicksley-Ellis and all his men would have died on the island out of despair. It was not my fault that the ships with food and medicine did not come. I could only beat my prisoners alive and save those that had it in them to live by beating them to greater effort. And now I am being killed for it, I do not understand where I went wrong except in the general wrong of us all. If I did another wrong please tell me how and why and I shall die happy.'

'I didn't know what to say,' Lawrence turned to me with a gesture of despair. 'He was only asking me what I had asked myself ever since these damned war trials began. I honestly did not understand myself. I never saw the good of them. It seemed to me just as wrong for us now to condemn Hara under a law which had never been his, of which he had never even heard, as he and his masters had been to punish and kill us for our transgressions of the code of Japan that was not ours. It was not as if he had sinned against his own lights: if ever a person had been true to himself and the twilight glimmer in him, it was this terrible little man. He may have done wrong for the right reasons but how could it be squared by us now doing right in the wrong way? No punishment I could think of could restore the past, could be more futile and more calculated even to give the discredited past a new lease of life in the present than this sort of uncomprehending and uncomprehended vengeance! I didn't know what the hell to say!'

The distress over his predicament became so poignant in this recollection that he broke off with a wave of his hand at the darkening sky. 'But you did say something surely,' I said. 'You could not leave it at that.'

'Oh yes I said something,' he said sadly, 'but it was most

inadequate. All that I could tell him was that I did not understand myself and that if it lay with me I would gladly let him
out and send him straight back to his family.'

'And did that satisfy him?' I asked.

Lawrence shook his head. He didn't think so, for after bowing deeply again and thanking Lawrence, he looked up and
asked: 'So what am I to do?'

Lawrence could only say: 'You can try to think only with all
your heart, Hara-san, that unfair and unjust as this thing which
my people are doing seems to you, that it is done only to try to
stop the kind of things that happened between us in the war
from ever happening again. You can say to yourself as I used to
say to my despairing men in prison under you: "There is a way
of winning by losing, a way of victory in defeat which we are
going to discover." Perhaps that too must be your way to
understanding victory now.'

'That, Rorensu-san,' he said, with the quick intake of breath
of a Japanese when truly moved: 'is a very Japanese thought!'

They stood in silence for a long while looking each other
straight in the eyes, the English officer and the Japanese
N.C.O. The moonlight outside was tense, its silver strands
trembling faintly with the reverberation of inaudible and far-
off thunder and the crackle of the electricity of lightning along
the invisible horizon.

Hara was the first to speak. In that unpredictable way of his,
he suddenly smiled and said irrelevantly: 'I gave you a good
Kurisumasu once, didn't I?'

'Indeed you did,' Lawrence answered unhappily, adding
instinctively, 'You gave me a very, very, good Christmas.
Please take that thought with you tonight!'

'Can I take it with me all the way?' Hara asked, still smiling
but with something almost gaily provocative in his voice. 'Is it
good enough to go even where I am going?'

'Yes: much as circumstances seem to belie it,' Lawrence ans-
wered, 'it is good enough to take all the way and beyond.' . . .
At that moment the guard announced himself and told
Lawrence he had already overstayed his time.

'Sayonara Hara-san!' Lawrence said, bowing deeply, using
that ancient farewell of the Japanese 'If-so-it-must-be' which is

so filled with the sense of their incalculable and inexorable fate,
'Sayonara and God go with you.'

'If so it must be!' Hara said calmly, bowing as deeply. 'If so
it must be, and thank you for your great kindness and your
good coming, and above all your honourable words.'

Laurens Van Der Post

TOWARDS MOZAMBIQUE

In peacetime winters, I remember best
Pacing the cold beach on a brilliant day,
With bouncing waves a-sparkle to the west
In the crisp wind that whips Sagami Bay,
And lifting clouds across the sea that stray
Leisurely upward over the smooth ice
Of Fuji's cone, and after them the play
Of shadows rising, and you feel, how nice
To cut this wedding cake and crunch it slice by slice.

Oshima's isle, rocked by Mihara's fires,
Warning to mariners, seamark by day,
At night a fitful flame that flares and tires,
The unwatched lamp that leads into the Bay—
Imai no hama, beach where the interplay
Of time and luck were for a moment such
That happiness for me was coiled away,
Taken for granted, brushed with casual touch,
As a thing preordained that didn't count for much.

Guns in the West. Across the enormous space,
The European, the Siberian plain
The Japan Sea, whose sky-coloured surface
You guess from mountains, where the rougher grain
Ends in a line of snow, a curving stain
Against what lies beyond, a blanker white—
As if it carried, we would stop and strain
To catch their whisper in the hurrying bright
Hubbub of high midday or the suspense of night.

The evening withers in the bitter chill
That breathes from the disasters in the West.
The news of France's fall seems to instil
One thought in every patriotic breast.
Geisha neglects her client, host his guest,
And all forget retort and song and act
In whispered strategy. (To us the best
Of our well-wishers, shortly to be tracked,
Whispers that Stahmer's here, and soon there'll be a Pact.)

This was the world in which we had to work.
Fixed at our post, forbidden to resign,
We, from Chuzenji, could but watch Dunkirk.
Then as the fuller moon began to shine
Over the saddles of the mountain spine,
The very stillness seemed to throb and ache.
Heaven forbid that *there* the night's so fine
Or this invasion moon—our thoughts must take
Wing to the Straits and leave our bodies by the Lake.

Cooling our fever with its wavering jet,
Into the dark there steals a wooden flute—
A bamboo's essence, fresh and dense and wet,
The inmost core of pole and brush and root,
Distilled in drops that nothing can dilute—
So sings the *shakuhachi*, full and round,
Each note complete and juicy as a fruit.
And, far away, the only other sound
Is where the huge cascade falls whispering underground.

Outside the iron gates, the buglers went
Blowing a springy quickstep, then a pair
Of mounted leaders, formal and intent,
And then a column, marching, marching—where?
Their get-up has an empire-snatching air,
Shirts for the jungle, helmets for the sun.
Not ours the empire anyway, for there
They'll find the fighter and the coastal gun
And fortress Singapore, the pride of '41.

Shipwreck, reverse, catastrophe and rout,
In that lean winter all headlines were bad,
Yet on Malaya's fortress holding out
We fixed our hope, or all the hope we had.
And then it fell. That night an ironclad,
Intensely lit in a prophetic dream,
Like a strange message on a signal-pad
(Transcribed elsewhere) was seen to make full steam
Through estuary or straits or narrowing tidal stream.

No circumnavigators ever came
More gladly towards Mozambique. But there grew
Queasy in us, while still at sea, the same
Fear of the present that Rip van Winkle knew.
Men are such egoists, when they've been through
Enough sensations in a given plot—
Love, suffer, yawn, no matter what you do—
So long as it recalls your private lot,
Remembrance makes of school or prison a beauty-spot.

Through the round ports the watery afternoon
Throws, on the ceiling, rays that swirl and gleam.
Rippling reflections, transient as the moon,
A flickering bioscope, vaguer than a dream,
And the small cabin lights with the dim beam
Of lantern images that shift and shake,
And all the harm goes fading down the stream:
Hate and despair and boredom and heartbreak,
Slipping astern and lost in the impermanent wake.
                                    Charles Hepburn Johnston

THE INTERROGATION OF JOHN LEONARD WILSON

On October 10th, 1943, soon after dawn, the civilians who
were interned in Changi Prison, Singapore, were called out to
parade in the main yard. They had no reason to suppose that
this was more than one of the routine roll-calls. However, it
soon became obvious that something very different was afoot.

The Japanese military police, the notorious Kampetai, had arrived in force and were taking over the camp. A number of the internees were called out by name, labelled and segregated from the main body, and taken away by the police to their headquarters in Singapore, which had been set up in a building which had formerly been the Y.M.C.A. centre. Here they were confined in appalling cell conditions, and the military police began their interrogations under torture. These interrogations went on for many months.

Leonard Wilson, then Bishop of Singapore, was taken by the police on October 17th, the day before he was to have held a Confirmation service in the camp. He was questioned under torture on that evening and during most of the day on October 18th and 19th. When he was returned to his cell on the third evening, he was in a semi-conscious state, in which he remained for three weeks.

This experience was in many ways central to Leonard Wilson's life. . . . he regarded these events as among the most significant moments of his own Christian experience, and a lasting proof of the reality of the Christian faith.

. . . In the evening of his arrival Leonard was questioned, the interrogation being punctuated with beatings, for between three and four hours. On the following morning he was again taken to the torture room, where he was made to kneel down. A three-angled bar was placed behind his knees. He was then made to kneel on his haunches. His hands were tied behind his back and pulled up to a position between his shoulder blades. His head was forced down and he remained in this position for seven and a half hours. Any attempt to ease the strain from the cramp in his thighs was frustrated by the guards, who brought the flat of their hobnailed boots down hard on to his thighs. At intervals the bar between his knees would be twisted, or the guards would jump on to one or both projecting ends. Beatings and kicks were frequent. Throughout the whole of this time he was being questioned and told that he was a spy. This was one of the times when he lost his nerve and pleaded for death.

Again, the next morning, he was brought up from the cells, and this time tied face upwards to a table with his head hanging over the end of it. For several hours he remained in that position while relays of soldiers beat him systematically from the ankles to the thighs with three-fold knotted ropes. He fainted, was revived with warm milk, and then the beating was continued. He estimated that he must have received over three hundred lashes. The beating, he said, was far easier to bear than the excruciating pain of the previous day. It was not long before he lost all sense of feeling. The blows had lost their power to hurt, so dead were the nerves of his body. Finally he was taken down to the cells and thrown on the floor. There was no skin left on the front of his legs from his thighs downwards. He had no medical attention while he was in that state, and he said that if it had not been for the help of Stephenson, a fellow internee in his cell, who subsequently died from the treatment he himself received, he would not have survived.

Roy McKay

LETTER TO HIS FRIENDS FROM BISHOP PAUL SEITZ

Please forgive my long silence. Since last I wrote to you much has happened, and much of it very distressing.

For thirty years in South Vietnam we were plunged into war, danger, destruction and misery of all kinds. Although we were agonized, no one, as late as December 1974, would have dared to predict that four months later it would all be over for that heroic little nation, finally submerged by triumphant communism.

Everything happened as in a nightmare; the crumbling of the South was murderous, immense and brutal. Nightmares pass with the night and with the new day comes reassurance, but this nightmare continues for the present generation without any apparent hope of it ever coming to an end.

The Montagnards, many of them situated in my former Diocese of Kontum, like the rest foundered in the storm. So another tragic turning in their History opens before them. We know what they are losing; we cannot tell when or how they will come out of it.

The towns of Ban Me Thuot, Plei-Ku and Kontum, in the Central Highlands, were the first to be 'liberated': Kontum on March 18th, 1975. One week later, the Doctors Edric Baker and Christian who had remained at their posts in the Minh-Quy hospital, were arrested and interned in a forest camp. The nursing nuns were submitted to 'psychological torture' by incessant, insidious interrogations. One of them was incarcerated in solitary confinement and finally the hospital was robbed and pillaged.

All the educational and social efforts for the Montagnard race, from the kindergarten to the university students' hostel in Saigon which was in the course of being established, right through the primary, secondary and technical schools all were closed or plundered.

The refugees, having fled from communism during the past years, were categorized as 'enemies of the people' and treated as such. Twenty thousand of them were obliged to return—on foot in the majority of cases—to their old villages, long ago reduced to ashes. Once more abandoning everything, and with only a simple basket on their back, they left for the hard labour of roadbuilding or the communal rice-fields. Under-nourished, without medical care, rediscovering with shock the cold of higher altitude at the start of the rainy season, they were ravaged by death; we know of 'villages' where the death rate rose to 30 and 40%.

As for the foreign nuns and missionaries, we were quickly put under 'house arrest' in Kontum; we were unable to circulate freely in the diocese any more and therefore unable to practise our ministry.

Not content with reducing us in this way to a powerless state, the new Masters sought to discredit us: accused us of spying, of political aims, of treason and liable therefore for the penalty of death, we were expelled—bishops, missionaries, nuns, doctors—we were all expelled almost in secret and expelled only 'thanks to the clemency of the people'.

Our own plans are still uncertain. I am at present visiting the many centres in Europe where our refugees are located.

I look forward to informing you of our future assignments. ... A Vietnamese Bishop with 65 priests has already taken over. Thus, the curtain falls at the end of one act and rises on another. 'God writes straight on crooked lines', says a Portuguese proverb; His designs are unfathomable!

Just as we set off at the Call of the Master at the time of our youth for the most beautiful adventure that it is given man to experience, so today we are ready to journey through a night without stars ... with heavy heart certainly, but without despair, in hope against hope that nothing is lost, that one day known to God, the star will shine again.

The essential thing that we have planted in the heart of these men is the knowledge of the God of Love: that will not perish.

Abide with us in this hope, praying as brothers who care, for all those of the crucified Churches.

In the name of all our people in South Vietnam and of their missionaries. I am sincerely yours in Christ.

✠ *Paul L. Seitz*

Vien reads from one of his long poems

It is not easy
to be a Vietnamese mother.
In the world one teaches children
how to pick flowers,
and here mothers teach children
how to enter an air raid shelter.
In the world one teaches children
to distinguish the singing of birds from noises,
and here mothers teach
how to distinguish
the sounds of jet fighters B7, A7, and F4.
Dear Mary, for 1969 years
you have borne your child in your arms.
Do you know that Vietnamese mothers
become older and more disconsolate day after day?

Vien

THE MIND OF A JUDGE

The Central Prisons are full of 'lifers', prisoners sentenced for life, and others sentenced to long terms. Most of these 'lifers' come in huge bunches in dacoity cases, and probably a fair proportion are guilty, though I am inclined to think that many innocent persons are involved also, as the evidence is entirely one of identification. It is obvious that the growing number of dacoities is due to the increasing unemployment and poverty of the masses as well as the lower middle classes. Most of the other criminal offences involving property are also due to this terrible prospect of want and starvation that faces the vast majority of our people.

Do our judges realize this, or give thought to the despair that the sight of a starving wife or children might produce even in a normal human being? Is a man to sit helplessly by and see his dear ones sicken and die for want of the simplest human necessities? He slips and offends against the law and the law and the judge then see to it that he can never again become a normal person with a socially beneficial job of work. They help to produce the criminal type, so-called, and then are surprised to find that such types exist and multiply. . . .

Must the State always be based on force and violence, or will the day come when this element of compulsion is reduced to a minimum and almost fades away? That day, if it ever comes, is still far off. Meanwhile the violence of the governing group produces the violence of other groups that seek to oust it. It is a vicious circle, violence breeding violence, and on ethical grounds there is little to choose between the two violences. It always seems curious to me how the governing group in a State, basing itself on an extremity of violence, objects on moral or ethical grounds to the force or violence of others. On practical grounds of self-protection they have reason to object, but why drag in morality and ethics? State violence is preferable to private violence in many ways, for one major violence is far better than numerous petty private violences. State violence is also likely to be more or less ordered violence, and thus preferable to the disorderly violence of private groups and individuals, for even in violence order is better than disorder except that this makes the State more efficient in its violence and powers of compulsion. But when a State goes off the rails completely and begins to indulge in disorderly violence, then indeed it is a terrible thing, and no private or individual effort can compete with it in horror and brutality.

'You must live in a chaos if you would give birth to a dancing star,' says Nietzsche. Must it be so? Is there no other way? The old difficulty of the humanist is ever cropping up, his disgust at force and violence and cruelty, and yet his inability to overcome these by merely standing by and looking on. That is the recurring theme of Ernst Toller's plays:

> The sword, as ever, is a shift of fools
> To hide their folly.
> By force, the smoky torch of violence,
> We shall not find the way.

Yet force and violence reign triumphant today everywhere. Only in our country has a noble effort been made to combat them by means other than those of force. The inspiration of that effort, and of the leader who lifted us out of our petty selves by his matchless purity of outlook still remains, though the ultimate outcome be shrouded in darkness.

But these are big questions beyond the power even of judges. We may not perhaps be able to find an answer to them in our time; or, finding an answer, be unable to impress it on wayward humanity. Meanwhile, the smaller questions and problems pursue us and we cannot ignore them. We come back to the job of the judge and the prison governor, and we can say this, at least with certainty: that the deliberate infliction of punishment or torture of the mind or body is not the way to reform anyone, that though this may break or twist the victim it will not mend him, that it is much more likely to brutalize and deform him who inflicts it. For the inevitable effect of cruelty and torture is to degrade both the sufferer and the persons who cause the suffering.

Jawaharlal Nehru

THE WOMAN WHO COULD NOT DIE (1)

'It is morning, the day is here again, Citizen. Get up. You must get up. We must take you to the wash-place. Do get up. Wake up, it is morning.' The growing, wondering horror in his

eyes causes me to bound over the chasm that yawns between
us. The mental effort of the leap is so overpowering that it
makes the muscles of my body contract. I sit up with a jerk.
Bolt upright. My head swims. My breath comes in snatches.
But the sad and frightened child must be reassured immediately. I strive desperately to look ordinary, to sound quite
ordinary too.

'Yes. I thank you. I shall get dressed now. I shan't take
long.'

His eyes shudder all over my face once more. Then he goes.
Is this madness?

I try to look life squarely in the face.

They say they will kill us both. If they do—so much the
better after all—one gets so weary! But what if they do not?
Nicolay is not the man to get unhinged under any circumstances. He is also not the man to die easily or to be shattered
easily by anything. Yet if I let myself die of this, or if I go out of
my mind here, that will shatter him profoundly: for life, no
matter how long he may live.

So it is clear that I must not die unless they kill me, and
above all I must not lose my reason. But if I refrain from
dreaming dreams that are speedily becoming my masters
instead of remaining my slaves, I shall have to think as *they*
want me to. I refuse to do that! I refuse to be forced into self-
torture. My mind and spirit are free. Why should they torment
themselves or me? Perhaps I could make objective stories of my
too vivid subjective dreams. It seems the only thing.

Having come to this resolution, I drowse all day in the
hushed grey twilight of my cell.

When evening comes and the light is switched on, anxiety
and foreboding awaken in the Inner. Above me, to the right of
me, to the left of me, wherever I direct my attention in this
immense building, men, agonized by what the Russians call
smértnaya toska (the agony that overshadows the soul when
death is very near), pace their cells. To and fro. To and fro.
The hopeless restlessness of caged tigers and lions is upon
them. . . . How could I enjoy going to the Zoo? How could I
study the movements of caged animals? Sketch them! Some of
the pacing men are wearing heavy boots, others creaky shoes.

That thud-thud over there is the sound of a heavy man walking
in his socks.

Somewhere in this stony maze Nicolay too is pacing ...
pacing, thinking ... thinking.

Iulia de Beausobre

PRISON

The waves are dancing on the sea
To the wind's free song.
The cell I have to dance in
Is ten feet long.

Longing trembles from the heavens
That makes hearts still.
My hole is dim with muddy glass
And barred with a grille.

Love with pale and gentle fingers
Softly marks a bed.
My door is made of iron:
To wooden planks I'm wed.

A thousand riddles, thousand questions
Make fools of those who try.
One only have I to answer:
Why I'm here? oh why?

Erich Mühsam

> *Erich Mühsam, German revolutionary poet, in 1934 ... was murdered by*
> *Nazis at the Oranienburg concentration camp.*

THE WOMAN WHO COULD NOT DIE (2)

'He knew a lot, St Seraphim of Sarov! He knew that Russia
would come to *this*. He knew, as many others have known, still
know and will know until the Dark Ages are over, that those
who have become corruptible and cowardly, must suffer. But
with the help of Christ, out of this chaos will be born a race of
men and women utterly incorruptible and perfectly unafraid.
To them, no moral values will be priced and they will look into

the eyes of life and into the eyes of death with equal and uncompromising courage. . . .

'Of this race, incorruptible and unafraid, there will be born another, a race of saints steeped in wisdom and in love. Among them will be born a leader, a man of will, as wise and full of love as the whole of his people, and Christ Himself will point him out and anoint him Czar, the Czar of Holy Russia, by the Grace of God.'

. . . We are so alertly silent that our silence engenders a gentle flutter as of hushed wings. Is it the wings of our soaring hearts that are beating?

Then, through the window there comes another sound. A man is singing. It is a trained voice, low-pitched and very beautiful, without the trace of an effort in it. The song is one of the innumerable plaintive melodies that float over the steppes of Russia.

*   *   *

A Mother in a Siberian prison sings despairingly over her dying child:

It will be warmer anon now,
warmer from day to day,
and the wolves will be slouching away now,
further and further away.
We shall spin songs for our sons now,
strange songs of love and hate,
of their fathers shot dead on the white snow
of their mothers cursed by fate.
All will grow stranger anon now,
stranger from year to year,
and our hearts will grow crystal clear now
the colour of frozen tear.

*   *   *

The door opens. Softly, Severity tells Natalia to 'get ready'. She will be taken before the examining officer.

Ever since she was arrested she had longed for this. You always hope to glean something from a cross-examination. Something about the whereabouts of your husband, or the actions of your parents and friends, or the fate of your children. No such knowledge need ever reach you, but you always hope it might. Natalia had longed for a cross-examination as everyone does, longed to know at last what it was all about, but now she is almost sick with apprehension. She tidies her hair instinctively, throws a shawl over her shoulders and goes to the door, pale as death but unresentful and erect as a good and beautiful queen out of a fairy-tale. Our hearts go with her.

The twilight deepens. The window is shut. We go to the wash-place. We come back. Natalia is still being cross-examined. Sonia sighs: 'Poor Guinea Pig. Poor, poor Guinea Pig!' Caterina goes to the window and surreptitiously makes the sign of the cross out into space, then lies down to pray. Hours pass. Many hours. Sonia and Zoia drop off to sleep. Caterina and I keep the vigil.

At last the door is unlocked and locked again as soon as Natalia has crossed the threshold. Her face is white and drawn. Her eyes immense, haunted, unfathomable. Very erect, she appears to glide towards the table, then pours some cold tea out of the kettle into her mug. She drinks long, with half-closed eyes, as though it were the wine of oblivion. As she moves softly in the direction of her bed our eyes meet. She closes hers and shudders deeply.

'Impossible,' she breathes. 'Oh, impossible.'

'Quite,' I say, just as softly; 'you never could. We must be cut out for villainies if we are to undertake them honestly, intending to carry them through. You couldn't.'

'But, Mother! Is it not her comfort, her happiness that I am kicking away haughtily, smugly placing the comfort *I* derive from "honesty" above her physical well-being, her peace of mind, her happiness?'

'*Happiness*, Natalia?'

'She would never know.'

'Can any of us or ours *not know* anything that matters, ever again? Surely, never again can we think or judge as others do— as if *we did not know*.'

'True.'

'Try to sleep, Natalia.'

'The Christ be with you.'

Next morning, early, while we are still drinking our tea,

Natalia is taken to the examiners again and does not come back
until lunch. Then she sinks down on her bed, exhausted in
body and soul. The smell of food makes her sick. I induce her
to eat a little of my white bread, to drink a sip of yaourth.
Every now and then she shudders uncontrollably from head to
foot. Her hands are hot and parched. This agony is giving her a
temperature. She too will be a physical wreck soon. Her
beautiful face will become haggard, her softly moulded body
will wither. Already she has become perceptibly thinner and is
acquiring the indescribable fixed gaze of the inhabitants of the
Inner.

We have barely finished lunch when the Gollywog comes for
her again. He looks quite upset. We know that he likes Natalia
very much. We all have our favourites among the jailers, as
they have among us, and we seem to have known each other
for very long now, though somewhat one-sidedly.

Shocked and horrified at the protracted torturing of Natalia,
we can neither read nor speak all the long hours that she is
away. She is brought back for dinner, which she does not eat,
then is led away again and remains absent very long.

. . . When Natalia re-enters the cell at last she is startlingly
thin and white, with dark circles as large as saucers under
immense eyes that look as though they were a frozen howl of
pain. She undresses quickly, lies down and turns to the wall
without a word to anyone, without even a look. Caterina and I
beseech each other mutely not to sleep. This child is being led
on to her Mount of Olives. It is right that we should watch
with her.

. . . Natalia opens her eyes wide, stares at the spyhole, listens,
drops her feet to the floor and—is crouching beside me.

'Should I,' she gasps, 'Oh, tell me only this—*should* I?'

'No you must not.'

'Mother will die in misery.'

'Possibly, but it would probably come to that anyhow in the
end. You could do the thing once. You could not do it over and
over again. And the moment you failed or even wavered—
where would she be? Besides . . . Christ Himself does look after
the utterly helpless in this country. We know and cannot
doubt, Natalia. Would you fail, betray your heritage?'

. . . They let us sleep quite late in the morning. As we drink our tea, Natalia appears to be miles away, but perfectly peaceful, unflinching and firm.

She is taken before the examining officer again before lunch, but not for long. She comes back with the square under-lip and the treading-on-air step of the indomitable conqueror, ready to accept the most ghastly material consequences of her spiritual victory.

. . . Next day we have a new senior jailer, slight of build, dark and very pale, with immense almond-shaped eyes. Natalia calls him Pearl of the East. The juniors are new too. All except my old fair-haired friend with the eyes of a Byzantine Madonna. But even he is new to the other women. He has not been here since the day that I scared him so. I am relieved to see he is less delicate-looking now. He has filled out a bit and is very tanned. My interest and solicitude amuse Sonia, and she calls him my Son.

The change of jailers coinciding with Zoia's disappearance makes us feel very lonely and brings the four of us extremely close together. Next day all our jailers are utter strangers to us again. And the next. And the next after that. No hope. Every man in all four watches is new, and we mind it very much. We feel forlorn.

Rocking dreamily on her bed, Natalia sings Zoia's little tune just above a whisper:

Not even the wind may know,
not even the gently falling snow . . .

'The affection that binds us is quite unlike any other affection, and no one may know of its intensity. No one could understand. . . . Only the string beneath the bow . . . may know . . . that I love you so.'

'But little child,' says Caterina, 'no one *can* know except those who understand. And those who understand *may* know because they *do* understand. How beautiful is life in all its strange diversity, complexity and fullness, when you *understand*.'

                                                      Iulia de Beausobre

WHY?

   'My God, My Father, why?'
   That was Thy piteous cry,
   Sweet Lord, on Calvary.

   In all perplexity,
   Echoing agelessly,
   Cometh that cry to me;

   When I must stand and see
   Some one apparently
   Suffering uselessly;

   Or worse than any pain
   Look on a life insane
   Where death would seem a gain;

   'Tis then Thy questioning cry,
   'My God, My Father, why?'
   Comforteth me greatly.

   If Thou could'st question so,
   I can through darkness go,
   Contented not to know.

   Yea, I can also see
   How life's dark night may be
   Love's opportunity.

Father Andrew

MARIE AVINOV: HER AMAZING LIFE

Before my return trip to Moscow, a friend in Tambov gave me a most magnificent present: a large, thick sausage. In those hunger-stricken days it was a priceless and mouth-watering gift. But I resisted the temptation of eating it on the spot. I carried it back with me on the train, treasuring it all the way as a surprise with which to regale Nika. Upon my return home I found a telegram: DISCARD SAUSAGE STOP EXPLANATORY LETTER

FOLLOWS. The letter, when it came, brought us frightful news: in Tambov, a gang had been apprehended manufacturing sausages from freshly dug-up corpses and selling them at fantastic prices in the market.

Such acts were merely symptomatic of the appalling conditions that resulted from the communists' enforcement of their land reforms, conditions which I believe were never reported outside of Russia. During the winter of 1920–21, famine and concomitant cannibalism broke out not only east of the Volga where the land was poorer, but even in the Ukraine, that land of magnificent crops. Even Nika, usually so self-controlled, boiled over with outrage when he first heard the news.

Finally, he grew calm and looked at me gravely: 'I can't help remembering that party we gave in early 1917, when Struve gave us his analysis of Marxism.' (Nika was speaking of Peter Struve, the famous Socialist who had been attracted to the Bolsheviks but had shied away upon closer acquaintance.) 'Do you remember Struve's last words, that all his listeners took for hyperbole? "Any country that is trapped by Communism will end up eating human flesh".' Nika fell silent and stared vacantly into space. It would have seemed callous to try to comfort him. How could one smooth over this overwhelming destruction of individual dignity, this rape of the spirit of man?

'Do you recall that case of the priests who were executed in 1919?' Nika murmured. 'Thirty of them were arrested and imprisoned in Moscow, and the old prison guards began treating the holy men with every possible consideration. They were even allowed to celebrate Mass for the other prisoners and the prison staff. But when the Bolsheviks got wind of the situation, they decreed a summary execution without trial. The same night the other prisoners heard the priests being marched out in procession, singing a funeral chant. But when all thirty of them were lined up in the prison yard, still dressed in their ecclesiastical robes, the troops refused to fire. So the Bolsheviks had them returned to their cells, shaved, and dressed in civilian clothes. The following night, they were executed by a Chinese firing squad.

'Now our dead aren't allowed to rest in peace. They are ploughing up cemeteries to make room for new buildings and

sports stadiums. The family down the street has been told "If
you want your dead, come and collect them". It's no rare sight
to see people dragging old coffins through the streets in their
frantic search for new burial places.'

*   *   *

'Yes,' he said, 'I remember November 1937! It was a terrible
month.'

'That's when they took Nika!'

'Yes . . . One hundred thousand of us were rounded up at
that time. I was taken to the Lubyanka, thrown into a crowded
cell, and grilled for nights on end . . . But, ahem! I daresay you
know all about that sort of thing.'

'Yes, but go on. Where did you find *him*? And what condition was he in?' My visitor leaned forward, and in his unexpectedly bright smile I saw a reflection of the Leonid I could
remember.

'. . . You see, our cell was so crowded we could hardly find
room to sit down. We all groaned when the guards opened the
door and pushed in this new group. The new arrivals were all
university professors, scientists, journalists, or literary men—
but, my God! They'd been bruised, beaten, and torn, though I
did not notice all this right away. When I first caught sight of
your husband, he was helping an old professor who was in a
state of hysteria. The poor man could no longer stand on his
own. Your husband must have been badly mussed up himself,
yet somehow he looked as if he'd just stepped out of his room,
freshly groomed. I don't know what it was that gave him his
unruffled, unselfconscious air. When I called his name, he
turned round and his whole face lit up. "Leonid, my poor
friend, are you in this too!" He was about to say more, but at
that moment the stricken professor was deprived of Avinov's
strong arm, and sank sobbing to the floor.' He sighed.

I sat motionless. 'What was his message,' I managed to murmur at last. 'Was it . . . was it a death message?'

Leonid inclined his head. 'All of the new arrivals were shot
that same night.' But just before the fatal call had come, it
seemed that Nika had managed to give Leonid what amounted
to his last words on earth. I shut my eyes, closing myself in to
keep out the shock and absorb the message:

'If you ever get out of here alive, promise me one thing: Find my wife, Maria Yuryevna—my Masha. Tell her I love her, and that my thoughts are with her. Tell her that for me, death comes as a release and a blessing. And tell her to believe this, and to treasure it in her heart.'

'Believe me, Maria Yuryevna,' added Leonid in a low voice, 'the final bullet was a blessing in disguise. With his unusual physique, Avinov might have survived years of torture.'

My face must have gone very white, for he glanced at me anxiously. But how was I to explain the complexity of my emotions—the deathblow of my last hope of ever seeing my beloved again; the distress at my seeming selfishness in holding him in a concentration camp all these years, as if willing him to live on in agony; and the quiet joy of having him, through that final message, back with me and never again to be taken away. But oh! What a long and arduous road a woman has to travel before she can accept as a blessing the brutal murder of the man she has loved above all else in life!   *Paul Chavchavadze*

Extract from a letter written by Marie Avinov's niece reflecting on the above passages:

Depressing as is the thought of 'man's inhumanity to man' which was too often the reason behind someone's incarceration, it is always a reassuring miracle to me that there is something about human nature that not only survives or overcomes adversity but also at times experiences a growth or expansion which might never have developed unless pushed to extremity.

Zoric Ward

THE GULAG ARCHIPELAGO (I)

Throughout the grinding of our souls in the gears of the great Nighttime Institution, when our souls are pulverized and our flesh hangs down in tatters like a beggar's rags, we suffer too much and are too immersed in our own pain to rivet with penetrating and far-seeing gaze those pale night executioners who torture us. A surfeit of inner grief floods our eyes. Otherwise what historians of our tortures we would be! For it is certain they will never describe themselves as they actually are.

But alas! Every former prisoner remembers his own interrogation in detail, how they squeezed him, and what foulness they squeezed out of him—but often he does not even remember their names, let alone think about them as human beings. So it is with me. I can recall much more—and much more that's interesting—about any one of my cellmates than I can about Captain of State Security Yesepov, with whom I spent no little time face to face, the two of us alone in his office.

There is one thing, however, which remains with us all as an accurate, generalized recollection: foul rot—a space totally infected with putrefaction. And even when, decades later, we are long past fits of anger or outrage, in our own quieted hearts we retain this first impression of low, malicious, impious, and possibly muddled people.

There is an interesting story about Alexander II, the Tsar surrounded by revolutionaries, who were to make seven attempts on his life. He once visited the House of Preliminary Detention on Shpalernaya—the uncle of the Big House—where he ordered them to lock him up in solitary confinement cell No. 227. He stayed in it for more than an hour, attempting thereby to sense the state of mind of those he had imprisoned there.

One cannot but admit that for a monarch this was evidence of moral aspiration, to feel the need and make the effort to take a spiritual view of the matter.

But it is impossible to picture any of our interrogators, right up to Abakumov and Beria, wanting to slip into a prisoner's skin even for one hour, or feeling compelled to sit and meditate in solitary confinement.

Their branch of service does not require them to be educated people of broad culture and broad views—and they are not. Their branch of service requires only that they carry out their orders exactly and be impervious to suffering—and that is what they do and what they are. We who have passed through their hands and feel suffocated when we think of that legion, which is stripped bare of universal human ideals.

Although others might not be aware of it, it was clear to the interrogators at least that the *cases* were fabricated. Except at staff conferences, they could not seriously say to one another or to themselves that they were exposing criminals. Nonetheless they kept right on producing depositions page after page to make sure that we rotted. So the essence of it all turns out to be the credo of the blatnye—the underworld of Russian thieves: 'You today; me tomorrow.'

They understand that the cases were fabricated, yet they kept on working year after year. How could they? Either they forced themselves *not to think* (and this in itself means the ruin of a human being), and simply accepted that this was the way it had to be and that the person who gave them their orders was always right. . . .

But didn't the Nazis, too, it comes to mind, argue that same way? There is no way of sidestepping this comparison: both the years and the methods coincide too closely. And the comparison occurred even more naturally to those who had passed through the hands of both the Gestapo and the MGB. One of these was Yegeny Ivanovich Divnich, an émigré and preacher of Orthodox Christianity. The Gestapo accused him of Communist activities among Russian workers in Germany, and the MGB charged him with having ties to the international bourgeoisie. Divnich's verdict was unfavourable to the MGB. He was tortured by both, but the Gestapo was nonetheless trying to get at the truth, and when the accusation did not hold up, Divnich was released. The MGB wasn't interested in the truth and had no intention of letting anyone out of its grip once he was arrested.

. . .'Just give us a person—and we'll create the *case!*' That was what many of them said jokingly, and it was ther slogan. What we think of as torture they think of as good work. The wife of the interrogator Nikolai Grabishchenko (the Volga Canal Project) said touchingly to her neighbours: 'Kolya is a very good worker. One of them didn't confess for a long time— and they gave him to Kolya. Kolya talked with him for one night and he confessed.'

What prompted them all to slip into harness and pursue so zealously not truth but *totals* of the processed and condemned? Because it was *most comfortable* for them not to be different from the others. And because these totals meant an easy life, supplementary pay, awards and decorations, promotions in rank, and the expansion and prosperity of the *Organs* themselves. If

they ran up high totals, they could loaf when they felt like it, or
do poor work or go out and enjoy themselves at night. And that
is just what they did. Low totals led to their being kicked out,
to the loss of their feedbag. For Stalin could never be convinced
that in any district, or city, or military unit, he might suddenly
cease to have enemies.

That was why they felt no mercy, but instead, an explosion
of resentment and rage toward those maliciously stubborn
prisoners who opposed being fitted into the totals, who would
not capitulate to sleeplessness or the punishment cell or hunger.
By refusing to confess they menaced the interrogator's personal
standing. It was as though they wanted to bring *him* down. In
such circumstances all measures were justified! If it's to be war,
then war it will be! We'll ram the tube down your throat—
swallow that salt water!

Alexander Solzhenitsyn

IN MEMORIAM: OLIVER FITZROY

Time is a passing bell that tolls and tolls
The ephemeral moment in the Tower of Now,
Tolls for all lovely things that flower and fade
As voices of evening die on darkening air.

Time tolls and tolls
The darling buds of May and the heart's loves,
The birds whose wings the dawn has dipped in light,
And soon that dawn and light and the flyer fallen,
The heart itself grown cold
And the beauty stolen.

Oh, hear the sorrow for what's past and past,
For the lovely young who died before they knew
Why their brief candles had been lighted up;
For the leaves fallen in the world's cold wood,
For the body fallen by bomb, torture and shellfire,
Or simply for food,
Simply for food.

Oh, hear the tolling for the flower faded,
The hawthorn over;
The floure de luce dead in the moist medowes,
The golden floure of Peru, and the Day Lillie,
Soone ripe, soone rotten, stinking by the night.

Oh, hear the sorrow for the lovers parted,
Oh, hear the tolling for the loved house desolated,
The dear wood blackened and the bird's flight.
Hear too, the dreadful tolling for the hope
That died as night-time with the quick Day Lillies:
And for the dew;
And joy in the green-leaved morning;
And for the turquoise butterfly the child killed
At noon, not caring;
Hear too, the tolling for the singing,
The singing.

But know, you lovers who part
In the dark, obliterating fog of sorrow,
Know, you visionaries, you dreamers,
You mothers who weep at evening for your dead,
Know, you who break from your bodies
In terror, agony and hunger,
You who lament the spring leaves and the Golden Flower,
You who mourn the lost home,
The butterfly, and the child gone,
Know; be comforted—
For with these shadows
Now builds the invulnerable Tower.

Dorothea Eastwood

ONE WORD OF TRUTH

This twentieth century of ours has proved crueller than the
preceding ones, nor did all its terrors end with its first fifty years.
The same old primitive urges rend and sunder our world—
greed, envy, licence, mutual malevolence—though now they
adopt euphemistic pseudonyms as they go, such as 'class
struggle', 'racial struggle', 'the struggle of the masses', 'the

struggle of organized labour'. The primitive refusal to compromise has been elevated to the status of a theoretical principle: it is considered the virtue of orthodoxy. This refusal to
compromise claims millions of victims in eternal internecine
wars, tediously hammering home its message that there is no
stable, universal human conception of goodness and justice,
that all such conceptions are fluid and changeable, so that you
should always act to the advantage of your own party. Whenever any group of workers sees a chance to seize an extra slice—
never mind if they don't deserve it, never mind if it's more than
they need—they up and grab it, and ruin take society. The
extent of the violent swings to and fro within Western society
—or so it seems to an onlooker from without—is so great that
the stage must shortly be reached when the system will become
unstable and must collapse. Violence, less and less restrained by
the legal system built up over the centuries, strides bold and
victorious through the world, caring not a jot that its sterility
has been amply demonstrated and proven throughout history.

It is not only mere brute force that is triumphant, but its
strident justification also. The world is flooded with the brazen
assurance that might is omnipotent while right is powerless.
Dostoevsky's 'Possessed'—figures in a gruesome nineteenth-
century provincial fantasy, one would have thought—are
spreading through the world, reaching countries where hitherto
people could not conceive of such creatures. See how in recent
years they have hijacked aircraft and seized hostages, caused
explosions and started fires, signalling thereby their resolve to
shake and destroy civilization! And they may very well succeed
in their aim. Young people, at an age when the only experience
they have is sexual, at an age when they have no years of
personal suffering and self-awareness to draw on, are enthusiastically repeating the discredited platitudes of our Russian nineteenth century in the fond belief that they've come up with
something novel. The inhuman degradation of human beings
practised by the Chinese Red Guards not long ago has been
accepted by the young as a splendid example to be followed.
The superficiality, the failure to understand the timeless essence
of human nature! The naïve confidence of these young people
who don't know life! 'We'll chuck out this crop of cruel, venal,

oppressive rulers, and we, their successors, will be just and understanding, once we've laid aside our bombs and guns.' But of course they won't. As for the people who've lived a bit and who know a thing or two . . . many of them dare not argue: they try to ingratiate themselves with the young—anything so as not to look 'conservative'. This is yet another Russian phenomenon of nineteenth-century origin! Dostoevsky called it 'being in bondage to advanced nations'.

The spirit of Munich is in no sense a thing of the past, for that was no flash in the pan. I would go so far as to say that the spirit of Munich is the dominant one in the twentieth century. The civilized world quailed at the onslaught of snarling barbarism, suddenly revitalized; the civilized world found nothing with which to oppose it, save concessions and smiles. The spirit of Munich is an illness of the will-power of the well-to-do, it is the usual state of those who have surrendered to materialism as the main aim of our life on earth. Such people—and how many there are today—choose passivity and retreat just so that normality can last a bit longer and the onset of brutishness be put off for another day; as for tomorrow, you never know, it may turn out all right. (But it won't! The price of cowardice will be all the higher. Courage and victory come to us only when we are prepared to make sacrifices.)

Alexander Solzhenitsyn

A STAIRCASE OF SILENCE

A crack ran through our hearthstone long ago.
And from the fissure we watched gently grow
The tame domesticated danger,
Yet lived in comfort in our haunted rooms.
Till came the Stranger
And the great and little doom.

Since Muir wrote the lines, themselves part of his own *mystique*, we have seen the cracked hearthstone give place to the gas-ovens and the holocaust, seen the fissure widen to engulf the ignorant and the learned, the poor and the wealthy, the primitive and the cultured. We have it today in its more

obvious forms equipped with Distant Early Warning devices.
Whether we have faced it in terms of *la perdition* is another
matter. Faced as never before in human history by the need to
rethink on a global scale the social and political relations of
mankind and to observe them more attentively not only across
continents but in the narrower conditions of our factories and
cities, it becomes plainer that the problem is spiritual. Such
things present themselves as the raw material out of which a
new *mystique* must be embodied. They are the primitive soil, 'la
première argile, la première terre', to which Péguy as poet was
constantly moved to return. They hold promise enough of
being fit clay for such enterprise only if the *mystique* is powerful
enough to release the spiritual energy needed for the task of
providing in the approaching unification of mankind for the
freedom of men to grow up as persons.

'A ladder of increasing complexity' is Bronowski's description of the movement of the evolutionary process. It is no less
true of the ladder of devotion. It may well be that great mul-
titudes of men and women have no great wish to exercise the
freedom that John Stuart Mill was eager to give them or to be
greatly concerned with their duties as citizens of a new world.
The problem is as old as Moses. The Hebrew answer was that it
was to be solved not by Leadership of Law external to the
personal lives of men but by the writing of a Law of Love in
their hearts and by the nurturing of personal relations in their
society. Confronting them by a redemptive act of God, it
required men to respond in faith in the working out of that
embodied answer.

Hebrew spirituality rose to that task in declaring a bond
uniting this people with one God and Father of all who loved
righteousness in the minutest details of daily life, who desired
mercy and pity to transform men's dealings with each other.
Christian spirituality imaged the unity of that Godhead as
plurality of Persons whose equality of dignity and mutuality of
love presented themselves as the pattern upon which human
life could and indeed must be shaped. However secularized
that pattern and the demands which it makes upon men may
be today—and the secularization may well be an important
aspect of its entry into human life—the Christian operation

seen in a vastly widened way continues the age-long attempted answer to the problem. Today it must call into its resources not only those that ecclesiastical tradition has retained but what physics, politics, poetry and sociology and a host of other fields of insight may afford.

Alan Ecclestone

DANE-GELD

It is always a temptation to an armed and agile nation
To call upon a neighbour and to say:—
'We invaded you last night—we are quite prepared to fight,
Unless you pay us cash to go away.'

And that is called asking for Dane-geld,
And the people who ask it explain
That you've only to pay 'em the Dane-geld
And then you'll get rid of the Dane!

It is always a temptation to a rich and lazy nation,
To puff and look important and to say:—
'Though we know we should defeat you, we have not the
     time to meet you.
We will therefore pay you cash to go away.'

And that is called paying the Dane-geld;
But we've proved it again and again,
That if once you have paid him the Dane-geld
You never get rid of the Dane.

It is wrong to put temptation in the path of any nation,
For fear they should succumb and go astray;
So when you are requested to pay up or be molested,
You will find it better policy to say:—

'We never pay *any*-one Dane-geld,
No matter how trifling the cost;
For the end of that game is oppression and shame,
And the nation that plays it is lost!'

Rudyard Kipling

THE GULAG ARCHIPELAGO (2)

So what is the answer? How can you stand your ground when you are weak and sensitive to pain, when people you love are still alive, when you are unprepared?

What do you need to make you stronger than the inter-rogator and the whole trap?

From the moment you go to prison you must put your cozy past firmly behind you. At the very threshold, you must say to yourself: 'My life is over, a little early to be sure, but there's nothing to be done about it. I shall never return to freedom. I am condemned to die—now or a little later. But later on, in truth, it will be even harder, and so the sooner the better. I no longer have any property whatsoever. For me those I love have died, and for them I have died. From today on, my body is useless and alien to me. Only my spirit and my conscience remain precious and important to me.'

Confronted by such a prisoner, the interrogation will tremble. Only the man who has renounced everything can win that victory. But how can one turn one's body to stone?

Well, they managed to turn some individuals from the Berdyayev circle into puppets for a trial, but they didn't succeed with Berdyayev. They wanted to drag him into an open trial; they arrested him twice; and (in 1922) he was sub-jected to a night interrogation by Dzerzhinsky himself. Kamenev was there too (which means that he, too, was not averse to using the Cheka in an ideological conflict). But Berdyayev did not humiliate himself. He did not beg or plead. He set forth firmly those religious and moral principles which had led him to refuse to accept the political authority estab-lished in Russia. And not only did they come to the conclusion that he would be useless for a trial, but they liberated him. A human being has *a point of view*!

N. Stolyarova recalls an old woman who was her neighbour on the Butyrki bunks in 1937. They kept on interrogating her every night. Two years earlier, a former Metropolitan of the Orthodox Church, who had escaped from exile, had spent a night at her home on his way through Moscow. 'But he wasn't the former Metropolitan, he was the Metropolitan! Truly I was worthy of receiving him.' All right then. To whom did he go when he left Moscow? 'I know but I won't tell you!' (The Metropolitan had escaped to Finland via an underground railroad of believers.) At first the interrogators took turns, and then they went after her in groups. They shook their fists in the little old woman's face, and she replied: 'There is nothing you can do with me even if you cut me into pieces. After all, you are afraid of your bosses, and you are afraid of each other, and you are even afraid of killing me.' (They would lose contact with the underground railroad.) 'But I am not afraid of anything. I would be glad to be judged by God right this minute.'

There were such people in 1937 too, people who did not return to their cell for their bundles of belongings, who chose death, who *signed* nothing denouncing anyone.

Alexander Solzhenitsyn

SOLZHENITSYN'S PRAYER

How easy it is for me to live with you, Lord!
How easy it is for me to believe in You!
When my mind is distraught
and my reason fails,
when the cleverest people do not see further
than this evening and do not know
what must be done tomorrow—
You grant me the clear confidence,
that You exist, and that You will take care
that not all the ways of goodness are stopped.

At the height of earthly fame I gaze
with wonder at the path
through hopelessness—
to this point, from which even I have been able to convey
to men some reflection of the light which comes from You.

And you will enable me to go on doing
as much as needs be done.
And in so far as I do not manage it—
that means that You have allotted the task to others.

Religion in Communist Lands

THE VOICE THAT THE JUNTA COULDN'T KILL

Victor Jara—a dark, happy Chilean, famous in his own country as a theatrical producer and folk-singer—was killed two weeks before his 35th birthday.

He was tortured. His hands were broken. He was machine-gunned to death.

The circumstances of his untimely and terrible end and the passion of his songs have combined to transform Victor Jara into a growing international legend.

A new Che Guevara who carried a guitar instead of a gun.

In modern Chile, ruled by a Right-wing military junta, it is forbidden to mention Victor Jara's name. But throughout that narrow strip of mountainous land his music is played in secret. In Europe, too, the myth of Jara grows yearly. The Italian city of Turin recently hosted the first international festival devoted to Jara's songs of hope and courage.

A biographical book of Jara songs, published in London, surprised everyone by practically selling out its first printing in under a year.

And in a quiet, white-walled mews house in North London, the English wife of the murdered singer lives with her two dark-eyed daughters and the memory of their father's cruel death.

Joan Jara is a gentle, self-effacing ex-ballet dancer who went to Chile 20 years ago and joined that country's National Ballet.

She met and married Victor Jara there. Their union was short but happy.

'For the rest of my life,' she told me, 'I shall go on where Victor left off. That has become the keystone of my life.'

Victor Jara was born in abject rural poverty in September 1938. He was the son of a Chilean ploughman, but, unlike most children of peasant families, Victor Jara received a full education.

He was fired from early youth by the injustice of Chile's social and political structure. When Dr Salvador Allende led Chile's new Left-wing government in 1970, Jara quit the theatre to dedicate himself to writing and singing songs in the cause of social change.

His credo was simple: 'Whether they are songs of love, of

accusation, of laughter or of struggle, my songs are rooted in the reality of my people, the peasants and workers of Chile.'

In mines, schools and factories Jara's tender resonant voice reflected the spirit and romanticism of the new Chile.

In September 1973, Allende was murdered in the Right-wing coup. Victor Jara and thousands of others were arrested and herded into the giant boxing stadium in Santiago.

During his imprisonment, Jara continued to sing and play for the other prisoners until the guards shattered the bones of his wrists and hands.

A few days later grief-stunned Joan Jara identified her husband's bruised, half-naked corpse in the city's makeshift mortuary . . . 'I was just an ordinary little girl, born in Highbury,' she told me. 'My father was a rather eccentric antique dealer who never actually sold anything. We never had any money.

'I was the last of six children. It was not a happy childhood. I was very shy. I didn't know how to talk to people. When I discovered I could dance, well, it was nice, because I could say things without talking. I never identified with classical ballet. For me, dance had to have meaning, something to say.

'Victor was 22 when I met him. It wasn't a sudden, over-night thing. I only gradually became aware of him. Once I displaced three spinal discs and was in traction for months.

'I thought I would never dance again. Victor came to see me all the time. He was cheerful and patient and refused to allow me to lose faith in myself as a dancer.

. . .'After he was killed, after I saw his body there in the mortuary, full of machine-gun wounds with his hand hanging from his wrist, I was too hurt to feel things properly.

'Now, nearly four years later, I find I can talk to the girls about their father with humour. Victor was a warm and funny person.

'As a father he had a deep belief in the power of example. The years have been very hard, but we've turned a corner somehow . . . we look more to the future.

'They killed Victor because of his music. But they could not silence his voice because it contains the voices of all those who were tortured and murdered with him. When people have seen closely, as I have, what Fascism really means, it is something that changes your whole life.

'Victor's songs are sung around the world, and I know in my heart that the girls and I will return to Chile . . . one day.'

Herbert Kretzmer

THE SIGNIFICANCE OF AUSCHWITZ

After Auschwitz we meet with a common resolution to abandon everything remotely connected with mythology. We must see and apprehend the conflict in its factual light. But the result of our front against all mythical tight-rope walking is not without its own dangers, for it induces a simple, sceptical silence. Even orthodox Christian thought once talked, and still talks, of the 'mystery' of evil, implying thereby that nothing useful can really be said on the subject. We may now go further and drop the word 'mystery' and give no explanation of our ills because we are convinced that there is none. As Job observed centuries ago, without being refuted, we are in a world which cares not for our well-being. The mountains and the sea are notorious for their silence. Some men take heavy knocks while others escape, but only for a time.

Yet this scepticism, too, remains intolerable when we walk over the camp today. Perhaps it may even be the root of our ills, for it paves the way to that moral relativism which suspends all judgements of right and wrong and thereby sustains the rule of terror. A belief in the rule of chance, coupled with that in the survival of the fittest and made respectable by our awareness of the almost endless varieties of custom among the peoples of the world, creates the mentality which understands, condones, and pardons all. Viewed in this light the conflict tends to be relegated to an issue of regional preferences and local climate.

It can hardly be denied that this so-called liberal substitute for traditional theodicy is one of the causes of Auschwitz. Paradoxically this hell was the last thing that any progressive thinkers ever intended. But their ideology came to buttress the slogan 'Everything is permitted'. Even in the nineteenth century Dostoevsky showed, especially in *Crime and Punishment* and in the *Devils*, that by blurring the dividing line between right and wrong and condoning criminal nihilism by means of psychological sympathy, the well-meaning encourage and finally help to establish the power of criminals and demons. When 'everything is permitted' any student may dream of becoming a Napoleon and may consequently justify the killing of a hoarding miser to pay his way. Every aspirant to power may trap and kill his adversary, since the means justifies the end, all being free to pursue their urges . . .

This breakdown of the liberal ethic is not a matter of fiction but highlights the nature of the conflict. Auschwitz was its logical consequence and physical apex. The serious contention that 'all things are lawful' was there seriously carried out. Auschwitz demonstrates the deadly potency of a moral relativism which attracts Christian theologians in their flirtation with the world. Even in the post-Auschwitz era the demand for toleration in all things can be discerned as the precursor to new forms of terrorism. It asks for, and obtains, theological sanction for a new morality which is tailored to all the destructive instincts. Thus the sincerity of progressive reformers enhances the peril to the world and to themselves.

The particular danger of this abuse of tolerance lies in the acceptance of evil as a natural phenomenon. One might almost say that the conflict ceases to be one once it is deprived of a court of appeal.

. . . The lasting significance of Auschwitz for humanity lies in its disclosure of the human condition as something incomprehensible and insoluble in merely human terms. The conflict occurred on a dimension which cannot be understood according to any theories or myths.

Ulrich Simon

Standing naked
Where they have placed me,
Nailed to the target
By their first arrows.

Again a bow is drawn,
Again an arrow flies,
—and misses.

Are they pretending?
Did a hand shake,
Or was it the wind?

What have I to fear?
If their arrows hit,
If their arrows kill,
What is there in that
To cry about?

Others have gone before,
Others will follow.

Dag Hammarskjöld

THE SHEPHERD AND THE WOLVES

In mid-Greece there is a group of small monasteries perched
precariously on steep, spiky outcrops of rock. Until recently the
only way in which supplies from the world and visitors could
reach them was by being hauled up in a net attached by a hook
to a stout rope.

... The Bishop of this rural area was, until his death in
January 1970, Dionysius Charalambos. He was a monk,
because in the Orthodox Church of the East it is the custom for
bishops to be chosen from among the monks, although parish
priests may be married men.... By 1942 he had become Abbot
of his monastery, and as such came into conflict with the
German occupying forces. Against their orders, posted all over
the island, he gave hospitality to an Englishman on the run
from the enemy.

... For all their efforts it proved impossible to get the
English soldier away from the island. He was caught by the
Nazis, and as a result the Abbot was arrested, and interrogated
at Mytilene.

'Have you received any English soldier in the Monastery and
taken care of him?'

I think carefully. Before I have time to answer, a blow on the
head comes my way. My monk's hat falls off and rolls along the

floor. I dare not stoop to pick it up. I admit that I gave him,
the Englishman, hospitality, and try to prevent them knowing
about the others who may have been mixed up in the affair. It's
chiefly this that rouses the Interrogation Officer's rage. He
launches into hitting me without restraint or reason. Much
more he hits me on the hands. Soon they become swollen and
bruised. Still he keeps on. He pulls my beard. He slaps me on
the face. He gives me vigorous punches in the stomach.

When I'm unconscious, they throw me into a prison cell.
Sometime or other I come to. I am completely alone in the
darkness, and the darkness speaks to me with such eloquence.
So what I feared is now a reality. I beseech the Lord to give me
courage and strength. The drama is developing into a tragedy,
because in addition to the beating we have humiliations, spiritual martyrdom, as well today. The humiliations are the kind
only monsters of faithlessness and Godlessness can inflict on a
servant of the Most High.

They take my cassock off me; then the under-robe also. They
leave me in my blood-stained underclothes. They thrash me.
They jeer at me. They hurl abuse at me. Whatever evil they
have heard of any clergyman whatsoever, they heap it all on
me. 'This is what you do . . . and this . . .' Obscenities pour
over me like a torrent. This makes me feel much more pain
than the bodily torture. They satisfy their hatred of the Greek
clergy on my person.

They pick up something they were wiping one of the guns
with. It was done in an instant. They dip it into a black liquid
and daub my face with it. They just kill themselves with laughing.

I fight to keep always clear before me the martyrdom of Him
who 'emptied himself' to stop myself giving way. What an
effort it is too!

O God, can it be that it is drawing near? Is my own 'emptying' drawing near? Help me, Lord, to endure to the end.

After this I am alone again in the pitch-dark cell. 'But woe to
that man by whom . . .'

I confess that I have given hospitality to this person, and I
have helped him as well. But it doesn't satisfy them. They are
trying to force me to open my mouth and to give something

away. In this way they could fill the prison cells and shoot a whole line of victims. Then they could keep putting bodies into sacks and feeding the fish lavishly with human flesh. But if a priest is bound to keep a trifling offence secret, how can he reveal something on which the life of one of his brethren depends?

But think again of the thrashing, the torments, the humiliations. How am I going to endure all that? Supposing they make me give in? Supposing words escape me which can bring others to ruin? You must stand firm, I tell myself. On and on till everything's over? I can't do anything else. Well go on and do it, I tell myself again, do it once for all—in a single go. Yes, I will do it. I will do just that. Once for all—I will shut my mouth. That will mean escape not for me but for the others. My spirit struggles hopelessly. Somewhere it looks for an anchor. In the darkness of its agony, a light begins to shine: 'Forsake me not, O Lord my God: be thou not far from me. Haste thee to help me: O God of my salvation.'

A new character comes on to the scene of the drama—the Commandant of the Gestapo. A real werewolf. It seems they had told him how I had invoked the help of God while they were beating me. So he threatens me, brandishing his stick:

'Gott, eh? By Gott!' And he aims his whip at me.

He doesn't scare me. The day before yesterday Top Brass had said the same sort of thing—and even worse—to me, when he had reached the limit of his fury and had got to the point where he must lash out at someone. My lips had been shut tight from the excessive pain. They only opened enough to whisper, 'My God . . . my God . . .'

Then, full of fury, he says to me, 'Gott in Himmel, there is no Gott there! By Gott!'

Then he shows me the picture of Hitler. But I have not yet endured the whole of my pain.

'God does exist,' I tell him, 'and the time will come when you will seek His mercy.'

The Commandant is a . . . very courteous gentleman. So he asks me through the interpreter, 'Where would you like me to thrash you?'

As if there is any part left unthrashed or unstained with

blood. So much so that I can neither lie down nor stand on my feet. I go to speak to him and he turns his face away. So Mr Lochner laughs sarcastically and says, 'He does not want you to look at him when you are speaking to him, in case your spit showers dirt on him.'

Now the Commandant gets down to it in person and thrashes me himself wickedly showing no mercy.

Thrash as much as you like! We have already passed the frontier of feeling.

It was early evening when I opened my eyes a little. My blood-stained cassock was mattress, bed-cover and pillow all in one.

Death is not far off. They will kill me. I will go to heaven. And there—there is the Lord, surrounded by a choir of Witnesses for the Faith.

Sleep overtook me a little. I woke refreshed. And today's torment was somewhat less . . .

At 9 what has now become the regular interrogation begins. . . . In the end:

'Why did you commit this crime, when you knew the consequences of it?'

'It was my duty as a Christian.' But still they wrote in capital letters: 'BECAUSE I WAS ON THE SIDE OF THE ENGLISH.'

Let it be. I don't want another beating now. I sign.

Bishop Dionysius Charalambos

NOTES FROM THE RED HOUSE

'You'll never get out of here.'
'Out from the madhouse?'
'Yes.'
'Oh well, we'll see.'
'No, you won't get out.'

*   *   *

Now it was the fifteenth. After dinner I would be in the third day of my hunger-strike. I was finding it quite easy. But something else was difficult: to try to get rid of the inner anxiety, the shameful worry about what was going to happen to me. 'Will they let me out or not?' That was what I was wholly engrossed in: not outwardly, but inwardly. And however much I realized that my faint-heartedness was not sensible, that God in heaven saw everything, I could not entirely concentrate on eternity and become quite calm: the madhouse, anxiety for my family, nerves . . . all these things had their effect . . . A nurse came up and asked me to help her with her 'social study': she had an exam tomorrow, and had not been to lectures nor looked at a book. I told her about Campanella, about surplus value, and about Lenin's story of revolution: but inside something was gnawing at me all the time: would I be let out or not? . . . Now they had let out all those due for discharge today . . . It was already two o'clock . . . three . . .

A patient whom I knew ran up: 'I've just seen the list of those going out, you're not on it!' Well, if it isn't, it isn't! Oh the skunks . . . the torturers! It was four o'clock now. They were getting ready for exercise, and I was putting on my coat too. No one was discharged at this time of day. I went into the yard with everyone else.

'Genmikh!'—I heard Alla's voice. Where was she? I looked round. She was sitting on the bench at the entrance to our red house.

'Genmikh! Herman Leonidovich told me that perhaps they would still be able to let you out today. He's with Maslyayeva—has taken her some papers about you . . .'

They wouldn't allow me to speak to her any more, they took me away with the other patients to the enclosure used for exercise. I walked in this enclosure, sometimes bumping into someone, irritated, tired, anxious.

Would these skunks let me out? After about 20 to 40 minutes a window on the first floor opened and someone shouted:

'Shimanov—go and get dressed quickly! In a quarter of an hour the office will be shut!'

'Shimanov! Shimanov! Run to the doctor! Get dressed!' The nurses walking with us shouted.

But I didn't feel like running. I went slowly up the stairs to the first floor, to 'my' ward, a sister coming after me.

'Run to the office,' said Shafran in his room. 'Your wedding ring and money are there. Hurry, it will be shut in ten min-

utes!' He was, once again, it seemed, adressing me as 'vy'
(polite form of address. Cf. Fr. 'vous') ... at least in Alla's
presence. She was there too.

Accompanied by a nurse I went to the other block, where
the office was. I got my ring and money and went back. In the
section I was given my clothes. I dressed in the empty corridor.
From the 'cheerful' half a sound of loud crying was coming—a
new patient had been brought in in the morning—he had
thrown everything off, and sat on his bed stark naked and
howled without stopping. I dressed and went into Shafran's
office to get the medical certificate.

'Well, I hope you will remember what we've talked about
here?' said Herman Leonidovich as he held out the certificate
to me.

'Yes, of course, Herman Leonidovich,—I will remember
those conversations.'

Alla and I went out of the hospital. Everywhere there were
people; it was the end of the working day. The sun was still
warm, there were queues for kvass (ice-cream sellers) ... There
were the little tubs filled with the cold white ice-cream, 48
kopecks each, which once we had to make.

I was unpleasantly hot in my warm pullover, and still under
the strain of the past days ... In my pocket were papers, notes
from the red house, which I would have to get into shape and
publish. I had written them, hiding them as well as I could
from the doctors and nurses, because these notes were my only
weapon ... If I landed up here again, they would allow no
message to get through to the outside world.

Alla would come to visit—they would bring out an imbecile
Genmikh, dribbling, giggling ... 'There's been some progress!'
the doctor would say. 'He no longer believes in God. He can
only think with difficulty of course, and can hardly speak ...
but even before, his logic was only on the surface. In reality he
talked nonsense.'

Who knows? Perhaps this is it, the longed-for and unique
happiness on earth—to become just such a dribbling, giggling
idiot who has risen above all misfortune, suppressed all sadness,
found the ultimate wisdom in the simplest and most pathetic
idiocy. To look upon one's doctor as one's priest, to confess to

him one's feelings and thoughts and receive in exchange miraculous pills . . . wasn't it an alluring prospect . . .

God's will be done in everything! Let them drive me out of my mind, or leave me in my senses, all is well and good under the High Heaven. I accept everything that God sends, as a child accepts from the hands of his father: sweetness and bitterness; reason and madness; light and darkness; any evil and every good.

In the madhouse I often thought how everything in our world is done through the will of God, which is so wonderful that it preserves absolutely human freedom, but at the same time leads a man and all humanity along its own mysterious paths. It is not possible to explain this completely by intellectual effort; but sometimes one has insights and can believe it.

So it was that wicked people put me, a defenceless person, into a madhouse, thinking to frighten me in this way, and to stop the preaching of Christianity . . . Naturally the question arises: are they all-powerful? It seems, at first glance, that they are . . . But . . . they did not succeed in frightening me . . . On the contrary, they disgraced themselves once again before everyone who reads this account . . . Well, they will shut me up again, and it will have the same effect . . . And if they do destroy me, a saint may indeed be made of me, for all I know. Not by my deserts—I have none—but through the crimes of my tormenters. And it is not even certain which would be worst for them—to kill me, shut me up in a madhouse or leave me in peace. Where is their absolute power?

This tiny example will not explain the infinite mystery of everything, but it gives me a transparent hint about the relation of human freedom to the Divine Purpose. Every activity gives birth to a mysterious counteractivity, which one may not understand, may not even notice, but which nevertheless balances and directs the course of things, so that everything goes along the mysterious path pre-ordained by God.

G. M. Shimanov

THE MOTHER'S SON

I have a dream—a dreadful dream—
    A dream that is never done.
I watch a man go out of his mind,
    And he is My Mother's Son.

They pushed him into a Mental Home,
    And that is like the grave:
For they do not let you sleep upstairs,
    And you aren't allowed to shave.

And it was *not* disease or crime
    Which got him landed there,
But because They laid on My Mother's Son
    More than a man could bear.

What with noise, and fear of death,
    Waking, and wounds and cold,
They filled the Cup for My Mother's Son
    Fuller than it could hold.

They broke his body and his mind
    And yet They made him live,
And They asked more of My Mother's Son
    Than any man could give.

For, just because he had not died,
    Nor been discharged nor sick.
They dragged it out with My Mother's Son
    Longer than he could stick . . .

And no one knows when he'll get well—
    So, there he'll have to be:
And, 'spite of the beard in the looking glass,
    I know that man is me!

Rudyard Kipling

Men of great sanctity have sometimes been formed in conditions aimed at their destruction. The Soviet labour camps which in the 1930s swallowed up thousands of human beings, also produced some of the twentieth-century's saints. Few of the Russian Orthodox bishops active in the 1920s were still alive at the end of the 1930s. 'No one lives through life without his Gethsemane or his Golgotha,' wrote Bishop German whilst in exile. He was able to see his situation as the way of salvation, of fulfilment, and in his letters encouraged his spiritual daughter to accept all the problems and difficulties surrounding her life as God-given, for 'God leads man to his spiritual goals by paths which from outside have an unpleasant and unhappy character'.

. . . Bishop Afanasi is another saintly man whose life continues to inspire the faithful in the USSR.

In June 1921 he was made a bishop. Between March and September 1922 he was arrested four times and then exiled for two years. In exile he celebrated the liturgy every day, and every day he wrote to his mother in Vladimir letters which upheld her and many of his flock. In January 1925 he returned to Vladimir, but at the end of 1926 the local authorities advised him to retire. He refused and was arrested in January 1927. Accused of belonging to a counter-revolutionary organization, he was sentenced to three years in a labour camp. In January 1929 he was moved to the appalling conditions of a typhus-ridden camp in the Solovetsky Islands. Miraculously he survived and at the end of February, having been pronounced fit, was sent to the Turukhansky region for three years of hard labour. By this time, after suffering from typhus and dreadful hunger, he was hardly recognizable—thin, shaven. After his release he returned to his beloved diocese of Vladimir, where he found another bishop in office and the cathedral transformed into an anti-religious museum. He retired quietly to a small village and served humbly in the local church. In 1936 the authorities began to search for him. He was arrested, accused of creating a secret house-church and sentenced to five years in the White Sea labour camps. Now he had to fell trees. He spent August to October 1937 in the isolation cell, from which a few prisoners were taken and shot every night.

Strangely he survived and at the end of November returned to felling trees. After another spell in the isolation cell he emerged an invalid, weak and coughing. In this condition he had to walk 400 kilometres in July 1941 to a labour camp in the Arkhangelsk region where he remained until June 1942. In November 1943 he was again arrested, moved from one prison to another until, in July 1944, he was transferred to Siberia. Only in 1954 was he finally freed. But the old people's home which he entered proved to be another form of imprisonment. At last in 1955 he was able to retire to a small town, Petushki, in the Vladimir region.

Those who knew him described him as the embodiment of love. He was peaceful, good, kind. He laughed and enjoyed teasing people. During his years of imprisonment he kept all the Church's festivals . . . He would continually repeat the words of John Chrysostom 'God be praised for everything': he would think of all that the prophets suffered and found great comfort in the example of Maximus Confessor. In one letter he wrote:

> There is no change in my situation. I sit by the sea and wait for the weather. I look at all this calmly, in the firm know-ledge that our fate does not depend on earthly rulers, but on Him, who holds in his hands the fate of the rulers themselves. I am comforted by the words of the psalmist: 'I will lift up mine eyes unto the hills, from whence cometh my help. My help cometh even from the Lord, who hath made heaven and earth.'

In his last years his favourite verse from the psalms was 'I am thine, O save me'. He died in 1962.

Religion in Communist Lands

THE TRIAL OF AIDA OF LENINGRAD

On Monday 15 July the third and last day of her trial takes place. Here is what Aida said in her final speech:

First of all I want to say . . . Citizen judges! Everyone knows what a joy it is to have a loving mother. People have different conceptions of happiness and joy in life. For some happiness is a life free of cares, for others their idea of joy is to go to a theatre, etc. But none of this can be compared to the happiness of having a loving mother. This is a special, higher conception of happiness, as everybody knows. I'm telling you this so that you realize that I have the same kind of happiness in being able to call God my Heavenly Father—and suddenly I have come to understand the meaning of this relationship more clearly than ever before. Heavenly Father—this means that I can turn to Him with my needs, tell Him everything, ask Him about everything and entrust my life to Him. The fact that I can call God my Father is very precious to me ... We are God's slaves because we desire to serve God humbly and put ourselves at His disposal. Christ said, 'Henceforth I call you not servants; for the servant knoweth not what his Lord doeth: but I have opened up the way for you. You are friends!' Yes we are slaves and friends and children. Atheism, now there's a really evil slavery. Take this trial. What have I seen in this trial? Once again I have seen that people are increasingly losing an understanding of what is just and reasonable. I've already quoted Lenin's words in my defence speech: 'Of the European countries, only in Russia and Turkey were shameful laws against religious people still in force. These laws either directly prohibited the open profession of faith or forbade its propagation. These laws are the most unjust, shameful and oppressive.' At one time people realized that it is unjust to forbid the propagation of a faith, now they don't understand this. Now they say, 'Believe yourself and pray, but don't dare talk about God to anyone.' To silence one's ideological opponent by force is no ideological victory. This has always been called barbarism.

Procurator: À propos of what is she introducing this quotation from Lenin? Lenin was talking about Tsarist times.

Aida: I don't know whether any parents ever before used to be forbidden to bring up their children according to their convictions, or if so, when. Now they are encroaching on this sacred right of parents. This trial is horrifying but not because you're going to pass sentence on me and take me off to prison. It's horrifying because many of those sitting in the court-room will not realize that it is unjust. I have been telling you why I sent the magazines *Herald of Salvation* and *Fraternal Leaflet* abroad. What is happening in the life of our church is a miracle. In the twentieth century, when atheists are shouting about the extinguishing of faith, a fire like this suddenly flares up. And I wanted everybody to know about this miracle of awakening. The Church upholds truth and fights for the truth.

Judge: You are not to talk about the church; talk about yourself.

Aida: I'll talk about myself in a minute. The Church's struggle is not to be understood as some political battle. The Church's struggle is to stand in the way of truth and follow the Lord straight-forwardly, regardless of everything else. When the church is fighting I can't remain uninvolved. One can be a militant atheist or a non-militant atheist, one can be simply a non-believer, indifferent towards both faith and atheism, but for the Christian there is only one course. The Christian can't be anything but militant. Once you know the truth, this means following it, upholding it and if necessary suffering for it. I can't be different, I can't act any differently. . . . I'm not in any way an important figure, and I'm not a heroine. I love freedom and would very much like to be free now with my family and friends. But I can't buy freedom at any price; I don't want to act against my conscience. I love freedom, but what good is freedom to me if I can't call God my Father? In prison one particular verse became especially dear to me and precious:

> Oh no, no one in the whole universe can rob the faithful of freedom,
> Though flesh fear the prisoner's chain and prison fill it with dismay,
> For the God of love gave freedom to Thought enslaved by darkness,
> And hitherto the world has not forged chains for her, the liberated one.

The knowledge that my soul and thoughts are free encourages and strengthens me. That is all I wanted to say to you.

Michael Bourdeaux and Xenia Howard-Johnston

PAULINUS TO HIS BELOVED MASTER AUSONIUS

I, through all chances that are given to mortals,
    And through all fates that be,
So long as this close prison shall contain me,
    Yea, though a world shall sunder me and thee,

Thee shall I hold, in every fibre woven,
    Not with dumb lips, nor with averted face
Shall I behold thee, in my mind embrace thee,
    Instant and present, thou, in every place.

Yea, when the prison of this flesh is broken,
    And from the earth I shall have gone my way,
Wheresoe'er in the wide universe I stay me,
    There shall I bear thee, as I do today.

Think not the end, that from my body frees me,
    Breaks and unshackles from my love to thee;
Triumphs the soul above its house in ruin,
    Deathless, begot of immortality.

Still must she keep her senses and affections,
    Hold them as dear as life itself to be.
Could she choose death, then might she choose forgetting:
    Living, remembering, to eternity.

                                                    Helen Waddell

CORRECTIVE LABOUR CAMP 'CHAPECHANKA'

I noticed in the camp that the families of many of those who
found themselves in prison would break up. You would see how
first one man would receive an official divorce from his wife,
and then another's wife would write that she was no longer
waiting for him and had a new family. It was hard to watch the
increasing spiritual suffering of these men.

Yes, it is certainly hard to live without the Lord. However
the example of faith and steadfastness of the wives of the

Christian prisoners called forth the wonder and admiration of many prisoners. Even in their letters the believers' wives not only did not reproach their husbands with the increase of their family troubles in connection with their arrest, but on the contrary, they encouraged them, and urged them to be faithful to the Lord until death. And when the wives of our prisoner brothers came to visit them in the distant northern camps, the whole camp and the entire guard used to talk about it, often with admiration.

Georgi Vins

FRONTIERS OF FREEDOM LIE INSIDE EACH ONE OF US

It has become part of our tradition to state that it is there, across the Berlin Wall, that the islands of the Gulag Archipelago begin, where oppression and violence begin, a world where there is no freedom. Whereas here, on this side of the Wall, we enjoy the ideals of freedom and democracy.

But in reality the frontiers of freedom and lack of freedom are much more complicated. They lie inside each one of us. True, over there we are in a prison. But a man can retain freedom of choice, can he not, even in prison? He can leave prison if he pays the price of betrayal. He can try to escape. He can demean himself to obtain some small favour, or he can fight. There is this freedom in prison.

A man who is not free within himself can find a mass of self-justifying arguments. The temptations of his captive state are created, he may tell himself, by noble aims and humane aspirations.

There is one of these which can calm even the conscience of a hangman: 'If I do not, someone else will. And that someone else will do more harm than I am doing.' How often I have heard this argument from warders, interrogators and prison psychiatrists. I have heard it here from West German industrialists. 'If I do not sell pipes to the Soviet Union my competitors will get the orders. And I have 1,500 men working with me.'

There were 1,500 men 'with me' in the labour camp. But

many of them understood things differently: 'If I do not, who
will? And if not now, when?' If I do nothing now, while they
beat my friend, tomorrow I will accept when they offer me the
job of executioner. Every day in my country a man's entire
experience of life repeats to him, 'Say nothing'. However, in
spite of decades of terror, more and more people are emerging
who refuse to say nothing, because it is exactly here that the
frontier exists between freedom and captivity.

Vladimir Bukovsky

THE SPRING OF LOVE

The mainspring of a clock provides the motive power which
over the days and the years keeps the clock ticking. It is so
finely adjusted, and exerts such a beautifully regulated pressure, that the clock will keep perfect time with the movements
of the sun and stars. Gradually, as we grow and develop, we
become aware that there is such a centre of authority within us,
which lays claim upon us, and keeps us in a true relation to the
rest of the universe. But it has this further character, that when
we are 'compressed, bent, coiled or otherwise forced out of our
normal shape' it gives us 'the property of returning to it'. This
property of resilience is found to underlie some of the most
remarkable human experience, and to throw further light on
the interlocking of good and evil.

In the slums of Calcutta families live in apparent
hopelessness, and in such degradation that their own human
excreta, beyond the resources of the sanitary department to
clear away, ooze out of their closets and block the paths between their houses. Yet in these slums may be seen crowds of
laughing children playing games, and a visitor may be received
into a home where three generations are living together with a
dignity and mutual respect which we in the affluent West have
lost.

In his book, *The First Circle*, Alexander Solzhenitsyn describes the life of political prisoners under the Stalin terror.
They are tortured into confessing imaginary crimes. 'No need
for a detailed study of how his torturers beat him, starved him,

kept him without sleep, perhaps spread-eagled him on the floor and crushed his genitals with their boots . . . "The fact that he confessed proves his guilt"—the epitome of Stalinist justice!' Their wives are harried into divorcing them. Their prison sentences are suddenly and illogically doubled at the moment they should have been released. Yet it is these men who know freedom, and not their jailers or the whole regiment of officials from Stalin downwards who live in perpetual fear. ' "You can shout at your colonels and your generals as much as you like," says the prisoner Bobynin to the minister Abakumov, "because they've got plenty to lose . . . I've got nothing, see? Nothing! You can't touch my wife and child—they were killed by a bomb. My parents are dead. I own nothing in the world except a handkerchief. These denims and this underwear—which hasn't even got any buttons"—he bared his chest to show what he meant—"is government issue. You took my freedom away a long time ago and you can't give it back to me because you haven't got it yourself. I'm forty-two years old. You gave me twenty-five years. I've done hard labour, I know what it is to have a number instead of a name, to be handcuffed, to be guarded by dogs, to work in a punitive brigade—what more can you do to me?" '

The next day a group of prisoners in the special prison, a research establishment for highly qualified technicians, are celebrating the birthday of one of their number with a little alcohol purloined from the chemical laboratory and coloured with cocoa. ' "Think how fortunate we are to be sitting here round this table, able to exchange ideas without fear or concealment. We couldn't have done this when we were free, could we? . . . I will never forget the real human greatness that I have come to know only in prison . . . let's drink a toast to the friendship which thrives between prison walls." '

This same resilience is to be found in the great crises of human history. When Jerusalem was captured by the Babylonians, in 589 BC, the king's sons were killed in his presence, and his eyes were then put out. He was sent with his people into slavery, and it was out of that context of darkness and humiliation that about fifty years later an insight dawned upon one of the Jewish exiles. He began to understand that a

man might perhaps suffer for another man, a nation for
another nation, and be to them a source of healing.

> He was . . . tormented and humbled by suffering;
>   we despised him, we held him of no account . . .
> Yet on himself he bore our sufferings,
>   our torments he endured . . .
> The chastisement he bore is health for us
>   and by his scourging we are healed.

We can all point to individual people who in our experience
have shown this same resilience. A middle-aged woman with a
weak heart whose husband is dying, nursing him for three
months, sitting up with him night after night, and discovering
within herself reservoirs of strength. A sailor in the war, whose
ship had gone down, and when he lands his wife meets him
with the news that their house has been bombed—they have
lost all their belongings and they laugh together with a new
sense of freedom and of belonging to each other. These are
scenes from real life. They point to a spring within the spirit of
man—a motive power—a resilience—a tension which is not a
tension of his own ego, but is able to operate most powerfully
when he 'goes beyond what he knows how to do', and can feel
and know and respond to the tension of the spring within him.

Stephen Verney

NIGHT VOICES IN TEGEL (2)

> Suddenly I sat up,
> As if, from a sinking ship, I had sighted land,
> As if there were something to grasp, to seize,
> As if I saw golden fruit ripen.
> But wherever I look, grasp, or seize,
> There is only the impenetrable mass of darkness.
>
> I sink into brooding;
> I sink myself into the depths of the dark.
> You night, full of outrage and evil,
> Make yourself known to me!

Why and for how long will you try our patience?
A deep and long silence;
Then I hear the night bend down to me:
'I am not dark; only guilt is dark!'

Guilt! I hear a trembling and quaking,
A murmur, a lament that arises;
I hear men grow angry in spirit.
In the wild uproar of innumerable voices
A silent chorus
Assails God's ear:

'Pursued and hunted by men,
Made defenceless and accused,
Bearers of unbearable burdens,
We are yet the accusers.

'We accuse those who plunged us into sin,
Who made us share the guilt,
Who made us the witnesses of injustice,
In order to despise their accomplices.

'Our eyes had to see folly,
In order to bind us in deep guilt;
Then they stopped our mouths,
And we were as dumb dogs.

'We learned to lie easily,
To be at the disposal of open injustice;
If the defenceless was abused,
Then our eyes remained cold.

'And that which burned in our hearts,
Remained silent and unnamed;
We quenched our fiery blood
And stamped out the inner flame.

'The once holy bonds uniting men
Were mangled and flayed,
Friendship and faithfulness betrayed;
Tears and rue were reviled.

'We sons of pious races
One-time defenders of right and truth,
Became despisers of God and man,
Amid hellish laughter.

'Yet though now robbed of freedom and honour,
We raise our heads proudly before men.
And if we are brought into disrepute,
Before men we declare our innocence.

'Steady and firm we stand man against man;
As the accused we accuse!

'Only before thee, source of all being,
Before thee are we sinners.

'Afraid of suffering and poor in deeds,
We have betrayed thee before men.

'We saw the lie raise its head,
And we did not honour the truth.

'We saw brethren in direst need,
And feared only our own death.

'We come before thee as men,
As confessors of our sins.

'Lord, after the ferment of these times,
Send us times of assurance.

'After so much going astray,
Let us see the day break.

'Let there be ways built for us by thy word
As far as eye can see.

'Until thou wipe out our guilt,
Keep us in quiet patience.

'We will silently prepare ourselves,
Till thou dost call to new times.

'Until thou stillest storm and flood,
And thy will does wonders.

'Brother till the night be past,
Pray for me.'

The first light of morning creeps through my window pale
   and grey,
A light, warm summer wind blows over my brow.
'Summer day,' I will only say, 'beautiful summer day!'
What may it bring me?
Then I hear outside hasty, muffled steps;
Near me they stop suddenly.
I turn cold and hot,
For I know, oh I know!
A soft voice reads something cuttingly and cold.
Control yourself, brother; soon you will have finished it,
Soon, soon.
I hear you stride bravely and with proud step.
You no longer see the present, you see the future.
I go with you, brother, to that place,
And I hear your last word:
'Brother, when the sun turns pale for me,
Then live for me.'

Dietrich Bonhoeffer

MAN'S SEARCH FOR MEANING (5)

When we spoke about attempts to give a man in camp mental courage, we said that he had to be shown something to look
forward to in the future. He had to be reminded that life still
waited for him, that a human being waited for his return. But
after liberation? There were some men who found that no one
awaited them. Woe to him who found that the person whose
memory alone had given him courage in camp did not exist
any more! Woe to him who, when the day of his dreams finally
came, found it so different from all he had longed for! Perhaps

he boarded a trolley, travelled out to the home which he had
seen for years in his mind, and only in his mind, and pressed
the bell, just as he had longed to do in thousands of dreams,
only to find that the person who should open the door was not
there, and would never be there again.

We all said to each other in camp that there could be no
earthly happiness which could compensate for all we had suffered. We were not hoping for happiness—it was not that
which gave us courage and gave meaning to our suffering, our
sacrifices, and our dying. And yet we were not prepared for
unhappiness. This disillusionment, which awaited not a small
number of prisoners, was an experience which these men have
found very hard to get over and which, for a psychiatrist, is also
very difficult to help them overcome. But this must not be a
discouragement to him; on the contrary, it should provide an
added stimulus.

But for every one of the liberated prisoners, the day comes
when, looking back on his camp experiences, he can no longer
understand how he endured it all. As the day of his liberation
eventually came, when everything seemed to him a beautiful
dream, so also the day comes when all his camp experiences
seem to him nothing but a nightmare.

The crowning experience of all, for the homecoming man, is
the wonderful feeling that, after all he has suffered, there can
be nothing he need fear any more—except his God.

Viktor Frankl

THE CAGE

Air knows as you know that I sing in my cage of earth,
And my mouth dry with longing for your winsome mouth of
    mirth,
That passes ever my prison bars which will not fall apart,
Wearied unweariedly so long with the fretful music of my
    heart.
If you were a rose, and I, the wandering invisible air
To feed your scent and live, glad though you knew me not
    there,

Or the green of your stem that your proud petals could never
    meet,
I yet would feel the caresses of your shadow's ruby feet.

O splendour of radiant flesh, O your heavy hair uncurled,
Binding all that my hopes have fashioned to crown me King
    of the World,
I sing to life to befriend me; she sends me your mouth of
    mirth,
And you only laugh as you pass me, and I weep in my cage
    of earth.

                                Isaac Rosenberg

THE REAL ENEMY (5)

My attempt at escape had failed. . . . It was ten o'clock on a
sultry night in August. I was awake, listening to the faraway
voice of the loud-speaker at the Gare d'Austerlitz. . . . I heard
hurried footsteps approaching my room. The key was thrust
into the lock and the light was switched on. My visitors were
Adolf, several members of the hospital guard and some plain-
clothes Gestapo men.

   . . . As they approached my bed they made abusive remarks
about me in a sneering, rather than an aggressive, tone. I
caught the word '*Franzose*'. For a moment I thought this was
some kind of heavy German practical joke. But before I knew
what had happened they had handcuffed both my hands to the
iron frame of my bed. When they had made sure that I could
not move, they left the room with an ironical 'Bonsoir,
Monsieur!' . . .

The hour which followed was one of the blackest of my life.
How could I get through the night stretched out in this position? If I had let myself go and struggled perhaps I would have
driven myself mad by the next morning. It was clear that my
plot had been discovered. And as I realized my chance had
gone, despair overcame me. For a long time I lay with dry
eyes, turning over in my mind every possibility of getting out
alive and assessing the chances. Having made every sort of
calculation, having peered into all the slightest possibilities, I

saw that it was hopeless. At that something gave way inside me. Left utterly alone with the wreck of my plans I did what I should have done before, I turned my face to God and asked for help.

It is difficult to describe exactly what I felt. Beneath everything, beyond everything, I felt myself humiliated and defeated. I had been so confident and now my pride had been laid low. There was only one way of coming to terms with my fate if I was not to sink into an abyss of defeatism from which I knew I could never rise again. I must make the gesture of complete humility by offering to God all that I suffered. I must not only have the courage to accept the suffering He had sent me; I must also thank Him for it, for the opportunity He gave me to find at last His truth and love. I remember the relief of weeping as I realized that this was my salvation. Then the inspiration came to me to kiss the chains which held me prisoner, and with much difficulty I at last managed to do this. I am not a credulous person, but even allowing for the state of mind I was in that night, there can be no doubt in my mind that some great power from outside momentarily entered into me. Once my lips had touched the steel I was freed from the terror which had possessed me. As the handcuffs had brought the terror of death to me, now by kissing my manacles I had turned them from bonds into a key. Many times since, when I have thought of death, I have failed to conceive of it as anything other than the end. But in the blackness of that night my faith gave me light. Peace returned to me and I slept quietly, accepting the death which would bring me life.

Pierre d'Harcourt

IN A GESTAPO PRISON IN POLAND 1942

Looking through the bars of my cell window, I saw a gathering of about fifty people, fellow prisoners, Poles. They were of all ages and dressed very scantily just as they had been hurriedly hustled out of their cells, although snow lay deep on the ground of the small courtyard and the temperature was well below zero. Pale and weak they hesitated, standing unsteadily in the unaccustomed freedom of the air and light.

The German guards heavily muffled in their fur coats, plied the metre long whips they carried and formed a straggling column before them. Harsh shouts broke the air and the men began to run around the courtyard, beating a path in the snow with their feet. Those who faltered, straggled, stumbled or attempted to walk, were savagely beaten with the whips and forced to continue. Those who, endurance at an end, fell, were beaten until they rose and staggered on. There was no sound except the shouts of the guards and the thud of the whips. This macabre race went on for fifteen minutes. Then all were made to lie flat on the snow and wriggle round the circuit flat on their bellies. Any who attempted to raise themselves on hands or knees were beaten till they lay flat. All were intent on the play. None of the guards spared a glance for my window where the sight of my face would have caused a shot. Another ten minutes and the prisoners exhausted, chilled, plastered with snow were herded in to lie in their cells and dry themselves as they could. The courtyard emptied ... only the track left remained as evidence that I had not dreamed the scene.

Peter Winton

In November 1941 I was living 'incognito' in a certain town in Poland. ... The Polish armies had long since disappeared, but the people carry on the war. In the concentration camps and prisons, in the gangs of forced labour, or face to face with the firing squads, they remain true to their ally, England. Will England remain true to them?

Grismond Davies-Scourfield

GOING UNDERGROUND

Though still prostrate I had by this time looked around me, to find all my company wearing Ku-Klux-Klan-style white hoods. Their purpose, among others, is undoubtedly to terrify. Yet with the curious calm which had invaded me since this upheaval of my existence began I was not in the least intimidated but even mildly amused and faintly disgusted; ever since then I have found newspaper pictures of masked men somehow obscene. As time went by my captors themselves grew oddly self-conscious of their triangular and slit-eyed hood, and a day was to come when they would ask me to restyle it for them.

By this time material preparations seemed to have ceased, and the soft voice went on to question me. Even at the time many of his questions seemed so irrelevant or inconsequential that I wondered if I was not simply being tried out for consistency and for my reactions to a truth drug. Many questions related to what was hinted might be my almost immediate return to Britain. Was there a direct flight to Britain from Montevideo? By what line? How often a week, and on what days? I dedicated myself to the consciously verbose type of reply, and flooded them with elaborate detail of British United's current overflight of Carrasco Airport, of our hopes for future services, and such further detail till my questioner wearied and changed the subject.

He wanted to know my views on the internal situation, on the personality of the President of the Republic, and on other items on which, I explained, he simply might not expect a foreign diplomat to comment. I went on to repeat more extensively to them what I had already said briefly during my comfortless transit to my present whereabouts—that as proven by the case of my colleague Cross in Canada, my government did not follow the practice of paying ransoms or promoting the exchange of prisoners; that on this precedent the most they could expect in return for my person was the ultimately self-cancelling outcome of a safe-conduct and their own eventual expatriation; that they had made a great mistake by getting me in their hair; that my government knew that these were my views too, and that my wife would by now already have restated them as hers. Meanwhile I would like to know if my personnel were safe and well after the assault, and for what extremity I should brace myself.

Another and somewhat harder voice replied, dealing with my first question by what I came to recognize as a standard Tupamaro technique, which was totally to ignore it. When I insisted and repeated it he simply replied flatly that he could say nothing about my driver and my other staff. As for myself, I could simply satisfy myself with the certainty that the Tupamaros were not assassins. Definitions, I replied, could vary—he knew it, I knew it, but did the dog know it? And in frankness, I added, precedent was not wholly reassuring for my present case. The voice replied that he was glad that I was facing my problem squarely. It was as well that I should know that, though I would not be murdered, my physical existence could not be guaranteed, in a variety of contingencies.

At this point I decided that there had better be a closer understanding. So far as I was concerned, I said, I was dead already. When I felt two bullets go by me in the car I had got my dying behind me; at this point I should add, the voice effectively apologized, and stated that the young gunman had been disciplined by what I later found was the standard system of taking him off operations and downgrading him in the weaponry hierarchy.

'So you don't mind dying?' enquired anew the soft voice. 'Very much so, but a man can only die once. A poet of ours said "I fear not death, yet I fear much to die", and that part of it is behind me. I'm at peace, my family are safe and will be taken care of. So every moment now is a "yapa", a bonus, the baker's dozen.'

My interrogator was intensely amused. 'So you're a fatalist then?' 'Not at all—just a philosopher.' 'And what might be the difference?' he asked. 'Free will,' I answered, on which he declared that this would suffice for my present interrogation, but that I must prepare myself for another and much more substantial one shortly.

Geoffrey Jackson

THE CHARACTER OF A HAPPY LIFE

This man is freed from servile bands
Of hope to rise, or fear to fall:
Lord of himself, though not of lands
And having nothing, yet hath all.

Henry Wotton

If radiance you desire,
Sunshine to the eyes;
Go forth, create it out of nothingness.
Go carve it even from the very rocks.
Draw it from the misty depths.
Of your own heart . . .

Simon Hacoben

Towards the end of the war usually the sermons quite fittingly dealt with some aspect of our return to civilization. The Editor was profoundly impressed by one such sermon delivered by the Non-Conformist 'Padre', Capt. the Reverend E. Platt. Incidentally the padre was successively an infantry Captain in the last war, a lawyer and then he took the cloth. The Germans chucked him into IVC not to minister to our souls (which he did very well) but because he was such a stinking nuisance to the authorities in the Stalags.

Extract from Padre Platt's sermon:

'*I am concerned about the general approach to life which I believe will prevail in the post-war world.* My reason for saying this is the fact of my having lived through two World Wars. I knew the fathers of the men who are fighting the present war. I knew the girls they married who became your mothers. I heard their conversation, and if you are not their natural born sons, then they themselves are here again, doing and saying the same things in the same way as yesteryear. The only way in which you men of this generation can make a better job of your post-war than we made of ours, is by being better than we were. And quite frankly I do not think you are—nor are you more intelligent—nor have you more or higher ideals—or fewer or worse vices. You know things your fathers did not know, but only about theories, sciences, formulae and the like: not about heroism or cowardice, honour, pain, hatred, love, success, failure, happiness, satisfaction, discontent, hope, determination or any of those primal things that constitute immediate reality. At the close of the First World War which your fathers fought and won, one of the politicians coined the phrase "A World fit for Heroes". It sounded fine and appeared to mean something —indeed for many people it became the focal point of all hope and faith. I wondered then and am still wondering what precisely it did mean. If it meant a country from which all perplexity and difficulty were removed by Act of Parliament— if it meant a country which called its sons to deeds of heroism and sacrifice once in a lifetime and afterwards each hero had an assured income, perhaps a pension, and was superannuated from all danger and enterprise, and wrapped for the rest of his life in social cotton-wool: if it meant those things, then such a country would never sire another hero, having plucked from the nation's womb the very seed of heroism. Yet I fear, that was the kind of future visualized by many; and there were some who unashamedly asked for a life of that kind. And is it not true that you have heard much the same wish expressed in this camp? And is there not something in all of us that plans a future on golden shores by a sunlit sea? But it is a level of life with which no healthy-minded man could long be satisfied, and which would revolt an idealist, and which a Christian could only regard as vice. Nowhere in the teaching of the N.T. could such living be justified—"If a man would follow after me, let him deny himself and take up his Cross."

. . . 'Pardon a very trite phrase from moral philosophy, which in spite of its triteness is worthy of notice. It is: "The true norm of living is where the best that is in man confronts the highest that is required of him." That aphorism is not higher than Christian teaching, it is just a philosopher's way of saying in words what Jesus taught in deeds.

. . . 'The call to be builders of the Realm of God has none of the spurious comfort of self-deception about it. Instead it has the hardness of self-discipline and the stern effort of self-denial. Western civilization may shortly have to choose between Karl Marx the Jew and the Jew Jesus of Nazareth. I think the choice finally will be Jesus of Nazareth.'

Ellison Platt

THE REAL ENEMY (6)

It is extraordinary to look back and see how so many men, who had withstood the physical and moral trials of captivity, disintegrated within a few weeks of beginning to live a life of so-

called liberty. Perhaps their whole moral personality had
become mysteriously transformed to face the challenge of the
camp, and, when that challenge had been withdrawn, it
proved incapable of resuming its normal, lower form. All I
know is that often when it became hardest of all for men to
behave like decent human beings they spread their wings and
rose to great heights; and when the strains and temptations
were removed, they sank into the mud.

In their heart of hearts they may have felt, as I did, that in
its way it was the life of the camp that was the true life, the life
that bore witness to what really counted in humanity, the
spirit. The life to which they had now returned was a sham.
They could no longer take it seriously, behave as though *its*
values were the ones that counted; but they had no wish to
challenge it, attack or improve it, and make the great majority
who believed in it disturbed and unhappy. So they tried to
escape from the contradiction, by every means from sex to
drink and drugs. And the drugs and drink killed many of them,
as, I suspect, many of them had hoped.

This, for me is the first lesson of the camp—that it made
beasts of some men and saints of others. And the second lesson
of the camp is that it is hard to predict who will be the saint
and who the beast when the time of trial comes. Men famous
and honoured in pre-war France, regarded as natural leaders,
showed neither spirit nor authority in the camp. Other men, of
seemingly mediocre brains and character, who would never
have been noticed in ordinary times, shone out like beacons as
the true leaders. Under the stresses and strains imposed by life
in the camp, only one thing prevailed—strength of character.
Cleverness, creativeness, learning, all went down; only real
goodness survived.

Sooner or later weakness of fibres was revealed in a man, and
sooner or later it destroyed him. Self-discipline was essential,
and this is the basis of character.

. . . It seemed to me that those men displayed most character
who had the capacity for living on their own and that these
men possessed something which is easiest described as religion,
faith, or devotion. I saw that leadership exercised by Christians.
I saw it in communists too. It was displayed by people who had

no religious faith or political creed in any formal sense, but who still had some inner core which gave them a belief in life, when the rest of us were lost. The camp showed that a man's real enemies are not ranged against him along the borders of a hostile country; they are often among his own people, indeed, within his own mind. The worst enemies are hate and greed, and cruelty. The real enemy is within.

Pierre d'Harcourt

Let me not pray to be sheltered from dangers but to be fearless in facing them.

Let me not beg for the stilling of my pain but for the heart to conquer it.

Let me not crave in anxious fear to be saved but hope for the patience to win my freedom.

Grant me that I may not be a coward, feeling your mercy in my success alone; but let me find the grasp of your hand in my failure.

Rabindranath Tagore

In French a book which gave me particular joy was a biography of the Czech–German poet Rainer Maria Rilke, not least for its 'two-for-the-price-of-one' quality, most of the copious quotations being in the original German. Rilke has always seemed to me a particularly interesting poet, having traits that extend from a fin-de-siècle, Art Nouveau, Beardsley connotation up to the 'Art Déco' and even to the early Existentialist vein of the twenties. More especially, I have always simply liked his verse; and it was with a particular pleasure, even poignancy, that I was able to re-read in captivity his beautiful poem, 'The Panther'. I have wondered since how many captives besides myself, and in how many prison, war, death, concentration-camps, have comforted themselves with this magnificent image of the caged beast, padding round and around behind his bars till, in the end, it is he who is still, whose eyes stare unblinking from some vast pivot of force, out on to a world of prison-bars that is spinning around him. By some curious extension of thought, this inversion of the captive's role by a great poet gave me much comfort, and the certainty that, in the midst of madness and fury, it was I who remained calm and sane.

Geoffrey Jackson

THE PANTHER

His eye has grown so weary with passing by the bars that it holds nothing more. He feels as though there were a thousand bars and behind these thousand bars no world.

The soft walk of lithe strong paces, which turns in the smallest of circles, is like a dance of energy around a centre in which a great will stands stupefied.

Only occasionally is the curtain of the pupil pushed open soundlessly—Then a picture enters, goes through the tensed stillness of his limbs and dies in his heart.

Rainer Maria Rilke

OLIVER PLUNKETT'S OTHER ISLAND

Our Irish neighbours will have cause to be grateful to their new saint for more than one reason. Especially now, he is a reminder of those other Irish, turning the image around to show a facet almost forgotten, yet real as any other, of gentleness, patience and forgiveness.

. . . For Oliver Plunkett spent his last months not simply with the acceptance of mortality, and what lies after it, which is our common lot. The threat, the likelihood alone of sudden death is an unpleasant enough cell-mate. His was the certainty. King David, that expert in the finer nuances of confinement, found his comfort in retrospection and in exhortation—'arrogant men have hidden a trap for me, And with cords they have spread a net—Let burning coals fall upon them! Let them be cast into pits, no more to rise!' But he also solaced his captivity and his fear of death in words that speak much more in the voice of

Oliver Plunkett that I hear—'My eyes are not raised too high; I do not occupy myself with things too great and marvellous for me. But I have calmed and quieted my soul, like a child quieted at its mother's breast.'

Oliver Plunkett never pleaded the status of a political prisoner. Nor however had he a drop of men's blood on his hands . . . there was no shattered flesh and bone save his own to spoil his last sleep, . . . so if there is a sanity as well as a sanctity in cruel death, we find it, in this year of Reconciliation, in this new saint of Tyburn Hill.

Geoffrey Jackson

UNCHANGING MISSION

I end with a reference to the Church in China, taking this from an article by Fr. Martin Jarrett-Kerr which appeared in the January 1965 *Prism*. It is about the Roman Catholic Church in a cruciform situation, down in a glorious way. Here is a prayer-poem written by a student in Chinese:

> *Lord, I am afraid of my fear,*
> *I am afraid of deserting Thee.*
> *Lord, I am afraid of my fear,*
> *I am afraid of not holding out*
> *   right to the end.*
> *Lord, I suffer, and I pray to Thee;*
> *Glorious Thou art, forget me not.*
> *The courage to give my life for Thee,*
> *Give Thou to me, and the love*
> *   which will make me one with Thee.*

The hero is the Catholic Bishop of Shanghai, Mgr. Kiung. In 1952 he addressed his clergy in retreat and these are some of his words. 'Fathers you must no longer entertain any illusory hopes . . . You are condemned. There is no emergency exit for you. Once and for all, you must now look at prison and death full in the face. That is your lot. That is what God, in his loving mercy, is reserving for you. What do you fear? You have nothing to lose, any more. If we deny our faith, we shall disappear, and there will be no resurrection. If we remain faithful, we shall disappear just the same—but there will be a resurrection.' Here is a Church in its Gethsemane—down. Three years later the bishop was arrested and imprisoned. After a time he was brought out before a large crowd in a sports stadium. He was dressed as a criminal, in shorts with his hands bound behind his back. For hours patriots came forward and testified against his imperial crimes, and there were torrents of denunciations. Finally the enemy of the people was pushed before the microphone. Physically ruined and morally broken they expected the usual confession. Raising himself very slowly, with a strong firm voice he pronounced one phrase: 'Long live Christ the King.'

Douglas Webster

Starr Daily, a Dante of modern times, has gone through the depths of sin and has suffered the purging fires before he could emerge from his wood of despair and see the stars. He, too, had a guide through the Nether Regions, one who had also become 'faint voiced through long silence'. The philosophy of Virgil is milk for lambs compared with the strong meat found in the virile philosophy of the old lifer. Here is a character who is as quickening to new life and as inspiring in moulding men as the good Bishop in *Les Misérables*. It is certainly a thrilling experience to sit humbly at the feet of a 'lifer' in a penitentiary to get one's greatest vision of the power of the Love of God that one has ever experienced. Yet that is exactly what the reading of this book will mean for many people.

In *Love Can Open Prison Doors*, Starr Daily shocked a sleeping Christendom into a new realization of the tremendous spiritual power lying latent in Jesus' way of life if we only practise it. It is difficult for those raised in sheltered Christian homes to appreciate how difficult it is to help those who come from the deepest valley of sin and suffering, those who have been immersed in the ditches of Malobolg. In this new book, Starr Daily covers the whole gamut of human needs. Out of the deepest pit of sin and the darkest valley of suffering, he comes to tell us of what he has seen and heard, in words that guide us safely over paths which he, himself, has trod. For not only has

he travelled the road, but he has recorded his experiences and
charted the way.

THIS MODERN DANTE

He saw all, suffered all, was
   healed of all.
Out of the deepest pit of sin
   and the darkest vale of
Sorrows he comes to point
The Way to the Stars.   *Glenn Clark*

The percentage of corrections among first offenders is not
available, but this is certain: every first offender who is not
corrected by the prison system becomes an old offender. Personal
experience and observation have revealed to me that a year in
prison, the most abnormal environment in the world, is just as
likely to confirm as it is to heal the beginning criminal. If he
has sufficient strength of character, nothing the prison can do
for or against him will make much difference. He will check off
his months, go out, and return no more. But if his conscience is
blunted and his character weak, everything connected with
prison life, both good and bad, is likely to contribute to his
further degradation, convince him that he was born to crime,
and thus furnish him with an excuse for anti-social conduct
rather than with an incentive to strive, struggle, and believe in
his inherent possibilities and essential goodness.

I agree with the penologist, however, that nothing can be
done for the old offender—by the prison system alone. In fact,
my experience of many years in prison contains no record of a
single confirmed criminal who was corrected only by punitive
methods. *On the other hand my memory is crowded with confirmed
criminals who were healed while in prison. In every case this was accomplished through the power of religion. . . .*

Prison religion is the square peg in a round hole. But in spite
of the fact that most chaplains are untrained and inadequate,
and that prison religion speaks to convicts in an unknown

tongue, it is the one and only power behind prison walls which can and does redeem the hardened old offender.

But let us return to that cell house we recently inspected. There is a long, straight path of boards, flanked on the outside by an iron railing and on the inside by a stone face in which has been left a string of square holes and barred doors. It is the second of four tiers up. Its name: 'Receiving gallery'.

Behind one of these barred doors is an almost barren cell. Here is where the convict begins his stretch. The impressionable first offender may be made or broken during the two or three days he is confined in one of these receiving cells.

I should say that the greatest opportunity offered the prison system to make a lasting impression on the life of a first offender is to be found on this receiving gallery. Alone in one of these drab, bare cells the unhardened new arrival is certain to become pensive and reflective. The conscience pricks him into shame and grief. Thoughts of his crime press in upon him. He thinks of his parents, friends, relatives, and of the disgrace and sorrow his misdeed has brought to these dear ones. Still tender and responsive to the finer sentiments, he is likewise pervious to constructive sympathy and wise understanding. If ever the touch of Christ was needed in the life of a first offender it is when he finds himself in a cell on the receiving gallery—alone with his thoughts and feelings in a strange abnormal environment—face to face with his conscience on the one hand and the threatening terrors of prison life on the other, both of which he is apt to magnify out of all proportion.

Vividly I recall this situation in my career of crime. I am convinced now, and always have been, that my criminal activities, even with the start I had, could have been ended on the first day and night I spent in the cell of a major prison. Had I heard the right voice then, I am certain that society would have been saved a mountainous toll, and I many years of bitterness and wasted life.

But whose was the first voice to reach me? A stupid guard who jeered at my fear and grief; a keeper who leaned against my cell door and taunted and mocked and menaced me; a free man who sought to wear away my self-control; a paid attendant who tried to infuriate me into an act of insolence, so that he might have an excuse for reporting me and thus getting me started off on the wrong foot. He did arouse my anger and hatred, but he failed to topple my self-control. The hate he invoked in me was so violent that it absorbed all my fears and griefs, along with all my good impulses and intentions.

The next voice I heard was that of a convict who was in charge of this, the most important of all the galleries from the standpoint of official opportunity. But who was this fellow in charge? And how could such a man secure this kind of job? The receiving gallery being the least populated, it became at once the softest of the cell house jobs. Favours have to be shown and special privileges given to stool pigeons, the lowest and foulest of men who feed upon the misfortunes of their own kind. And this fellow, a stool pigeon and degenerate, had thus been favoured with a resultant cost to society in bloodshed, rape, and money beyond any possible computation.

He was a five-time loser to prison; was utterly without conscience or a sense of responsibility. He, too, made a sordid pastime out of my predicament, and sought to influence me in all the pernicious ways familiar to him. In bland, confidential tones he told me how to 'do' time—but not a word of how to 'use' time. During my stay on the receiving gallery this man gave me a thorough education in the deadly convict philosophy of life. I swallowed it. And there was not a word of it which was not aimed at my destruction at society's expense.

Starr Daily

To Tessa, Niederschonenfeld, 30.1.22

Dear,

It is dreadful to be exposed day after day to the monotonous, constantly repeated noises of this place, where the walls are so thin that from the cells above and both sides and below the sound comes to you. Noise in the corridors, bunches of keys rattling, the doors, with their heavy bars of iron, slamming home, roll-calls of names by the warders, shutting of doors, stamping of hob-nailed boots on the stone-tiles or, more dreadful still, the shuffling of rubber-soles. Day after day chains of sound are strangling you with their dissonance.

During the first year I could, by mere will, by a slight effort keep all the noises away and insulate my cell from the sea of noise like an island of calmness. During the second year it was harder: as the psychologists say, one's point of irritability gets lower. During the third year the day came when in helplessness I felt every noise like the lash of a whip on a wounded head. Every time it cost me a tremendous effort to overcome the many hostile noises and to eliminate them from my consciousness—and that takes a good deal of nervous energy.

On his fellow prisoners

. . . Life has grown ugly. There are only a few who want to talk to one another. Do you know that passage in Nansen's book, where he describes how his ship lay for months frozen in the ice; and his men bound round their faces cloths with eye-holes, so that they need not look at one another.

I live with two men, dear comrades, a quiet industrious life.

Hatred rages between the prisoners. And I have no talent for hatred. One would have to enquire into the different reasons for this.

Even to share the same political opinions does not build a bridge over class differences due to upbringing, differences felt strongly when men are living in intimacy. The man to whom that cursed order of society did not open the way of educating himself in the things of the spirit hates the man who possesses that education. Hatred of the 'intellectuals' isn't any longer a rational thing but has become merely instinctive.

Then the man is hated who gets more parcels, more money, who has more clothes, more books, who can earn money from his work in a way that the rest can't manage. (And it does no good to share what he gets with the others.)

Another cause of hatred is membership of different groups in the revolutionary associations; a most important reason is the different attitude to the well-known twenty-one points of Moscow. The adherents in here take the same attitude to their opponents which was so evident outside in the struggles of the day; its character you will certainly have got to know from the newspapers.

The deepest cause is uncontrolled outburst of emotion: the prison-psychosis. It is horrible how it breaks down and lays waste men's souls. One of the most disgusting manifestations I had forgotten. Every revolution attracts people who have not the slightest sympathy for the revolution, but who join it out of lust for adventure, out of muddled, confused moods, out of joy in mere action, out of a passion of self-intoxication, an aimlessness which believes that it has finally found an aim, and from motives whose 'filthiness' I do not want to describe here. In gaol these men become dangerous. They talk to the comrades as if nothing were radical enough for them and it is difficult to oppose them since naïve, trusting comrades come to their assistance, and help them. They want 'something to be done' every day; they accuse the moderate men of treachery. Towards the authorities they take quite another attitude; servile, sneaking, they protest that it is some unfortunate, regrettable accident which has brought them into such company. They are ready to give information on everything which occurs among the prisoners. Yes, even if something is done which slightly traverses the regulations, it is immediately after it has been distorted and perverted, brought by these fellows to the notice of the prison authorities who, in spite of all, *cannot*, I believe, feel any respect for the informers.

But, outside, once they are released? With flags flying they march in the ranks of the darkest reaction. With a useful point of view that some wretched little paper is glad to publish. One of them had a proclamation in the *Augsburger Postzeitung*:

I am healed. In what confusion I was living! *Such* are the famous revolutionary workers, *such* the leaders and so on. Socialism the bane of the Peoples.

Ernst Toller

FIVE STEPS: MOABIT 1934

Five steps forward, Five steps back,
So we go around.
You, man in front, you, man behind,
Don't speak aloud, speak low.

A warder here, a warder there,
Careful, let us not speak,
Have we not learned to understand
When our mouths are shut?

A warder here, a warder there,
Will not discourage us,
And are we caught, no force or fear
Will make our spirit break.

You, man in front, you, man behind
We have much to say to each other,
Yet even when silently walking we know
That the future marches with us.

Kurt Schwartz

THE WALKER AND THE CAGE

I hear footsteps over my head all night.

They come and they go. Again they come and they go all night. They come one eternity in four paces and they go one eternity in four paces, and between the coming and the going there is Silence and the Night and the Infinite.

For infinite are the nine feet of a prison cell, and endless is the march of him who walks between the yellow brick wall and the red iron gate, thinking things that cannot be chained and cannot be locked, but that wander far away in the sunlit world, each in a wild pilgrimage after a destined goal.

... Throughout the restless night I hear the footsteps over my head.

Who walks? I know not. It is the phantom of the jail, the sleepless brain, a man, the man, the Walker.

One–two–three–four: four paces and the wall.

One–two–three–four: four paces and the iron gate.

He has measured his space, he has measured it accurately, scrupulously, minutely, as the hangman measures the rope and the gravedigger the coffin—so many feet, so many inches, so many fractions of an inch for each of the four paces.

One–two–three–four. Each step sounds heavy and hollow over my head, and the echo of each step sounds hollow within my head as I count them in suspense and in dread that once, perhaps, in the endless walk, there may be five steps instead of four between the yellow brick wall and the red iron gate.

But he has measured the space so accurately, so scrupulously, so minutely that nothing breaks the grave rhythm of the slow, fantastic march . . .

All the sounds of the living beings and inanimate things, and all the noises of the night I have heard in my wistful vigil.

I have heard the moans of him who bewails a thing that is dead and the sighs of him who tries to smother a thing that will not die;

I have heard the stifled sobs of the one who weeps with his head under the coarse blanket, and the whisperings of the one who prays with his forehead on the hard, cold stone of the floor;

I have heard him who laughs the shrill, sinister laugh of folly at the horror rampant on the yellow wall and at the red eyes of the nightmare glaring through the iron bars;

I have heard in the sudden icy silence him who coughs a dry, ringing cough, and wished madly that his throat would not rattle so and that he would not spit on the floor, for no sound was more atrocious than that of his sputum upon the floor;

I have heard him who swears fearsome oaths which I listen to in reverence and awe, for they are holier than the virgin's prayer;

And I have heard, most terrible of all, the silence of two hundred brains all possessed by one single, relentless, unforgiving, desperate thought.

All this I have heard in the watchful night.

And the murmur of the wind beyond the walls,

And the tolls of a distant bell,

And the woeful dirge of the rain,

And the remotest echoes of the sorrowful city,

And the terrible beatings, wild beatings, mad beatings of the One Heart which is nearest to my heart.

All this I have heard in the still night;

But nothing is louder, harder, drearier, mightier, more awful than the footsteps I hear over my head all night . . .

All through the night he walks and he thinks. Is it more frightful because he walks and his footsteps sound hollow over my head, or because he thinks and speaks not his thoughts?

But does he think? Why should he think? Do I think? I only hear the footsteps and count them. Four steps and the wall. Four steps and the gate. But beyond? Beyond? . . .

He does not go beyond. His thought breaks there on the iron gate. Perhaps it breaks like a wave of rage, perhaps like a sudden flow of hope, but it always returns to beat the wall like a billow of helplessness and despair.

. . . Only one thought—constant, fixed, immovable, sinister, without power and without voice.

A thought of madness, frenzy, agony and despair, a hell-brewed thought, for it is a natural thought. All things natural are things impossible while there are jails in the world—bread, work, happiness, peace, love.

But he thinks not of this. As he walks he thinks of the most impossible thing in the world.

He thinks of a small brass key that turns just half around and throws open the red iron gate.

. . . That is all the Walker thinks, as he walks throughout the night.

And that is what two hundred minds drowned in the darkness and the silence of the night think, and that is also what I think.

Wonderful is the supreme wisdom of the jail that makes all think the same thought. Marvellous is the providence of the law that equalizes all, even in mind and sentiment. Fallen is the last barrier of privilege, the aristocracy of the intellect. The democracy of reason has levelled all the two hundred minds to the common surface of the same thought.

I, who have never killed, think like the murderer;

I, who have never stolen, reason like the thief;

I think, reason, wish, hope, doubt, wait like the hired assassin, the embezzler, the forger, the counterfeiter, the incestuous, the raper, the drunkard, the prostitute, the pimp, I, I who used to think of love and life and flowers and song and beauty and the ideal.

A little key, a little key as little as my little finger, a little key of shining brass.

All my ideas, my thoughts, my dreams are congealed in a little key of shiny brass.

All my brain, all my soul, all the suddenly surging latent powers of my deepest life are in the pocket of a white-haired man dressed in blue.

He is great, powerful, formidable, the man with the white hair, for he has in his pocket the mighty talisman which makes one man cry, and one man pray, and one laugh, and one cough, and one walk, and all keep awake and listen and think the same maddening thought.

Greater than all men is the man with the white hair and the small brass key, for no other man in the world could compel two hundred men to think for so long the same thought. . . . I shall call him Almighty, for he holds everything of all and of me in a little brass key in his pocket.

Everything of me he holds but the branding iron of contempt and the claymore of hatred for the monstrous cabala that can make the apostle and the murderer, the poet and the procurer, think of the same gate, the same key and the same exit on the different sunlit highways of life.

. . . My brother, do not walk any more.

It is wrong to walk on a grave. It is a sacrilege to walk four steps from the headstone to the foot and four steps from the foot to the headstone.

If you stop walking, my brother, no longer will this be a grave, for you will give me back that mind that is chained to your feet and the right to think my own thoughts.

I implore you, my brother, for I am weary of the long vigil, weary of counting your steps, and heavy with sleep.

Stop, rest, sleep, my brother, for the dawn is well nigh and it is not the key alone that can throw open the gate.

Arturo M. Giovanitti

Arturo Giovanitti was an Italian priest living in America who left the Church and interested himself in the Labour Movement. In 1912 he was arrested during a strike at Lawrence (Mass.) and charged with 'Constructive Murder'. His speech was made at the Salem Court House on 23 November 1912. While awaiting trial he wrote The Walker and the Cage. *His trial resulted in his acquittal by Jury.*

THE ARREST OF OSCAR WILDE AT THE CADOGAN HOTEL

He sipped at a weak hock and seltzer
    As he gazed at the London skies
Through the Nottingham lace of the curtains
    Or was it his bees-winged eyes?

To the right and before him Pont Street
    Did tower in her new built red,
As hard as the morning gaslight
    That shone on his unmade bed.

'I want some more hock and seltzer,
    And Robbie, please give me your hand—
Is this the end or beginning?
    How can I understand?

'So you've brought me the latest *Yellow Book*:
    And Buchan has got in it now:
Approval of what is approved of
    Is as false as a well-kept vow.

'More hock, Robbie—where is the seltzer?
    Dear boy pull again at the bell!
They are all little better than *cretins*,
    Though this *is* the Cadogan Hotel.

'One astrakhan coat is at Willis's—
    Another one's at the Savoy:
Do fetch my morocco portmanteau,
    And bring them on later, dear boy.'

A thump and a murmur of voices—
    ('Oh why must they make such a din?')
As the door of the bedroom swung open
    And two PLAIN CLOTHES POLICEMEN came in:

'Mr Woilde, we 'ave come for tew take yew
  Where felons and criminals dwell:
We must ask yew tew leave with us quoietly
  For this *is* the Cadogan Hotel.'

He rose, and he put down the *Yellow Book*.
  He staggered—and, terrible eyed,
He brushed past the palms on the staircase
  And was helped to a hansom outside.

John Betjeman

(1) Success as Punishment

People point to Reading Gaol and say, 'That is where the artistic life leads a man.' Well, it might lead to worse places. The more mechanical people to whom life is a shrewd speculation depending on a careful calculation of ways and means, always know where they are going, and go there. They start with the ideal desire of being the parish beadle, and in whatever sphere they are placed they succeed in being the parish beadle and no more. A man whose desire is to be something separate from himself, to be a member of Parliament, or a successful grocer, or a prominent solicitor, or a judge, or something equally tedious, invariably succeeds in being what he wants to be. That is his punishment. Those who want a mask have to wear it.

But with the dynamic forces of life, and those in whom the dynamic forces become incarnate, it is different. People whose desire is solely for self-realization never know where they are going. They can't know. In one sense of the word it is of course necessary, as the Greek oracle said, to know oneself: that is the first achievement of knowledge. But to recognize that the soul of a man is unknowable, is the ultimate achievement of wisdom. The final mystery is oneself. When one has weighed the sun in the balance, and measured the steps of the moon, and mapped out the seven heavens star by star, there still remains oneself. Who can calculate the orbit of his own soul? When the son went out to look for his father's asses, he did not know that a man of God was waiting for him with the very chrism of coronation and that his own soul was already the soul of a king.

(2) Clapham Junction

Everything about my tragedy has been hideous, mean, repel-
lant, lacking in style; our very dress makes us grotesque. We are
the zanies of sorrow. We are clowns whose hearts are broken.
We are specially designed to appeal to the sense of humour. On
November 13th, 1895, I was brought down here from London.
From two o'clock till half-past two on that day I had to stand
on the centre platform of Clapham Junction in convict dress,
and handcuffed, for the world to look at. I had been taken out
of the hospital ward without a moment's notice being given to
me. Of all possible objects I was the most grotesque. When
people saw me they laughed. Each train as it came up swelled
the audience. Nothing could exceed their amusement. That
was, of course, before they knew who I was. As soon as they
had been informed they laughed still more. For half an hour I
stood there in the grey November rain surrounded by a jeering
mob.

*   *   *

Well, now I am really beginning to feel more regret for the
people who laughed than for myself. Of course when they saw
me I was not on my pedestal, I was in the pillory. But it is a
very unimaginative nature that only cares for people on their
pedestals. A pedestal may be a very unreal thing. A pillory is a
terrific reality. They should have known also how to interpret
sorrow better. I have said that behind sorrow there is always
sorrow. It were wiser still to say that behind sorrow there is
always a soul. And to mock at a soul in pain is a dreadful thing.
In the strangely simple economy of the world people only get
what they give, and to those who have not enough imagination
to penetrate the mere outward of things, and feel pity, what
pity can be given save that of scorn?

*   *   *

ACCEPTANCE

To regret one's own experiences is to arrest one's own
development. To deny one's own experiences is to put a lie into
the lips of one's own life. It is no less than a denial of the

soul. . . . The important thing that lies before me, the thing that I have to do, if the brief remainder of my days is not to be maimed, marred, and incomplete, is to absorb into my nature all that has been done to me, to make it part of me, to accept it without complaint, fear, or reluctance.

THE BALLAD OF READING GAOL

I never saw a man who looked
    With such a wistful eye
Upon that little tent of blue
    Which prisoners call the sky.

Yet each man kills the thing he loves,
    By each let this be heard,
Some do it with a bitter look,
    Some with a flattering word.
The coward does it with a kiss,
    The brave man with a sword!

Like two doomed ships that pass in storm
    We had crossed each other's way:
But we made no sign, we said no word,
    We had no word to say.

The Governor was strong upon
    The Regulation Act:
The Doctor said that Death was but
    A scientific fact:
And twice a day the Chaplain called,
    And left a little tract.

And once, or twice, to throw the dice
    Is a gentlemanly game,
But he does not win who plays with Sin
    In the secret House of Shame.

Something was dead in each of us,
    And what was dead was Hope.

And the wild regrets, and the bloody sweats,
  None knew so well as I:
For he who lives more lives than one
  More deaths than one must die.

I know not whether Laws be right
  Or whether Laws be wrong;
All that we know who lie in gaol
  Is that the wall is strong;
And that each day is like a year,
  A year whose days are long.

How else but through a broken heart
  May Lord Christ enter in?

Surely there was a time I might have trod
  The sunlit heights, and from life's dissonance
  Struck one clear chord to reach the ears of God.

Oscar Wilde

AN HOUR AT EVENING

Scene: A room in the Manor House. The Queen of Scots and
Mary Seton sit with their embroidery.

Marie. Hark at that curlew, Seton, singing in Spring,
      Pouring his soul in a bubbling long Te Deum
      Of Spring, and his love, and the winds and the wide sky
        space.
      Oh! to ride on a blowing day again! To see
      The bending grasses, the cloud shadows racing:
      To hear the plovers and the curlews calling!
      Precious it is to hoard the happy hours
      As children do, forgetting the dark and the cold—
      To tell them lovingly, bead by shining bead,
      Slipping them through the fingers of the mind . . .
      I have known so much, so much, of happiness.

Seton. Little enough, dear Madame, overmuch
        Of dule and strife and all adversity.

Marie. Happiness lies at the inner root of being—
        We have it or have not, and such as I
        Draw happiness through every living sense.
        Life is my love, and till the vital spark
        Is quenched, I'll feed my soul with little joys.

Seton. I would some brush could paint you now, lit
        With the flowing moment! They are not you, these
          charts
        Of your features men have made. They had as well
        Confine the winds of heaven in a box
        Or trap the laughing seas.

Marie.   I' faith, my Seton
        You are turned poet. Is this the fruit of love?

Seton. Of love for you. I need no stimulus
        To see what all men see—even your foes:
        I who would leave you never.

Marie.   Listen, dear heart:
        My life is over. Nay, question not—I know
        A lion-hearted prince, who shall be nameless,
        Is dreaming, even now, high knightly dreams.
        Myself, I dream and strive and wrestle endlessly,
        Beating my wings against the prison bars—
        How else could I live? How face the nothingness,
        Stark night succeeding sterile day, gaunt year
        Succeeding year? But half my given span
        Is yet accomplished: I, a queen, am queen
        While life endure, and must not seek content
        But ever fight and fall and fight again
        In that high lonely office to which my God
        Has called me. I must be resolute
        Even unto death. This is the weird
        Of the royal-born: only the coward or cheat

Shall dally or turn aside from destiny.
But, Seton, long ago hope fled the field
And left but acquiescence in the fight
And stubborn pride. You are not queen, but woman,
And need the benison of love. Yours not
The baneful destiny, the battle politic.
It is our will that you should leave us now, to seek
That thing for which God made your loving heart.
The bounty of love.

Seton.   Dear Madame, did you then
Find love so sweet?

Marie.   Love is no Lotus Land
Of dream. Love is a stronghold builded, stone
By stone, with patient hands; a sanctuary
Where pride and self are yielded up forever.
What chance had I to build? What chance to learn
That one-ness born of close-shared chequered years
Of joy and sorrow? Love is a giving out
Of self to other self through nights and days
Of passion and tenderness. The lifted cup
Only, was mine; but you may drain the wine.
Your faithful heart was fashioned for the joys
Of home and children, husband and happy love.
                                        Dorothy Margaret Paulin

A SLEEP OF PRISONERS

Adams. Pinioned here, when out of my body
  I made them both, the fury and the suffering,
  The fury, the suffering, the two ways
  Which here spreadeagle me.

                    *   *   *

Adams. How ceaseless the earth is. How it goes on.
  Nothing has happened except silence where sound was,
  Stillness where movement was. Nothing has happened,

But the future is like a great pit.
My heart breaks, quiet as petals falling
One by one, but this is the drift
Of agony for ever.

David.   Now let's hope
There will be no more argument,
No more half-and-half, no more doubt,
No more betrayal. You trouble me,
You trouble me.

Meadows (*in his sleep*). Cain.

                    (David *hides*.)

Cain.   Where is
Your brother?

David.   How should I know? Am I
His keeper?

Adams.   Where is keeping?
Keep somewhere, world, the time we love.
I have two sons, and where is one,
And where will now the other be?
I am a father unequipped to save.
When I was young the trees of love forgave me:
That was all. But now they say
The days of such simple forgiveness are done,
Old Joe Adam all sin and bone.

Meadows.   Cain: I hear your brother's blood
Crying to me from the ground.

David.   Sir, no: he is silent.
All the crying is mine.

Meadows.   Run, run, run. Cain
Is after you.

David.   What shall I do?

Meadows.   What you have done. It does it to you.
Nowhere rest. Cage of the world
Holds your prowling. Howl, Cain, jackal afraid.
And nowhere, Cain, nowhere
Escape the fear of what men fear in you.
Every man's hand will be against you,
But never touch you in quietness.
Run! Run!

David.   The punishment
  Is more than I can bear. I love life
  With a good rage you gave me. And how much better
  Did Abel do? He set up his heart
  Against your government of flesh.
  How was I expected to guess
  That what I am you didn't want?
  God the jailer, God the gun
  Watches me exercise in the yard,
  And all good neighbourhood has gone.
  The two-faced beater makes me fly,
  Fair game, poor game, damned game
  For God and all man-hunters.
Meadows.   They shall never kill you.
David.   Death was a big word, and now it has
                          come
  An act so small, my enemies will do it
  Between two jobs. Cain's alive,
  Cain's dead, we'll carry the bottom field:
  Killing is light work, and Cain is easily dead.

                    *   *   *

Peter (*asleep*). Why did you call me? I'm contented here:
  They say I'm in prison. Morning comes
  To a prison like a nurse:
  A rustling presence, as though a small breeze came,
  And presently a voice. I think
  We're going to live. The dark pain has gone,
  The relief of daylight
  Flows over me, as though beginning is
  Beginning. The hills roll in and make their homes,
  And gradually unfold the plains. Breath
  And light are cool together now.
  The earth is all transparent, but too deep
  To see down to its bed.
            (David, *the dream figure of Abraham, stands beside* Peter.)
David.   Come with me.
Peter. Where are we going?
David.   If necessary
  To break our hearts. It's as well for the world.

Peter. There's enough breaking, God knows. We die,
   And the great cities come down like avalanches.
David. But men come down like living men.
   Time gives the promise of time in every death,
   Not of any ceasing. Come with me.
   The cities are pitifully concerned.
   We need to go to the hill.
Peter.   What shall we do?
David. What falls to us.
Peter.   Falling from where?
David. From the point of devotion, meaning God.
   Carry this wood, Isaac, and this coil
   Of rope.
Peter. I'm coming.
David.   There has to be a sacrifice.
   I know that. There's nothing so sure.
Peter. You walk so fast. These things are heavy.
David. I know. I carry them too.
Peter.   I only want
   To look around a bit. There's so much to see.
   Ah, peace on earth, I'm a boy for the sights.
David. Don't break my heart. You so
   Cling hold of the light. I have to take it
   All away.
Peter. Why are you so grave?
   There's more light than we can hold. Everything
   Grows over with fresh inclination
   Every day. You and I are both
   Immeasurably living.

                  *   *   *

David.   Keep close to me.
   It may not be for long. Time huddles round us,
   A little place to be in. And we're already
   Up the heavy hill. The singing birds
   Drop down and down to the bed of the trees,
   To the hay-silver evening, O
   Lying gentleness, a thin veil over
   The long scars from the nails of the warring hearts.
   Come up, son, and see the world.

God dips his hand in death to wash the wound,
Takes evil to inoculate our lives
Against infectious evil. We'll go on.
I am history's wish and must come true,
And I shall hate so long as hate
Is history, though, God it drives
My life away like a beaten dog. Here
Is the stone where we have to sacrifice.
Make my heart like it. It still is beating
Unhappily the human time.
Peter. Where is the creature that has to die?
    There's nothing here of any life worth taking.
    Shall we go down again?
David.   There is life here.
Peter. A flinching snail, a few unhopeful harebells.
    What good can they be?
David.   What else?
Peter.   You, father,
    And me.
David. I know you're with me. But very strangely
    I stand alone with a knife. For the simple asking.
    Noon imperial will no more let me keep you
    Than if you were the morning dew. The day
    Wears on. Shadows of our history
    Steal across the sky. For our better freedom
    Which makes us living men: for what will be
    The heaven on earth, I have to bind you
    With cords, and lay you here on the stone's table.
Peter. Are you going to kill me? No! Father!
    I've come only a short way into life
    And I can see great distance waiting.
    The free and evening air
    Swans from hill to hill.
    Surely there's no need for us to be
    The prisoners of the dark? Smile, father.
    Let me go.
David.   Against my heart
    I let you go, for the world's own ends
    I let you go, for God's will

I let you go, for children's children's joy
I let you go, my grief obeying.
The cords bind you against my will
But you're bound for a better world.
And I must lay you down to sleep
For a better waking. Come now.
> (*In mime he picks Isaac up in his arms and
> lays him across the front of the pulpit.*)

Peter (*in his bunk*). I'm afraid.
And how is the earth going to answer, even so?
David. As it will. How can we know?
But we must do, and the future make amends.
Peter. Use the knife quickly. There are too many
Thoughts of life coming to the cry.
God put them down until I go.
Now, now, suddenly!
David (*the knife raised*). This
Cuts down my heart, but bitter events must be.
I can't learn to forgive necessity:
God help me to forgive it.
> (*Adams appears as the dream figure of the Angel.*)

Adams. Hold your arm.
There are new instructions. The knife can drop
Harmless and shining.
David. I never thought to know,
Strange voice of mercy, such happy descending.
Nor my son again. But he's here untouched,
And evening is at hand
As clear and still as no man.
Peter. Father, I feel
The air go over me as though I should live.
David. So you will, for the earth's while. Shall I
undo the cords?
Adams. These particular. But never all.
There's no loosening, since men with men
Are like a knotted sea. Lift him down
From the stone to the grass again, and, even so free,
Yet he will find the angry cities hold him.
But let him come back to the strange matter of living

As best he can: and take instead
The ram caught here by the white wool
In the barbed wire of the briar bush:
Make that the kill of the day.
David.   Readily.
Peter. Between the day and the night
  The stars tremble in balance.
  The houses are beginning to come to light.
  And so it would have been if the knife had killed me.
  This would have been my death-time.
  The ram goes in my place, in a curious changing.
  Chance, as fine as a thread,
  Cares to keep me, and I go my way.

Christopher Fry

THE CHILDREN

These were our children who died for our lands: they were dear
  in our sight.
We have only the memory left of their home-treasured sayings
  and laughter.
The price of our loss shall be paid to our hands, not another's
  hereafter.
Neither the Alien nor Priest shall decide on it. That is our
  right.
But who shall return us our children?

At the hour the Barbarian chose to disclose his pretences,
And raged against Man, they engaged, on the breasts that they
  bared for us,
The first felon-strike of the sword he had long-time prepared
  for us—
Their bodies were all our defence while we wrought our
  defences.

They bought us anew with their blood, forbearing to blame us,
Those hours which we had not made good when the
  Judgement o'ercame us.

They believed us and perished for it. Our statecraft, our learn-
  ing
Delivered them bound to the Pit and alive to the burning
Whither they mirthfully hastened as jostling for honour—
Not since her birth has our Earth seen such worth loosed upon
  her.

Nor was their agony brief, or once only imposed on them.
The wounded, the war-spent, the sick received no exemption:
Being cured they returned and endured and achieved our
  redemption,
Hopeless themselves of relief, till Death, marvelling, closed on
  them.

That flesh we had nursed from the first in all cleanness was
  given
To corruption unveiled and assailed by the malice of Heaven
By the heart-shaking jests of Decay where it lolled on the
  wires—
To be blanched or gay-painted by fumes—to be cindered by
  fires—
To be senselessly tossed and retossed in stale mutilation
From crater to crater. For this we shall take expiation.
  But who shall return us our children?
                                        Rudyard Kipling

Chillon! Thy prison is a holy place,
  and thy sad floor an altar—for 'twas trod,
Until his very steps have left a trace
  Worn, as if thy cold pavement were a sod,
By Bonnivard! May none those marks efface!
  For they appeal from tyranny to God.
                                        Lord Byron

A WORLD AWAY. A MEMOIR OF MERVYN PEAKE

'Hallo ... Hallo ... Are you there? Oh are you there? Darling, are you there?'

The line was there ... The possibilities of communication were there, but he was not there.

'Hallo ... Hallo, I MUST go on saying it. I want to see you. I want to speak to you. I want you to answer me ... I want life to be as it used to be. Darling, I'm wilting from the need of you.'

The silence remained, but the line which had been connected for thirty years was frail, and only a few unintelligible sounds could be heard. Despair gave way to the hope which always lay in my mind.

'Darling ... I haven't seen you for twelve years ... Nearly a third of our life-time together. Answer me ... Say something, tell me.'

The silence remained. A crackling of sound ... Noises which were incomprehensible. Silence alone is better than incomprehension. 'Where are you? Where have you gone? I can see you, I can touch you, but you have gone. I am coming to see you. Each time before I see you, I flower ... Each time I have seen you, I die.'

Silence ... Always the silence of a foreign language. Unbelievable that what had been rich, funny, vibrant, had become vacant.

'I am coming to see you. I long to. I have forgotten all now, but the past. The intense joy of it. The madness and the love. I will be with you today.'

There was no sound, but a series of sounds that I have heard but do not understand. Sounds from a world so far away. Is it an empty world ... As desolate as I think it is, or is it peopled with visions. A world exclusive to you? Somewhere, may I share a little of that world?

The silence was now so white ... so untrammelled that speaking could do nothing but violate it.

There was a journey. There was fear that hope was unfounded. There were people. There was no silence. There was nothing, and there was hope clinging like a wet garment, so close to me.

The red buses . . . Strings of them . . . Not silent . . . Took me. There is the waiting and there is never silence. There are the black conductors, and the Cockney conductors, and the Irish conductors. Laughs sometimes, the lusty wit of the office cleaners. The pushing in the North End Road, the burdens of string bags full of cut-price detergents, vegetables, and sometimes even flowers, and I am making my way to you . . . Full of hope. I've forgotten about God. Once he was part of our universe, but he has gone, and the thin line has gone, and there is nothing left but what I know of you. Dark man . . . Funny man . . . Gentle man. Man that made life something new each day. Where are you? Please tell me where you have gone.

You said, 'Each day we live is a glass room.' It is, and it is so easily shattered. Every time when I see you, the glass is in one piece. Each time I leave you it is shattered.

Quickly. I want to see you. Slowly, the door is unlocked. The niceties of life are fulfilled. To the white-coated man 'How cold it is, what a lovely day' . . . 'Good morning' again. Pleasant people who do not know who they have in their possession, so lost and so alone are you.

I go down the cold stairs, and sometimes you have heard my voice, from above, as I say my platitudes. There is a shuffling. I am afraid you are going to fall. I'm always afraid for you. Sometimes there is no sound, and I open your door, to your room, but no longer to you.

Quiet empty room. Quiet empty man. Your eyes look, and do not see. Your ears hear, and do not hear. Your mouth opens and closes and says nothing. Your hands hold a pencil, and let it fall. Your feet move, but do not walk . . . Then suddenly the eyes focus, and they smile. Your voice speaks, and I understand, then it is all gone again. You try to lift a chocolate from the table, and it falls.

I show you your books—that you have written, and which *are* you but you don't see them. I read to you the wise words of the men who judge them, but those words fall upon stony ground. You have gone away and I can't find the way with you.

I want the vision of you, as you were. Are you *you*? Or have you gone?

We sit silently, and then you are restless. You want to move and cannot. You want to speak, and cannot, and the silence no longer has peace in it. The beautiful silence.

I give you a pencil, and I prop a sketch-book in your knee. The pencil falls, and the book drops off your knee.

Sometimes, I make a feeble joke, which used to make our children laugh when they were very small. You do and can still laugh. 'Mary Rose sat on a pin. Mary Rose.'

A Squirrel comes nervously in sharp little movements to stand with its hands crossed outside your window. I throw crumbs to it, and quick as a pickpocket they have disappeared, before the pigeons or the sea-gulls or the sparrows have a chance to battle for them.

Such small happenings now. So little to divert you. Now it is time to go. When I leave you I say 'Goodbye', but goodbye was said many years ago, before we knew we were saying it.

And now you sit amongst others, who sit because they are old. With their pasts known to themselves alone. Is it patience or tiredness which makes them so still? Are they empty of everything? Their eyes seem to be. Are their hearts too?

You look almost like them, and I want to say that you are not. But in the presence of such silent silence, I cannot think of you as any different from the other tired people.

You have gone. I long to see you again.

Maeve Gilmore

O God, who knowest the needs of every heart, look in mercy on all who are beyond human help, all those whose hope is gone, and all those whose sickness finds no cure, all who feel beaten by the storms of life. Grant them Thy strength, and uphold them with the assurance of Thy light and love.

The Bible Reading Fellowship

'These are they who have come out of the great tribulation.'
Revelation 7 : 14 RSV

PART II

FORGIVENESS

Forgiveness is the key that unlocks the door of resentment and the handcuffs of hate. It is a power that breaks the chains of bitterness and the shackles of selfishness. He who cannot forgive others, breaks the bridge over which he himself must pass.

Corrie ten Boom

THE SPIRIT OF HOPE

Those who have known what it is to be freed from great mental distress and brought out again into light and joy by God lose all desire to pass judgement and bear grudges. They feel the same if God has sent them someone to whom they can open their minds. They knew that helpless people are apt to resent the offer of help, don't want assistance. Nevertheless, they came to realize that the helping hand to freedom was fraternally given in God's name. All they want now is to help share their neighbour's troubles, to serve, help, forgive unconditionally and endlessly. It is experiences of this kind that encourages spiritual growth in those who are enabled to open out new horizons of forgiveness and hope for others, to understand their mental distress and help them bear it. Spiritual men of this kind, sealed with the spirit, have existed in Christianity from the beginning. They are an integral part of the Church. In a certain sense, each of us is a man of the spirit, for each of us sooner or later is called to alleviate the mental suffering of his brethren by the spiritual works of mercy, and thereby find relief for his own mind and spirit.

Ladislaus Boros

IMPRISONMENT AT THESSALONIKA

The Abbot Dionysius was sentenced to ten years for his part in helping the English soldier. For a time they remained in the prison at Mytilene and then were moved to another prison in Thessalonika. Here the conditions were harsh. The cells were cold and dirty. Food was scarce. By now the Abbot had made many friends among his fellow-convicts, but one of the terrifying features of the prison routine was the unexpected arrival of prison officers to take men out for execution. This happened almost daily and no one knew who would face the firing-squad next, or why the victims were chosen. One such loss the Abbot felt deeply—the execution of a village schoolmaster.

We wake in peace and quiet . . . Very shortly those condemned to death pass in parade . . . Out of the line goes the schoolmaster, I.P. from Pontus. I never expected him to go. I

am absolutely amazed. I got so angry I could not refrain from
saying something. 'You too then? You too?' I rush over to him.

'Yes,' he answers, and his voice does not tremble and his gaze
is steady. 'Goodbye. Pray that the Lord will give me strength.'

I let him go—without embracing him.

. . . I send Demetrius who's near to find out what he
can . . . They've gone, he says, 'they've taken them. I did
admire their self-discipline . . . Not one of them wept. Perfectly
quietly they turned out their things and handed them over.
Whatever any one had that was valuable, they put their
address on it so it could be sent back home. And when they got
into the Black Maria, Peter was the first to shout, "Courage,
lads, we are Christians. Now's the time for our faith to show
itself." In the end they all shouted together, "We are the brave
fellows. These men here are the cowards. They murder men
from inside prisons. Goodbye, chaps, good-bye." '

I can't wait to note down what I know of these men.

Take the schoolmaster—I.P. He was a good man, full of zeal
and high ideals. He became a teacher with a deep sense of his
sacred mission. He dreamed of an energetic awakening of the
nation from the spiritual lethargy into which it had sunk. With
conspicuous devotion he based his whole life upon the Law of
Christ in the Gospels. He was inspired by it both as head of his
family and as a father. . . . The result of all this was that he turned
up in the 'Lions Den'. And it all came to a sudden end before the
firing squad.

I remember once he pulled a small New Testament out of his
pocket. He opened it and gave it to me to read what was
written on the cover.

'It's my will,' he said. 'It seems to me that now we are in a
situation where we must be prepared for everything.'

I read it carefully two or three times, and thought it all
over—and still I marvelled at it.

To Greece, our motherland, I leave my children whom I
have brought up as Christians, and twenty-five years of con-
scientious work in the arduous but sacred calling of a schoolmaster.

To my beloved children I leave the holy Gospel which alone

can make men happy.

To my life's companion, my dear wife, I leave the care of our darling children.

To my enemies I leave my forgiveness.

There were many others too.

Bishop Dionysius Charalambos

Forgiveness breaks the chain of causality because he who forgives you—out of love—takes upon himself the consequences of what *you* have done. Forgiveness, therefore, always entails a sacrifice.

The price you must pay for your own liberation through another's sacrifice, is that you in turn must be willing to liberate in the same way, irrespective of the consequences to yourself.

. . . When I think of those who have preceded me, I feel as if I were at a party in the dead hour which has to be got through after the Guests of Honour have left.

When I think of those who will come after—or survive me, I feel as if I were taking part in the preparations for a feast, the joys of which I shall not share.

Dag Hammarskjöld

Oh Lord teach us to forgive with Thy forgiveness, Thy understanding, Thy compassion, as we hope to be forgiven. Day by Day.

E.B.

THE WOMAN WHO COULD NOT DIE (3)

The tramp-tramp of our feet sounds drear and hollow up and down and through the maze of passages and staircases. Some bits of the way are stifling-hot, others icy-cold. Some of it is lit up with astonishing brightness. Sometimes the light is very dim. But invariably within the living silence that throbs beyond the walls of the passage and staircases I can feel the tremor of

sme'rtnaya toska (the agony that overshadows the soul when
death is very near). However, as we proceed slowly on the way
back to my cell, the Leonardo insulates me from all this, wrap-
ping me up in the mantle of his thoughts.

A great bond is formed, he says, between the man who is
tortured day in, day out, and the man who day in, day out,
tortures him. Greater than there could possibly be between the
tortured man and a blithe free citizen who understands nothing
because he does not want to see or know a thing. If you ponder
on this you may find the justification for your apparently
absurd suffering.

But, Leonardo, surely there is no justification for a crowd of
well-fed, reasonably strong men bullying a weary, under-
nourished, half-demented woman who doesn't even know what
it is all about.

Don't you know?

Only in a most sweeping, general way. I was not alluding to
that knowledge. If you want to understand, to know the truth
about this sort of thing, you must rise higher and look deeper.
If you do, you can transform the ghastly bond into that magic
wand which changes horror into beauty . . .

It is unpardonable that anyone should be tortured, even
you—if *you* merely leave it at that. But, surely, when you overcome the pain inflicted on you by them, you make *their*
criminal record less villainous? Even more, you bring something new into it—a thing of precious beauty. But when,
through weakness, cowardice, lack of balance, lack of serenity,
you augment your pain, their crime becomes so much the darker, and it is darkened by you. If you could understand this,
your making yourself invulnerable would not be *only* an act of
self-preservation; it would be a kindness to *Them* . . . Look
down right into the depths of your heart and tell me—Is it not
right for you to be kind to them? Even to them? Particularly to
them, perhaps? Is it not right that those men who have no
kindness within them should get a surplus of it flowing towards
them from without?

The whole of me responds with a 'Yes!' like a throb of thun-
dering music. It is so shattering that it makes me stagger. The
jailer steadies me: 'Take care!' He looks concerned, he has the

gentle eyes of a puppy, 'All right?' 'Yes', and we move on.

Drowsily I think: Oh, Leonardo, what if we are both only mad after all, my dear?

Lying on my spiky bed in the glare of my cell. I cannot keep sufficiently awake to think, nor can I go to sleep entirely and let myself forget everything. My body is a long, thin object full of burning pain. Within the whole of the flaming width and depth and length of it an ice-cold pattern is gradually forming. It must be the nerves of this body of mine. They quiver incessantly and tingle as with the bite of frost. The contracted iciness of this network of nerves smarting within my expanding, burning body causes a feeling of pain so intolerably acute that with a jerk I fling the whole icy maze out of me.

Strange. With their iciness all heat has left my body, every vestige of warmth. I am a block of ice. But hovering above me is the network of my nerves, transformed into an intricate system of looking-glasses. In these looking-glasses the whole of my life is mirrored. Also the life of the Inner. The life of the examiners. The life of Russia. The life of Man. All is quite clear. All is most perfectly intelligible. And nothing matters. How can anything matter when all is cold and clear?

Then in one of the looking-glasses I catch the reflected image of the memory of Peace. The warm, the glowing memory of Delightful Peace.

This iciness that grips me is not peace, it is despair. Peace does not sting either with frost or flame. Peace may not give clear sight, perhaps, but it bestows profound insight. Out of the icy wilderness of utter indifference, out of the shattering, all-embracing, chill understanding that wrecks all feeling of security, one flame calls in a limitless dark universe. One flame that still hovers within my iced body, burning bright and straight as the flame of a taper before the Crucifix. Then all in me dies. All except my hearing. And to my hearing there comes a voice:

Out of the confines of eternity I flow to man as light. From man I flow to man as warmth. When the great sun rises in the heart of man, I flow back to the limits of eternity as love. I am the pivot of the human world. I am security. My breath is peace. Seek in the miracle of warmth flowing from harrowed man to harrowed man. Seek and you will find me.

Iulia de Beausobre

'What,' it will be questioned, 'when the sun rises, do you not see a round disc of fire somewhat like a guinea?' 'O no, no. I see an innumerable company of the heavenly host crying, "Holy, Holy, Holy is the Lord God Almighty!"'

William Blake

THE WOMAN WHO COULD NOT DIE (4)

The Governor comes. The door is shut after him, but not locked. A very blue eye stays glued to the spyhole.

Zoia was right. He had been here several times, but as he always asked about my health I thought he was one of the medical staff. It was absurd of me—he is in uniform and has tiny red enamel stars on the lapels of his coat. They indicate his rank—that of General.

He goes up to the window and twists his neck to see the little bit of sky, high, high up. Then he turns round and says, in a studied monotone: 'Have you any complaints to put before the prison authorities, any requests?' He has a large writing pad in one hand and a pencil in the other.

I am half sitting, half reclining on my bed. Zoia is lying on hers. He leaves the window and moves towards the head of her bed. She has to turn right round and lie on her stomach to see him. In a voice that is half annoyed, half perplexed he says: 'Surely you should stand up when I come into your cell.'

Zoia flushes a deep crimson and jumps up. She stands very straight, arms stiffened along the sides of her body.

I am so amazed at never having thought of this before and never having been told about it, that all I do is to say: 'Does one have to?'

He turns away towards the wall and kicks the wainscoting several times lightly with the toe of his boot.

Then in a voice that is hesitant and embarrassed: 'I come here *so* seldom. Don't you think you might?'

Astonished, I stand up with alacrity. My one desire is to put him at his ease. He turns round and comes towards me. There is only a corner of the table between us. We look at each other. And we see each other. In the moment's hush that follows we are both present at the eternal miracle, the lightning quick nativity of human understanding.

I see that it is not only Party discipline that keeps this old and saddened communist from giving up the distasteful work to which he has been appointed. I see that in the unavowed depths of his heart, in the subconscious luminous clarity of it, he knows that it is good and right for him to be Governor of the Palace of Torture, instead of the awful freaks who might be, if he were not. I see him realize with wonder and relief that I am not hostile to him, or to anyone, or anything. The barrier of cruel superficialities has fallen away, and we both know that all things in all eternity will be good and clear between us. If only—*we do not forget.*

And because miracles are sacred and must be veiled, he repeats: 'Any requests?' And I say: 'I forgot to take my sponge with me when I was brought here. Might I have a sponge?'

... After this we are very silent. Emma's all-embracing mood of hostility freezes us. In her presence Zoia and I hardly like to speak to each other, even lightly, of all the agonized tenderness that is breaking our hearts. At last Zoia can stand it no longer. Ever so softly she begins to sing:

Not even the wind may know,
not even the gently falling snow,
only the string beneath the bow
may know
that I love you so. . . .

'The song was written and composed by a young violinist sentenced to five years' hard labour. By chance he and the girl to whom he was engaged were sent to the same concentration camp. They had kept their engagement very secret for some reason. Even the G.P.U. knew nothing of their friendship, so no one stopped the wheel of fate that sent them both to the same camp, at the same time, for two quite different offences. Loose living, although said to be strictly forbidden, is often tolerated by the local camp chiefs, but affection is always persecuted and, when possible, killed. The violinist kept very silent. But his songs were so true to life that soon all men and women in the numerous hard-labour camps of Russia were singing them. Too

soon this drew hostile attention to the sad young violinist.
Someone guessed his secret and separated him from the girl he
loved. He hanged himself.'

Iulia de Beausobre

WE ARE SAD WITH A VAGUE SWEET SORROW

We are sad with a vague sweet sorrow
Whose touch is a scent of sighs;
A flower that weeps to a flower
The old tale that beauty dies.

Our smiles are full of longing,
For we saw the gold flash of the years.
They passed, and we know where they came from,
The deep-deep well of tears.

Isaac Rosenberg

THE SUFFERING OF JESUS

One of the most moving testimonies is that of the young
Danish sailor Kim Malthe-Bruun who belonged to a resistance
group and at the age of 21 was shot to death by the Gestapo on
April 6, 1945. During the four months of his imprisonment he
turned again and again to the figure of Jesus, trying to grasp
what his teaching and his life were all about. In a letter from
January 22, 1945, he wrote:

the teaching of Jesus should not be something that we follow
just because we have been taught to do so ... At this
moment there comes to me, as one of the profoundest truths
I have learned from Jesus, the perception that one should
live solely according to the dictates of one's soul.

The following letter, dated March 3, 1945, reports about
torture that he survived, torture that rendered him unconscious. On the next day he wrote:

Since then I have been thinking about the strange thing that actually has happened to me. Immediately afterward I experienced an indescribable feeling of relief, an exultant intoxication of victory, a joy so irrational that I was as though paralysed. It was as if the soul had liberated itself completely from the body . . . When the soul returned once more to the body, it was as if the jubilation of the whole world had been gathered together here. But the matter ended as it does in the case of so many other opiates: when the intoxication was over, a reaction set in. I became aware that my hands were trembling . . . Yet I was calm and spiritually far stronger than ever before.

However, though I am unafraid, though I do not yield ground, my heart beats faster every time someone stops before my door . . .

Immediately afterward it dawned upon me that I have now a new understanding of the figure of Jesus. The time of waiting, that is the ordeal. I will warrant that the suffering endured in having a few nails driven through one's hands, in being crucified, is something purely mechanical that lifts the soul into an ecstasy comparable with nothing else. But the waiting in the garden—that hour drips red with blood.

One other strange thing. I felt absolutely no hatred.

About three weeks later he wrote:

Since then I have often thought of Jesus. I can well understand the measureless love he felt for all men, and especially for those who took part in driving nails into his hands. From the moment he left Gethsemane, he stood high above all passion . . .

. . . Kim also speaks of a double experience he had when he was tortured: the Gethsemane 'time of waiting' and the death on the cross, which is easy and transports the soul into a kind of euphoria. It isn't the sacrifice that is difficult. That is something 'purely mechanical' . . . What is hard is the 'drops of blood' in the period of waiting. We know from reports of people who have survived torture that the torment of waiting for the crisis calls forth all doubts in the person being tortured.

The person's own identity is shattered, the pain takes away his consciousness of the cause for which he is suffering, and it leaves the person an empty shell. Why shouldn't one reveal the names of friends? Haven't they long since been arrested? Haven't they themselves long since come clean and confessed? Perhaps in his waiting for the scream Kim experienced the same thing. But for him what is decisive is winning the battle against death. He is now stronger, free of hatred. Love unbounded is nearer than before.

It is impossible to distinguish Jesus' suffering from that of other people as though Jesus alone awaited God's help. The scream of suffering contains all the despair of which a person is capable, and in this sense every scream is a scream for God.

All extreme suffering evokes the experience of being forsaken by God. In the depth of suffering people see themselves as abandoned and forsaken by everyone. That which gave life its meaning has become empty and void: it turned out to be an error, a delusion that is shattered, a guilt that cannot be rectified, a void.

Every suffering that is experienced as a threat to one's own life touches our relationship to God, if we use this expression in the strict theological sense. That is, if we don't think of it as an attribute that some people have, like music ability, but as something everyone possesses, as that 'which a person trusts' (Luther). This (non-explicit) relationship to God is called into question in extreme suffering. The ground on which life was built, the primal trust in the world's reliability—a reliability conveyed in many diverse ways—is destroyed.

The experience that Jesus had in Gethsemane goes beyond this destruction. It is the experience of assent. The cup of suffering becomes the cup of strengthening. Whoever empties that cup has conquered all fear. The one who at the end returns from prayer to the sleeping disciples is a different person from the one who went off to pray. He is clear-eyed and awake; he trembles no longer. 'It is enough; the hour has come. Rise, let us be going.' An angel came down to Jesus no more than one comes down to other people—or no less than that! Both perspectives are true; Mark and Luke are only using varied ways of putting the matter. One can say that in every prayer an angel waits for us, since every prayer changes the one who prays, strengthens him, in that it pulls him together and brings him to the utmost attention, which in suffering is forced from us and which in loving we ourselves give.

Dorothee Soelle

THE YOUNG CAPTIVE

Spared by the scythe, ripens the growing ear,
The grape-vine of the wine-press knows no fear,
    But takes what life can give;
And I, who am like them both young and fair,
Although the present moment has its care
    I too desire to live.

Though Stoics with dry eyes embrace their death
I weep and hope; and to the North Wind's breath
    I bow, and raise my head.
Some days are bitter, others sweet no less
And even honey has its bitterness
    And seas their tempests dread.

By prison walls in vain am I oppressed;
Illusion nurtures hope within my breast,
    Her wings remain to me.
Freed from the fowler's nets, the captive bird
More joyously far in the skies is heard
    Singing of liberty.

Is it for me to die? My quiet rest
And quiet waking never are distressed
    By terror of my fate;
But the oppressed, with laughter in their eyes
Seeing me greet the dawn, themselves arise
    With joy re-animate.

Far from its end my path. I cannot stay,
For of the shady elms that flank my way
    I have but passed these few.

The feast of my life hardly have I commenced,
One instant only have my warm lips sensed
   The cup that was my due.

I, who would live my harvest to behold
And like the sun see green leaves turn to gold,
   Ask that my days be long.
Pride of the garden, I have seen the fires
Of morning only, and my heart desires
   Its noon and evensong.

Death, thou canst wait for me. Get thee from here.
Go, and console those hearts which shame and fear
   And cold despair devour.
Pallas has still her verdant bowers for me,
Love, its embrace; the Muses, melody—
   It is not yet my hour.

André Chenier

> *André Chenier was one of the victims of Robespierre. In the prison of
> Saint-Lazare he was inspired by the beauty of Aimée de Coigny, Duchesse
> de Fleury, to write the stanzas of which we have given a very inadequate
> translation. He was sent to the guillotine at the age of thirty-one.*

What has Life lost by the happiness which might have been
his, had he been allowed to go on living? What has it gained by
the suffering he has escaped?

What nonsense I'm talking! Life is measured by the living,
and the number of a man's days are reckoned in other terms.

Dag Hammarskjöld

THE TRUTH IN ACCEPTANCE

The more strongly we affirm reality, the more we are immersed in it, the more deeply we are touched by these processes
of dying which surround us and press in upon us.

. . . Lusseyran depicts what being blind can mean, under
other circumstances when acceptance is not achieved.

'When I was fifteen I spent long afternoons with a blind boy

my own age, one who went blind, I should add, in circumstances very like my own. Today I have few memories as painful. This boy terrified me. He was the living image of everything that might have happened to me if I had not been fortunate, more fortunate than he. For he was really blind. He had
seen nothing since his accident. His faculties were normal, he
could have seen as well as I. But they had kept him from doing
so. To protect him, as they put it, they had cut him off from
everything, and made fun of all his attempts to explain what he
felt. In grief and revenge, he had thrown himself into brutal
solitude. Even his body lay prostrate in the depths of an armchair. To my horror I saw that he did not like me.'

The second situation in which Lusseyran experienced extreme suffering involves Buchenwald, the German concentration camp to which Jacques is deported when he, as a nineteen-
year-old high school student, is leading a resistance group. He
survives hunger, cold, and a period of illness that appears
hopeless and then undertakes tasks for the other prisoners, as in
the 'Defence of France' group. 'We had to make war on the
disease (of doubt and agony hitting the camp because of false
rumors) . . . how were we to hold on to the remnants of reason
in the swirling madness of deportation?'

These are very characteristic sentences. Jacques received
information about the military situation for his cell block. He
gathered, interpreted, and translated the reports. But more
than that 'I could try to show . . . (my fellow prisoners) how to
go about holding on to life. I could turn towards them the flow
of light and joy which had grown so abundant in me. From
that time on they stopped stealing my bread or my soup. It
never happened again. Often, my comrades would wake me up
in the night and take me to comfort someone, sometimes a long
way off in another block.

'Almost everyone forgot I was a student. I became "the blind
Frenchman". For many, I was just "the man who didn't die".
Hundreds of people confided in me. The men were determined
to talk to me. They spoke to me in French, in Russian, in
German, in Polish. I did the best I could to understand them
all. That is how I lived, how I survived. The rest I cannot
describe.'

. . . The affirmation of suffering, when it is not squeezed out of a person, has a mystical core that Philene's statement puts into words in a way that is at once ironic and profound. It is not by chance that mystical elements crop up in all Christian reflection on suffering. One can read Lusseyran's book as a commentary on the great mystical experiences: dying to self, poverty, light within the soul. What disgusts me about the banal theology of the devotional pamphlets is precisely its ignorance about this mystical core. These devotional pamphlets replace mysticism with masochism. They don't demand too much of people but too little, only the acknowledgement of a supreme potentate and not a love that has far surpassed the potentate and his ways, a love that 'despite even the residents of heaven' speaks the yes of faith, even against all experience.

Dorothee Soelle

FATHER AND SONS (John 20:17)

LET GOD
   be Father
   speak
   liberate me from my prisons
   direct my path
   infuse me with His grace and love.

LET ME
   be son
   listen
   walk out of my prisons through opened doors
   follow his guidance
   open up my being to His grace and love,

   Study and imitate
   the perfect sonship
   of Jesus Christ
   the universal brother
   of all other sons.

George Appleton

In the summer and autumn of 1968 K.G.B. officials were constant visitors to the camp. I was summoned to conversations lasting many hours. They suggested, cautiously at first, and then quite blatantly, that I should collaborate with them against the Church. There were threats, and also offers of an early release. But at what a price! The fee for an early release was betrayal of God and His works. At the end of September I took no food for ten days, demanding that the K.G.B. should leave me in peace. After my hunger-strike I wrote a poem addressed to my persecutors.

To My Persecutors

My persecutors, I do not curse you,
And at this hour under the burden of the cross
I pray for you and bless you
With the simple humanity of Christ.

I am pure before you: by word and deeds.
I have called you to good and to light.
I have so much wished that your hearts
Would be possessed by the lofty ideal of Love.

But rejecting this kind summons
You answered with rabid enmity.
My persecutors, I do not curse you,
But I am saddened by your fate.

The immortal examples of history
Speak of the futility of persecution—
The fires of love and abundant faith
Burn enthusiastically through the whole land!

My persecutors, I do not curse you,
And at this hour under the burden of the cross
I pray for you and bless you
With the simple humanity of Christ.

Georgi Vins

TO: SOLZHENITSYN

Perhaps more than the speech you did not say
This was the gesture which relieved who knows
How many millions on a Winter's Day
Who stood aside from violence and chose
To watch you turn away.

With unshed tears and no farewells I take
Your soap, a tooth brush, I go with the men
Who threatened you. Courage and keen heartbreak
Trembled the world to gentleness again
Yes, still one man can make.

Tormentors look at empty hands, the wild
And violent opportunists feel disgraced
Russia has given one more tragic child
To teach compassion to the wondering west
Make it a moment wild.

Elizabeth Jennings

PRAYER OF A MAN WHO DIED IN A CONCENTRATION CAMP

Peace to all men of evil will. Let vengeance cease and punishment and retribution. The crimes have gone beyond measure, our minds can no longer take them in. There are too many
martyrs . . . Lord do not weigh their sufferings on your scales of
justice, and let them not be written in their act of accusation
and demand redress. Pay them otherwise. Credit the torturers,
the informers and traitors with their courage and strength of
spirit, their dignity and endurance, their smile, their love, their
broken hearts which did not give in even in the face of death,
even in times of greatest weakness . . . take all this into account
Lord for the remission of the sins of their enemies, as the price
of the triumph of justice. Take good and not evil into account.
And let us remain in our enemies' thoughts not as their victims,
not as a nightmare, but as those who helped them overcome
their crimes. This is all we ask for them.

Anthony Bloom

MAN'S SEARCH FOR MEANING (6)

How is it possible that men of flesh and blood could treat others as so many prisoners say they have been treated? Having once heard these accounts and having come to believe that these things did happen, one is bound to ask how, psychologically, they could happen. To answer this question without going into great detail, a few things must be pointed out:

First, among the guards there were some sadists, sadists in the purest clinical sense.

Second, these sadists were always selected when a really severe detachment of guards was needed.

There was great joy at our work site when we had permission to warm ourselves for a few minutes (after two hours of work in the bitter frost) in front of a little stove which was fed with twigs and scraps of wood. But there were always some foremen who found a great pleasure in taking this comfort from us. How clearly their faces reflected this pleasure when they not only forbade us to stand there but turned over the stove and dumped its lovely fire into the snow! When the S.S. took a dislike to a person, there was always some special man in their ranks known to have a passion for, and to be highly specialized in, sadistic torture, to whom the unfortunate prisoner was sent.

Third, the feelings of the majority of the guards had been dulled by the number of years in which, in ever-increasing doses, they had witnessed the brutal methods of the camp. These morally and mentally hardened men at least refused to take active part in sadistic measures. But they did not prevent others from carrying them out.

Fourth, it must be stated that even among the guards there were some who took pity on us. I shall only mention the commander of the camp from which I was liberated. It was found after the liberation ... that this man had paid no small sum of money from his own pocket in order to purchase medicines for his prisoners from the nearest market town. An interesting incident with reference to this S.S. commander is in regard to the attitude toward him of some of his Jewish prisoners. At the end of the war when the American troops liberated the prisoners from our camp, three young Hungarian

Jews hid this commander in the Bavarian woods. Then they
went to the Commandant of the American Forces who was
very eager to capture this S.S. commander and they said they
would tell him where he was but only under certain conditions:
the American commander must promise that absolutely no
harm would come to this man. After a while, the American
officer finally promised these young Jews that the S.S. commander when taken into captivity would be kept safe from
harm. Not only did the American officer keep his promise but,
as a matter of fact, the former S.S. commander of his concentration camp was in a sense restored to his command, for he
supervised the collection of clothing among the nearby
Bavarian villages, and its distribution to all of us who at that
time still wore the clothes we had inherited from other inmates
of Camp Auschwitz who were not as fortunate as we, having
been sent to the gas chamber immediately upon their arrival at
the railway station.

But the senior camp warden, a prisoner himself, was harder
than any of the S.S. guards. He beat the other prisoners at
every slightest opportunity, while the camp commander, to my
knowledge, never once lifted his hand against any of us.

It is apparent that the mere knowledge that a man was
either a camp guard or a prisoner tells us almost nothing.
Human kindness can be found in all groups, even those which
as a whole it would be easy to condemn. The boundaries between groups overlapped and we must not try to simplify matters by saying that these men were angels and those were devils.
Certainly, it was a considerable achievement for a guard or
foreman to be kind to the prisoners in spite of all the camp's
influences, and, on the other hand, the baseness of a prisoner
who treated his own companions badly was exceptionally con-
temptible. Obviously the prisoners found the lack of character
in such men especially upsetting, while they were profoundly
moved by the smallest kindness received from any of the
guards.

I remember how one day a foreman secretly gave me a piece
of bread which I knew he must have saved from his breakfast
ration. It was far more than the small piece of bread which
moved me to tears at that time. It was the human 'something'

which this man also gave to me—the word and look which accompanied the gift.

... Life in a concentration camp tore open the human soul and exposed its depths. Is it surprising that in those depths we again found only human qualities which in their very nature were a mixture of good from evil, which goes through all human beings, reaches into the lowest depths and becomes apparent even on the bottom of the abyss which is laid open by the concentration camp.

Viktor Frankl

But they who love the greater love
Lay down their life; they do not hate.

Wilfred Owen

I PRAY THAT GOD FORGIVES THEM

Corrie ten Boom stood naked with her sister Betsie watching a concentration camp matron beating a prisoner. 'Oh, the poor woman,' Corrie cried. 'Yes may God Forgive her,' Betsie replied. And again Corrie realized that it was for the souls of the brutal Nazi guards that her sister prayed. Both women had been sent to the camp for helping the Jews. Christ's spirit and words were their guide: it was His persecuted people they tried to save—at the risk of their own lives: it was His strength that sustained them through times of profound horror.

*   *   *

Betsie and I were put to work levelling some rough ground just inside the camp wall. This too was back-breaking labour. Sometimes as I bent to lift a load my heart cramped strangely: at night spasms of pain gripped my legs.

But the biggest problem was Betsie's strength. One morning after a hard night's rain we arrived to find the ground sodden and heavy. Betsie had never been able to lift much; today her shovels-full were microscopic and she stumbled frequently as she walked to the low ground where we dumped the loads.

'*Schneller!*' a guard screamed at her. 'Can't you go faster?'

Why must they scream, I wondered as I sank my shovel into the black muck. Why couldn't they speak like ordinary human beings? I straightened slowly, the sweat drying on my back. I was remembering where we had first heard this maniac sound. The Beje. In Tante Jan's rooms. A voice coming from the shell-shaped speaker, a scream lingering in the air even after Betsie had leapt to shut if off . . .

'Loafer! Lazy swine!'

The guard snatched Betsie's shovel from her hands and ran from group to group of the digging crew, exhibiting the handful of dirt that was all Betsie had been able to lift.

'Look what Madame Baroness is carrying! Surely she will over-exert herself!'

The other guards and even some of the prisoners laughed. Encouraged, the guard threw herself into a parody of Betsie's faltering walk. A male guard was with our detail today and in the presence of a man the women guards were always animated.

As the laughter grew I felt a murderous anger rise. The guard was young and well fed—was it Betsie's fault that she was old and starving? But to my astonishment, Betsie too was laughing.

'That's me all right,' she admitted. 'But you'd better let me totter along with my little spoonful, or I'll have to stop altogether.'

The guard's plump cheeks went crimson. 'I'll decide who's to stop!' And snatching the leather crop from her belt she slashed Betsie across the chest and neck.

Without knowing I was doing it I had seized my shovel and rushed at her.

Betsie stepped in front of me before anyone had seen. 'Corrie!' she pleaded, dragging my arm to my side. 'Corrie! keep working!' She tugged the shovel from my hand and dug it into the mud. Contemptuously the guard tossed Betsie's shovel toward us. I picked it up, still in a daze. A red stain appeared on Betsie's collar; a welt began to swell on her neck.

Betsie saw where I was looking and laid a bird-thin hand over the whip mark. 'Don't look at it, Corrie. Look at Jesus only.' She drew away her hand: it was sticky with blood.

Corrie ten Boom

Prayer found on a scrap of paper near the body of a dead child in Ravensbrück.

O Lord, remember not only the men and women of good will, but also those of ill will. But do not only remember all the suffering they have inflicted on us, remember the fruits we bought, thanks to this suffering; our comradeship, our loyalty, our humility, the courage, the generosity, the greatness of heart which has grown out of this. And when they come to judgement, let all the fruits that we have borne be their forgiveness.

Anonymous

HOW TO LOVE (1 John 4:19)

> O Lord, you teach me
>> that there is only one cure
>> for hatred
>> namely love.
> But what if I have no love?
> 'Then, my child,
>> you must learn to love.'
> Lord, how do I begin?
> 'By accepting love,
>> my love, the Father's love.
>> When you accept love
>> you begin to love in return.
> 'Don't look so sceptical—
>> your mother loved you
>> before you were born
>> and when you were born
>> and when you were
>> a helpless scrap of humanity;

'Your Father loved you
    with protective, providing love.
'You felt secure,
    wanted, valued, care-free
    because of their love.
'Let your heavenly Father love you,
    my Father and yours,
    and you will love in return.
'Our love, the Father's and mine,
    must grow in you
    must move outward
    to all other children of his.
'And if it is true love
    selfless and undemanding,
    it will dissolve the other's hatred,
    sweeten his bitterness,
    disarm his aggressiveness,
    heal his pain
    and beget love in return.'
How long will it take, my Lord?
'It depends on you, my child,
    how deeply you have felt my love
    and responded.
'It cannot fail, because it was love
    which created the universe,
    begat man in love
    and kept the welcoming arms outstretched
    even on a cross.
'Love, my child,
    because you are so greatly
    so eternally loved.'

George Appleton

The work at Siemen's, however, was sheer misery. Betsie and I had to push a heavy handcart to a railroad siding where we unloaded large metal plates from a boxcar and wheeled them to a receiving gate at the factory. The gruelling workday lasted eleven hours. At least, at noontime we were given a boiled potato and some thin soup; those who worked inside the camp had no midday meal.

Returning to camp we could barely lift our swollen and aching legs. The soldiers patrolling us bellowed and cursed, but we could only shuffle forward inches at a step. I noticed again how the local people turned their eyes another way.

Back at the barracks we formed yet another line—would there never be an end to columns and waits?—to receive our ladle of turnip soup in the centre room. Then as quickly as we could for the press of people, Betsie and I made our way to the rear of the dormitory room where we held our worship 'service'. Around our own platform area there was not enough light to read the Bible, but back here a small light bulb cast a wan yellow circle on the wall, and here an ever larger group of women gathered.

They were services like no others, these times in Barracks 28. A single meeting might include a recital of the Magnificat in Latin by a group of Roman Catholics, a whispered hymn by some Lutherans, and a sotto-voce chant by Eastern Orthodox women. With each moment the crowd around us would swell, packing the nearby platforms, hanging over the edges, until the high structures groaned and swayed. At last either Betsie or I would open the Bible. Because only the Hollanders could understand the Dutch text we would translate aloud in German. And then we would hear the life-giving words passed back along the aisles in French, Polish, Russian, Czech, back into Dutch. They were little previews of heaven, these evenings beneath the light bulb. I would think of Haarlem, each substantial church set behind its wrought-iron fence and its barrier of doctrine. And I would know again that in darkness God's truth shines most clear.

At first Betsie and I called these meetings with great timidity. But as night after night went by and no guard ever came near us, we grew bolder. So many now wanted to join us that we held a second service after evening roll call. There on the *Lagerstrasse* we were under rigid surveillance, guards in their warm wool capes marching constantly up and down. It was the same in the centre room of the barracks: half a dozen guards or camp police always present. Yet in the large dormitory room there was almost no supervision at all. We did not understand it.

Another strange thing was happening. The Davitamon bottle was continuing to produce drops. It scarcely seemed possible, so small a bottle, so many doses a day. Now, in addition to Betsie, a dozen others on our pier were taking it.

My instinct was always to hoard it—Betsie was growing so very weak! But others were ill as well. It was hard to say no to eyes that burned with fever, hands that shook with chill. I tried to save it for the very weakest—but even these soon numbered fifteen, twenty, twenty-five . . .

And still every time I tilted the little bottle, a drop appeared at the tip of the glass stopper. It just couldn't be! I held it up to the light, trying to see how much was left, but the dark brown glass was too thick to see through.

'There was a woman in the Bible,' Betsie said, 'whose oil jar was never empty.' She turned to it in the Book of Kings, the story of the poor widow of Zarephath who gave Elijah a room in her home: 'The jar of meal wasted not, neither did the cruse of oil fail, according to the word of Jehovah which he spoke by Elijah.'

Well-but-wonderful things happened all through the Bible. It was one thing to believe that such things were possible thousands of years ago, another to have it happen now, to us, this very day. And yet it happened, this day, and the next, and the next, until an awed little group of spectators stood around watching the drops fall onto the daily rations of bread.

Many nights I lay awake in the shower of straw dust from the mattress above, trying to fathom the marvel of supply lavished upon us. 'Maybe,' I whispered to Betsie, 'only a molecule or two really gets through that little pinhole—and then in the air it expands!'

I heard her soft laughter in the dark. 'Don't try too hard to explain it, Corrie. Just accept it as a surprise from a Father who loves you.'

And then one day Mien pushed her way to us in the evening food line. 'Look what I've got for you!'

Mien was a pretty young Dutch woman we had met in Vught. She was assigned to the hospital and often managed to bring to Barracks 28 some stolen treasure from the staff room— a sheet of newspaper to stuff in a broken window, a slice of bread left untouched on a nurse's plate. Now we peered into the small cloth sack she carried.

'Vitamins!' I cried, and then cast an apprehensive glance at a policeman nearby. 'Yeast compound!' I whispered.

'Yes!' she hissed back. 'There were several huge jars. I emptied each just the same amount.'

We gulped the thin turnip water, marvelling at our sudden riches. Back at the bunk I took the bottle from the straw. 'We'll finish the drops first,' I decided.

But that night, no matter how long I held it upside down, or how hard I shook it, not another drop appeared.

Corrie ten Boom

POWERS OF GOOD

With every power for good to stay and guide me,
comforted and inspired beyond all fear,
I'll live these days with you in thought beside me,
and pass, with you, into the coming year.

The old year still torments our hearts, unhastening;
the long days of our sorrow still endure;
Father, grant to the souls thou hast been chastening
that thou hast promised, the healing and the cure.

Should it be ours to drain the cup of grieving
even to the dregs of pain, at thy command,
we will not falter, thankfully receiving
all that is given by thy loving hand.

But should it be thy will once more to release us
to life's enjoyment and its good sunshine,
that which we've learned from sorrow shall increase us,
and all our life be dedicate as thine.

Today, let candles shed their radiant greeting;
lo, on our darkness are they not thy light
leading us, haply, to our longed-for meeting?—
Thou canst illumine even our darkest night.

When now the silence deepens for our hearkening,
grant we may hear thy children's voices raise
from all the unseen world around us darkening
their universal paean, in thy praise.

While all the powers of good aid and attend us,
boldly we'll face the future, come what may.
At even and at morn God will befriend us,
and oh, most surely in each newborn day!

Dietrich Bonhoeffer

THE NIGHT OF THE NEW MOON (2)

'The depth of darkness into which you can descend, and still
live, is an exact measure, I believe, of the height to which you
can aspire to reach.'

I began by trying to describe to the Japanese doctor what life
had been like in a Japanese prisoner-of-war camp, because he
confessed that even after all this time he personally had taken
no interest in the matter and had read no literature about it. I
tried to make my description as factual as possible, and to keep
my own personal emotions out of it, which was not as difficult
as it may sound because I had for many years now looked
repeatedly and deeply into the experience and it had, I truly
believe, left nothing bitter or destructive in my mind. I barely
mentioned the physical brutalities we had experienced at the
hands of our Japanese guards and particularly at the hands of
their Korean converts who increasingly took over from them as

the war effort demanded more and more of the Japanese. But they, in the manner of all converts, became much more fanatical than their converters until they were caricatures of the worst kind of Japanese. I skimmed over the grimmest of my own experiences. For instance, I said little of how before I was brought into a so-called Japanese 'regular' prisoner-of-war camp I had been made to watch Japanese soldiers having bayonet practice on live prisoners-of-war tied between bamboo posts; had been taken to witness executions of persons of all races and nationalities, for obscure reasons like 'showing a spirit of wilfulness', or not bowing with sufficient alacrity in the direction of the rising sun.

It was amazing how often and how many of my men would confess to me, after some Japanese excess worse than usual, that for the first time in their lives they had realized the truth, and the dynamic liberating power of the first Crucifixion utterances: 'Forgive them for they know not what they do.'

I found that the moment they grasped this fundamental fact of our prison situation, forgiveness became a product not of an act of will or of personal virtue even, but an automatic and all-compelling consequence of a law of understanding: as real and indestructible as Newton's law of gravity. The tables of the spirit would be strangely and promptly turned and we would find ourselves without self-pity of any kind, feeling deeply sorry for the Japanese as if we were the free men and they the prisoners—men held in some profound *oubliette* of their own minds.

. . . The Japanese contempt for prisoners-of-war, all the greater because they themselves regarded captivity as the final degradation of the male spirit, and would, and indeed did take their own lives in hundreds of thousands rather than endure the disgrace of falling into enemy hands. This contempt was reinforced by the profound disregard of the importance of life on earth implicit in their culture, and their belief that the life of an individual man was of 'no more account than a feather'.

. . . Again, I could write a book on this aspect of our imprisonment alone, because I had already been aware of it on my first visit to Japan, as far back as 1926, and had come away from the Far East knowing that these forces, of the 'vengeance of history' as I called it to myself even then, had already been

set in motion by the Japanese victory in their war against the
Russians at the beginning of the century, and were steadily
gathering strength beneath the rough surface of the international scene.

So much were the Japanese themselves caught up in the
psychology of this aspect of their conquest that it completely
dominated their view of their European prisoners. They never
saw us as human beings, but as provocative symbols of a
detested past. They had only to look at us for this urge of
resentment to quicken in their blood to such an extent that I
still marvel not so much at the excesses they perpetrated as at
their restraint.

I remember saying to Nichols at the time that one of our
gravest dangers was that we were imprisoned at a moment
when not just the chickens but all the *pterodactyls* of our history
in the Far East had come home to roost. Throughout our
imprisonment this was, I believe, one of the elements most
threatening to our survival and the genuine cause of the gravest
excesses that were inflicted on us from time to time.

I myself had no doubt that in time the Japanese would be
defeated, but what I could not tell, in the light of all this, was
how they could ever be defeated in such a manner that they
themselves would be relieved of these overwhelming compul-
sions, of this unconscious sense of a duty, a mission of history to
carry the feud aflame in their blood to a final cataclysmic end
in which they and all the people they had captured would have
to perish.

I knew of no nation at the time for whom honour, however
perverted, was so great a necessity as for the Japanese. Honour,
and a life in which they did not lose honour with themselves
seemed to them as important as, if not more important than,
food. . . .

I was convinced of only one thing: that unless they could be
defeated in such a way that they were not deprived of their
honour by defeat, there was nothing but disaster for them and
us in the end. This, more, even, than starvation or disease, I
saw as the real danger that would threaten us every minute of
the days and nights of our long years of captivity, either
through a break-down in the restraint of an individual

Japanese commander and his guards, or through the deliberate
choice of the overall Japanese command to pull down their own
sprawling military temple, Samson-like, and to destroy the
European Philistine along with themselves rather than endure
defeat with ignominy.

Laurens Van Der Post

To suffer woes which Hope thinks infinite
To forgive wrongs darker than death or night;
　To defy Power, which seems omnipotent;
To love and bear; to hope till Hope creates
From its own wreck the thing it contemplates;
　Neither to change, nor falter, nor repent;
This, like thy glory, Titan is to be
Good, great and joyous, beautiful and free;
This is alone Life, Joy, Empire and Victory.

P. B. Shelley

THE NIGHT OF THE NEW MOON (3)

I felt strongly that if war had had any justification at all it
was only in the sense that at its end, it should leave victors and
vanquished free for a moment from the destructive aspects of
their past. Modern war appeared to me as a grim autonomous
state of life carrying within itself its own harsh system of reward
and punishment for those who waged it. It was as if war today
were a bitter form of penance for all our inadequate yesterdays.
Once this terrible penance had been paid, my own experience
suggested, it re-established men in a brief state of innocence
which, if seized with imagination, could enable us to build
better than before. To go looking for particular persons and
societies to blame and punish at the end of war seemed to me to
throw men back into the negative aspects of the past from
which they had been trying to escape, and to deprive them of
the opportunity they had so bitterly earned in order to begin
afresh.

In any case, I did not believe then as I do not believe now,

that you could punish whole peoples or even solitary
individuals into being better persons. This seemed a renegade,
discredited and utterly archaic concept. It has been tried
throughout history. Far from being an instrument of redemption, which is punishment's only moral justification, it is an
increasingly self-defeating weapon in the hands of dangerously
one-sided men. I only know that I came out of prison longing
passionately—and I am certain my longing was shared by all
the thousands of men who had been with me—that the past
would be recognized as the past and instantly buried before it
spread another form of putrefaction in the spirit of our time. I
thought that the only hope for the future lay in an all-
embracing attitude of forgiveness of the peoples who had been
our enemies. Forgiveness, my prison experience had taught me,
was not mere religious sentimentality; it was as fundamental a
law of the human spirit as the law of gravity. If one broke the
law of gravity one broke one's neck; if one broke this law of
forgiveness one inflicted a mortal wound on one's spirit and
became once again a member of the chain-gang of mere cause
and effect from which life has laboured so long and painfully to
escape.

The conduct of thousands of men in war and in prison with
me confirmed with an eloquence which is one of the most
precious memories of war, that the spirit of man is naturally a
forgiving spirit. I was convinced that if the cancellation of the
negative past which is forgiveness could take its place, it would
automatically be followed by the recognition that men could
no longer change the pattern of life for the better by changing
their frontiers, their systems and their laws of compulsion of
judgement and justice, but only by changing themselves.

I had learnt to fear the Pharisee more than the sinner; judgement and justice almost more than human error. I know judgement and justice had brought us far but that *far* was not far
enough. Only the exercise of the law of forgiveness, the declaration for ever of an unconditional amnesty for all in the warring
spirit of men, could carry us on beyond. This alone could be
the beginning of real change in life and it could only be by
example of patiently living out the change in ourselves that we
could hope to change for the better the societies to which we

belong. It had become axiomatic for me that we could take nobody and no people further than we had taken ourselves. To the extent to which I felt my own war experience could contribute to such a shift in the imagination of man, I responded as a matter of inner urgency—despite all the other preoccupations that beset me—and very soon after my return from Java, put it as well as I could into a story called a 'A Bar of Shadow' ... However as far as the day-to-day facts of what we had endured under the Japanese were concerned, I preferred to remain silent, because I was convinced that the inevitable use to which they would be put in this literal and two-dimensionally minded age of ours, would work against the whole truth of war and the meaning and consequences it should have for the world.

I would have remained silent even now if it had not been for the fact that I see another kind of one-sidedness being introduced into the thinking of our time, as dangerous as the other one-sidedness that I feared in ourselves at the end of the war. This one-sidedness results from the facts that more and more people see the horror of Hiroshima and Nagasaki out of context. They tend to see it increasingly as an act of history in which we alone were the villains. I have been amazed to observe how in some extraordinary way my own Japanese friends do not seem to feel that they had done anything themselves to provoke us into inflicting Hiroshima and Nagasaki on them and how strangely incurious they are about their own part in the war. I felt that it was extremely important for them as well as for us to maintain a view of this cataclysmic event as steady as it was whole. I had a feeling almost as if I had been placed in a special position by life to contribute in a small way to what should be the final wholeness of the concept of the history of the moment. Perhaps no particular event in history is fully accounted for until it has been seen also from the point of view of the persons who had a special relationship with it. It is precisely because I am convinced that the thousands of people who were in prison with me, and I in particular, had a special relationship with this terrible moment in time that I felt I had a duty to put my share of it on record.

This sense of duty has become more acute as the time left for me to do so has become less. There was, too, the obvious dan-

ger that something essential of the experience would be forgotten. The physical facts and the statistics of what happened to us
were perhaps not imperilled. But what seemed to me to be
increasingly in danger were the great imponderables of those
years that conceived our experience, gave it its own unique life
and clothed the bare bones of facts and statistics of our existence with something precious and irrevocable out of our per-
ishable flesh and blood.

Laurens Van Der Post

Hiroshima, Aug. 6. Hundreds of candles representing the
souls of Hiroshima's atomic bomb victims shone in the dusk
over a Japanese river tonight in a moving climax to ceremonies
commemorating the dropping of the bomb 31 years ago.

The candles, in small wood and paper lanterns with peace
messages on them, were set adrift in the Ota river from the
memorial park in the city centre. Flowers were piled high
round a cenotaph listing the names of 89,134 known victims of
the bomb.

The Times

Who would once more relight Creation's flame,
Turn back to sanity a world that goes insane,
To bridge this awful chasm of despair?
The faint small voice of Hope calls out,
Do you answer? Will you dare?

Qedrwl

BLESSED ARE THOSE WHO SUFFER

'After my year in the factory, before going back to teaching,
I had been taken by my parents to Portugal, and while there I
left them to go alone to a little village. I was, as it were, in
pieces, soul and body. That contact with affliction had killed
my youth. Until then I had not had any experience of afflic-

tion, unless we count my own, which, as it was my own, seemed to me to have little importance, and which moreover was only a partial affliction, being biological and not social.

'I knew quite well that there was a great deal of affliction in the world, I was obsessed with the idea, but I had not had prolonged and first-hand experience of it. As I worked in the factory, indistinguishable to all eyes, including my own, from the anonymous mass, the affliction of others entered into my flesh and my soul. Nothing separated me from it, for I had really forgotten my past and I looked forward to no future, finding it difficult to imagine the possibility of surviving all the fatigue. What I went through there marked me in so lasting a manner that still today when any human being, whoever he may be and in whatever circumstances, speaks to me without brutality, I cannot help having the impression that there must be a mistake and that unfortunately the mistake will in all probability disappear. There I received forever the mark of a slave, like the branding of the red-hot iron the Romans put on the foreheads of their most despised slaves. Since then I have always regarded myself as a slave.

'In this state of mind then, and in a wretched condition physically, I entered the little Portuguese village, which, alas, was very wretched too, on the very day of the festival of its patron saint. I was alone. It was the evening and there was a full moon over the sea. The wives of the fishermen were, in procession, making a tour of all the ships, carrying candles and singing what must certainly be very ancient hymns of a heart-rending sadness. Nothing can give any idea of it. I have never heard anything so poignant unless it were the song of the boatmen on the Volga. There the conviction was suddenly borne in upon me that Christianity is pre-eminently the religion of slaves, that slaves cannot help belonging to it, and I among others.

'Christianity exists for slaves. It is the religion of the oppressed, of those marked by affliction. It concerns itself with their needs. People are pronounced blessed not because of their achievements or their behaviour, but with regard to their needs. Blessed are the poor, the suffering, the persecuted, the hungry.'

The text above is also nothing else but a beatitude. It comes from a letter of Simone Weil's, written about May 15, 1942, prior to her emigration for America. The letter speaks about suffering, but above all it expresses a boundless affirmation of life, even the life of a slave. Those who are amazed when they are addressed without brutality, when they are not used and treated as commodities—the religion of slaves exists precisely for them. Not that they should remain slaves thereby, but that they should thereby stand, arise. I am not referring to the religion of slavery, which perpetuates slavery, but rather to the religion of those unfortunate for a time, to whom life is promised. Their suffering, their rights, their truth are expressed.

Dorothee Soelle

JOHN LEONARD WILSON'S PRISON MINISTRY

While Leonard did not suffer further physical torture, except for one brief period, the interrogation went on for months.

. . . During this time all those taken from Changi were in the most appalling cell conditions in the military police headquarters. The commission already referred to described them as follows:

The internees were crowded, irrespective of race, sex, or state of health, in small cells or cages. They were so crowded that they could not lie down in comfort. No bedding or covering of any kind were provided, and bright lights were kept burning overhead all night. From eight a.m. to ten p.m. inmates had to sit up straight on the bare floor with their knees up, and were not allowed to relax or put their hands on the floor, or talk, or move, except to go to the lavatory. Any infractions of the rigid discipline involved a beating by the sentries. There was one pedestal water-closet in each cell or cage, and the water flushing into the pan provided the only water supply for all purposes, including drinking. It should be recorded here that nearly all the inmates suffered enteritis or dysentery. No soap, towel, toilet articles or handkerchiefs were permitted, and inmates had no clothing other than that they were wearing. The food supplied, normally rice, occasional vegetables, and weak tea with no milk or sugar, was less than half of that supplied by our own prisons department as punishment diet for Asiatics.

... The three women taken from Changi prison were detained in exactly the same conditions as the men, and shared cells with the male prisoners of all races. They were afforded no privacy, even for their most intimate requirements, and any attempt on the part of European men to screen them was broken down by the guards ... The buildings resounded all day and night with blows, the bellowing of inquisitors, and the shrieks of the tortured ... In these conditions, and this atmosphere of terror, these men and women waited, sometimes for months, their summons to interrogation, which might come at any hour of the day or night.

For three weeks after his three days of torture, Leonard was in a semi-conscious state, but as his wounds began to heal and his physical condition improved, his spirit of faith and love rose to meet the suffering and evil of this cell life. His own words taken from the broadcast sermon already quoted, are the best description of this resurrection of faith.

It is true, of course, that there were many dreary and desolate moments, especially in the early morning. I was in a crowded and filthy cell with hardly any power to move because of my wounds, but here again I was helped tremendously by God ... There was a tiny window at the back of the cell and through the bars I could hear the song of the Golden Oriole. I could see the glorious red of the Flame of the Forest tree, and something of God's indestructible beauty was conveyed to my tortured mind. Behind the Flame tree I glimpsed the top of Wesley's church, and was so grateful that the church had preserved so many of Wesley's hymns. One that I said every morning was the first hymn we sang today *Christ Whose Glory Fills the Skies*. Do you remember the second verse?

Dark and cheerless is the morn
Unaccompanied by Thee;

> Joyless is the day's return
> Till Thy mercy's beams I see.

And so I went on to pray,

> Visit then this soul of mine
> Pierce the gloom of sin and grief.

And gradually the burden of this world was lifted and I was carried into the presence of God and received from Him the strength and peace which were enough to live by, day by day.

This spirit passed from Leonard to others. A number of those in the cells asked him about the meaning of prayer. It was impossible to talk during the day, but at night, by keeping a careful watch, they were able to talk in whispers. These exchanges grew into a rich fellowship, so that when people were taken out of the cell to the torture rooms, they knew that those behind would be praying for them and sharing in spirit their suffering.

In March 1944, Leonard was moved to a different cell. Here there was a Chinese, who had already been in touch with two Christians in other cells, a Presbyterian called Robert Burns, and a Lancashire man named Sam Travers. They had taught the Chinese a good deal about Christianity, and told him to get in touch with Leonard if he could. Leonard continued to instruct the Chinese at night, and on Maundy Thursday, in the early morning, he was baptized with water from the lavatory basin in the cell. Two further incidents are best described in Leonard's own words:

> Every Sunday after February, when I was moved to a less conspicuous cell, I began taking the communion service. On one occasion a most courageous woman, a Christian, who was Mrs Elizabeth Choy, a mission teacher, and was in because of her help to internees, was sweeping the corridor. She came past our cell and I stopped the service for a moment to tell her what we were doing. A few minutes later she came back and knelt outside the bars and received the Sacrament through the bars. She was not seen by the guards. Our cell was just round the corner, and, if the guards came,

we could see a shadow on the wall, so had to keep constant watch. We used a little rice which had been given to us some time ago, and had communion in one kind, and when we got our weak tea for breakfast, we used it as a Loving Cup.

The other incident concerned one of the military police who had taken part in the torturing to which Leonard was subjected. In a letter to Brigadier Sir John Smyth, v.c., written in April 1967 Leonard said:

> Before I left Singapore in 1945 I arranged for a Japanese-speaking evangelist from the School of Oriental Studies, Miss Hentie, to come out to Singapore to work amongst the Japanese and to preach the gospel of reconciliation. She had to work amongst what were known as the 'surrendered personnel', and also amongst those who were in prison for war crimes. When I got back in 1946 I found what splendid work she had done, and there were quite large classes going on in preparation for Christian baptism amongst both sets of people.
>
> In 1947 I took various services of baptism and confirmation in the cathedral for those who had been prepared, and I got permission for those who were serving sentences to be marched up from the prison. Among those that I baptized and confirmed was one of the men of the military police who had been responsible four years earlier, for taking part in my own torturing. I have seldom seen so great a change in a man. He looked gentle and peaceful, even though he was going back to serve a ten-year sentence, and later he received communion at my hands in the prison.

Roy McKay

BALLADE OF MISERY AND IRON

Haggard faces and trembling knees,
    Eyes that shine with a weakling's hate,
Lips that mutter their blasphemies,
    Murderous hearts that darkly wait:

These are they who are men of late,
Fit to hold a plow or a sword.
   If a prayer this wall may penetrate,
Have pity on these my comrades, Lord!

Poets sing of life at the lees
   In tender verses and delicate;
Of tears and manifold agonies—
   Little they know of what they prate.
   Out of this silence, passionate
Sounds a deeper, a wilder chord.
   If sound be heard through the narrow grate,
Have pity on these my comrades, Lord!

Hark, that wail of the distant breeze,
   Piercing ever the close-barred gate,
Fraught with torturing memories
   Of eyes that kindle and lips that mate.
   Ah, by the loved ones desolate,
Whose anguish never can pen record,
   If thou be truly compassionate,
Have pity on these my comrades, Lord!

   L'Envoi
These are pawns that the hand of Fate
   Careless sweeps from the checker-board.
Thou that know'st if the game be straight,
   Have pity on these my comrades, Lord!

George Carter

'FORGIVE THEM': JOHN LEONARD WILSON'S SERMON

Leonard never dwelt on the physical horror of the torture he
suffered. When he referred to this time, it was to make clear that
this experience had established for him once and for all the
truth of the Christian faith he confessed. As the story of his
earlier years unfolds, it will be seen that he did not always
possess that quiet assurance of those who can say, 'I am not
ashamed: for I know Him whom I have believed.' After the
experience of those days of horror, pain and darkness, he knew

that he had been upheld by God's love beyond the point of no
return, and whatever doubts and difficulties, failures and disappointments, later came his way, his spirit was never defeated,
for now he too could say with confidence, 'I know Him whom I
have believed.'

It was on October 13th, 1946, three years after these events,
that Leonard preached in the Sunday service of the B.B.C., and
first gave to the world some account of what the experiences of
those days had come to mean to him. He said:

I remember Archbishop William Temple in one of his
books writing that if you pray for any particular virtue,
whether it be patience or courage or love, one of the answers
God gives you is an opportunity for exercising that virtue.
After my first beating I was almost afraid to pray for courage
lest I should have another opportunity for exercising it, but
my unspoken prayer was there; and without God's help I
doubt whether I could have come through. Long hours of ignoble pain were a severe test. In the middle of that torture
they asked me if I still believed in God. When, by God's help, I
said, 'I do,' they asked me why God did not save me, and by
the help of his Holy Spirit, I said, 'God does save me. He does
not save me by freeing me from pain or punishment, but he
saves me by giving me the spirit to bear it.' And when they
asked me why I did not curse them, I told them, it was
because I was a follower of Jesus Christ, who taught us that
we were all brethren. I did not like to use the words, 'Father,
forgive them'. It seemed too blasphemous to use our Lord's
words, but I felt them, and I said, 'Father I know these men
are doing their duty. Help them to see that I am innocent.'
And when I muttered, 'Forgive them', I wondered how far I
was being dramatic and if I really meant it, because I looked
at their faces as they stood around and took it in turn to flog,
and their faces were hard and cruel and some of them were
evidently enjoying their cruelty. But by the grace of God I
saw these men not as they were, but as they had been. Once
they were little children playing with their brothers and
sisters and happy in their parents' love, in those far-off days
before they had been conditioned by their false nationalist

ideals, and it is hard to hate little children; but even that was
not enough. There came into my mind, as I lay on the table,
the words of that communion hymn:

> Look, Father, look on his anointed face,
> And only look on us as found in Him;
> Look not on our misusings of Thy grace,
> Our prayer so languid, and our faith so dim;
> For lo! between our sins and their reward
> We set the passion of Thy Son our Lord.

And so I saw them, not as they were, not as they had been,
but as they were capable of becoming, redeemed by the
power of Christ, and I knew it was only common sense to say
'Forgive'.

Roy McKay

THE EPITAPH IN THE FORM OF A BALLAD

> Men, brother men, that after us yet live,
>   Let not your hearts too hard against us be;
> For if some pity of us poor men ye give,
>   The sooner God shall take of you pity.
>   Here are we five or six strung up, you see,
> And here the flesh that all too well we fed
> Bit by bit eaten and rotten, rent and shred,
>   And we the bones grow dust and ash withal;
> Let no man laugh at us discomforted,
>   But pray to God that he forgive us all.

> If we call on you, brothers, to forgive,
>   Ye should not hold our prayer in scorn, though we
> Were slain by law; ye know that all alive
>   Have not wit alway to walk righteously;
>   Make therefore intercession heartily
> With him that of a virgin's womb was bred,
> That his grace be not as dry well-head
>   For us, nor let hell's thunder on us fall;
> We are dead, let no man harry or vex us dead,
>   But pray to God that he forgive us all.

The rain has washed and laundered us all five,
    And the sun dried and blackened; yea, perdie,
Ravens and pies with beaks that rend and rive
    Have dug our eyes out, and plucked off for fee
    Our beard and eyebrows; never are we free,
Not once to rest; but here and there still sped,
Driven at its wild will by the wind's change led,
    More pecked of birds than fruits on garden-wall;
Men, for God's love, let no gibe here be said,
    But pray to God that he forgive us all.

Prince Jesus, that of all art lord and head,
Keep us, that hell be not our bitter bed;
    We have nought to do in such a master's hall.
Be not ye therefore of our fellowhead,
    But pray to God that he forgive us all.

François Villon
Translated by A. C. Swinburne

Extract from a letter of Alfred Dreyfus to his wife (written on Jan. 3rd, 1895, after his conviction and two days before his public degradation).

The supreme humiliation, I am told, is to take place the day after tomorrow. I expected it, and was prepared, but, nevertheless, the blow has been violent. I will be strong, as I have promised you drawing the support I still need from your love, from the affection of all of you, from the thought of my darling children, and from the supreme hope that one day the truth will out. But it is absolutely necessary for me to feel your affection shining around me. I must feel you fighting by my side. So continue your search without ceasing.

I hope to see you soon and gather strength from your eyes. Let us help and support each other against all adversaries. I must have your love if I am to live. Without it the mainspring is broken.

When I am gone, urge everyone not to give up the search. From Saturday on I shall be at the Santé. Take all the necessary steps to see me there. It is there, above all, that I shall need your support.

... 4.15 Since four o'clock my heart has been beating as if it would break. You are not here, darling. Seconds seem like hours. I prick up my ears to hear if someone is coming for me, but I hear nothing. I keep on waiting.

5 o'clock. I am calmer. It has done me good to see you ... Once more a thousand kisses, my darling.   Alfred

From another letter written from the Santé a few days later.

Oh, why can't one open a man's heart with a surgeon's knife and see what is written upon it? All the good people who watched me walking past would be able to read there in letters of gold: 'This is a man of honour.' But I understand them, all the same. In their place I would have been unable to conceal my scorn at the sight of an officer who had been proclaimed a traitor to his country ...

Alfred Dreyfus

Thomas More, about to die for treason, speaks:

I am the King's true subject, and pray for him and for all the realm ... I do none harm, I say none harm, I think none harm. And if this be not enough to keep a man alive, in good faith I long not to live ... I have, since I came into prison, been several times in such a case that I thought to die within the hour, and I thank Our Lord I was never sorry for it but rather sorry when it passed. And therefore, my poor body is at the King's pleasure. Would God my death might do him some good.

Robert Bolt

'TO RECOVER THAT VISION'

'Tell me,' he said, 'what do you really mean when you talk about things which are permanent? We've agreed that Russia as a nation will last for ever. Is that all you mean?'

'It's something I came to see in my early times of imprisonment,' Stephan answered slowly. 'As a prisoner you live so close

to the rest that the boundaries disappear. The ordinary distinc-
tions don't operate because there's nothing to preserve them—
you've lost everything you took a pride in, what you're
ashamed of can't be hidden. So you know men far better than
you can in any other phase of life. You get to see how much you
have in common—being hungry the whole time for food and
women and nicotine, always rather frightened, frightened of
dying slowly or of some new, unthought-of humiliation.

   ... 'What struck me most about my fellow-prisoners,' he
said, 'was their stupendous goodness. Most of them were kind
without any reason, they shared whatever came their way, they
helped you all the time. ... you won't easily believe this, but
it's true, I swear it is. My feet were agonizingly cold one night
—it was in a frozen lumber camp, somewhere in Yatusk
Province—I dreamt they'd gone gangrenous and a surgeon was
sawing off the toes. Then after a while the torture passed and
my feet got blissfully warm. When it was light I found what
had happened—it was due to the man next me, a fresh arrival,
an old Jew from Vilna who hardly knew me at all. I suppose
he'd heard me squealing, I may have called out something
about my feet. At any rate he'd taken off his old coat and
wrapped it very carefully round my legs. And before morning
he'd died.'

   ... 'I was so young then,' he continued, ... 'so childish in
mentality, that I simply accepted those things—it was not till
later that I started to reason about them. I was doing my first
spell of solitary confinement—I'd been sent to Veslich after
getting wrong with the district soviet—and when you're in
darkness with no one to speak to all day long you follow your
thoughts as far as they go, just to use up time. That was when I
tried to see where it came from, this power I'd found in other
men of deserting themselves, surrendering their own advantage. I hunted in my own nature—where else had I to hunt?—
and there I saw nothing but a midden of appetites and self-
regard. Then I had an odd experience, I found myself crying
with pity—actually weeping—for one of my guards, a big ugly
bastard who'd done me out of a day's rations. That seemed so
senseless that I had to look outside myself for the reason. And
then I saw it quite plainly—as if I'd stumbled on the solution of

a problem in mathematics—I saw that the goodness of God can only work by means of His creation, it uses even the most degenerate and feeble, it can find a passage through every human absurdity and every corruption . . . I say it came like the answer to a problem. But it was also a vision. I did—in those days of endless darkness—I did see God's goodness as a thing entirely different from anything I'd learnt or imagined. It was a waterfall of light, but it was also close and personal—not a vague and misty thing but tangible, like Mussorgsky's music or the taste of wine . . .'

'What I lacked,' he said pensively, 'was the physical means to make a record of that experience there and then, for other people's use as well as mine. If I could have done that I'd have ceased to worry whether my life had any sense or purpose . . . The trouble is that one sees nothing so clearly in daylight— there are too many distractions. Too much noise and anger, too many voices, including one's own. I read a lot of books. I thought that other men's philosophy might lead me back to the truth I'd once held in my hands. It hasn't, up to now . . . So I make do with other occupations! But it's hard to take it seri- ously, this transient business of getting money for tobacco and food. What I really live for is to recover that vision—to go where it leads, to make it operate.'

R. C. Hutchinson

DUNGEON GRATES

But only the strange power
Of unsought Beauty in some casual hour
Can build a bridge of light or sound or form
To lead you out of all this strife and storm . . .
One moment was enough,
We know we are not made of mortal stuff.
And we can bear all trials that come after,
The hate of men and the fool's loud bestial laughter
And Nature's rule and cruelties unclean,
For we have seen the Glory—we have seen.

C. S. Lewis

FREEDOM, SUFFERING AND LOVE

What has enthralled me most in the long process of thinking
out and working out the argument of this book is that, starting
as I do from an evolutionary standpoint about man and looking particularly at the three mainstays of freedom, suffering
and love, there has emerged the fact (emerged is correct
because I did not try to organize it so) that the activity which
we call forgiveness occupies the central position in a discussion
of man as God-made in freedom and God-destined through
love. This is surely a hint of validity from the Christian point of
view. By forgiveness I do not mean exclusively the forgiveness
of man by God. Christianity has tended to lay so much emphasis on this cardinal necessity in Christian faith that it has
laid too little on the other aspect of forgiveness, that of one
human by another ... Christ made this quite central in the
Lord's Prayer, '. . . as we forgive them that trespass against us',
and in other parts of his teaching. It seems to emerge that
forgiveness in both its directions is the instrument by which the
defeat of the devil is brought about, and furthermore that the
forgiveness of man by man is in no way far behind that of man
by God as the instrument of man's liberation. People can
hardly believe at first hearing that it can be so, for forgiveness is
sometimes seen as affecting small things in which not much
sacrifice is required in order to forgive. But it is in fact the most
exciting exercise of love in the whole field of human relationship.

Forgiveness brings us face to face with pain, for, whatever else
it is made up of, it is centrally the matter of dealing with pain;
if you have not been hurt there is nothing to forgive. That is
why it is the most exacting exercise of love. The vital thing
which evolution tells us is that pain lies at the heart of that
massive array of equipments which have ensured man's survival and advance. Man's vulnerability is his safeguard, and it
is also the trigger for his aggressiveness, defensiveness and will
to dominate—and his refusal to forgive. Thus it is that evil is
enabled to proliferate and that a vicious circle of hurt, counter-
hurt and yet more hurt drives people and groups further apart
until they cease to see each other's need or the validity of each

other's point of view at all. Pain is indeed the single most significant experience of humanity.

It need not, however, be destructive or divisive; it need not proliferate or form vicious circles. What Christ was doing, in innermost meaning, in the crucifixion was to accomplish the dealing with pain in such a way that it could not be any of these things. In him love rose to its climax in meeting pain and injustice, to its most totally exacting dimension, and remained unbroken. That is forgiveness, because whom you go on loving you do not any more even desire to condemn or revenge yourself upon. So man's forgiveness was assured but, almost as vital, the trail of man's forgiveness of man was blazed. The evil of man's proliferating estrangements was shown to be terminable.

That laid before man the challenge to enter the exercise of love in this highest dimension. That entry into such a love requires absolutely the power of divine grace without which man succumbs before the instinct of self-protection and revenge. That forgiveness defeats evil and the love which powers it is the foundation of man's own growing in likeness to God.

Andrew Elphinstone

Enter my night as into my house . . .
    then must it be that my Paradise
Will be nothing but a great clear night which will fall on
    the sins of the world.

Alan Ecclestone

When Jesus prayed 'Father forgive them, they do not know what they are doing' he lifted up to God the whole tangled and unfathomable pattern of human ignorance and fear and injury and retaliation in which he was so hideously caught. He stated his faith again that it was all within that fatherly love whose purpose is to make a kingdom of forgiveness and reconciliation.

We have beautiful and important anticipation of that great forgiveness here and now, whenever one human being forgives another or is forgiven by man, woman or God. But there is a vast area of the unforgiven and the apparently unforgivable in this world. There are people who do not yet want forgiveness and die not wanting it. There are those who are incapable of forgiving, like the brutalized child who is so damaged that he grows into an inadequate or psychopathic adult; he cannot understand what forgiving means, and no one can forgive on his behalf. There are some situations of fantastic horror, like the Nazi attempt to exterminate the Jews, that seem to go beyond anything we can attribute to any known person or persons. And there may be a dark infinity of distress reaching out from some of our own smallest wrongdoings. No one can scour the world for all those who have been injured or will yet be injured by his cruelties and failures and make amends to them all. The fact is that the word of full forgiveness cannot be heard by anyone in this world. If this world is all there is it cannot be heard at all.

However, it is Christian faith that ultimately, beyond history, it will be heard by all. In the world of time the immeasurable wrongness of life must remain incomprehensible. Jesus finally referred this greatest mystery to God's purpose to transform all life in the fulfilment of his heavenly kingdom. That kingdom comes as men come to see God as forgiving love, always present, always overcoming evil with good ... As anxiety loosens they become free to give. The spirit of man in freedom is by a marvellous necessity a giver and lover.

As the Bible ends, in a bewildering dazzle of images and symbols for that which all its packed religion discerns ahead of us, there is a recurring image of a final gift which is an unending love, the gift of praise to him who will at last be seen to have done all things well.

J. Neville Ward

PART III

FREEDOM

Man is created free, and is free, even though he is born in chains.

Friedrich von Schiller

And I called to the Lord from my narrow prison and He answered me in the freedom of space.

Viktor Frankl

My free soul may use her wings.

George Herbert

Some Fancy they may achieve freedom by doing as they please, by living undisciplined uncontrolled lives. And they are surprised when they end up enslaved by some habit, some stronger mind, some malicious evil which resides within themselves or in society. As one writer put it, 'They think they are emancipated, when they are only unbuttoned.'

O. Carroll

Men rattle their chains to show they are free.

Anonymous

Jesus then said to the Jews who had believed in him, 'If you continue in my word, you are truly my disciples, and you will know the truth, and the truth will make you free.' They answered him, 'We are descendants of Abraham, and have never been in bondage to any one. How is it that you say, "You will be made free"?'

Jesus answered them, 'Truly, truly, I say to you, every one who commits sin is a slave to sin. The slave does not continue in the house for ever; the son continues for ever. So if the Son makes you free, you will be free indeed.'

John 8:31–6 RSV

PRAY FOR THEM

Inside most of the readers of this page there lives a small light of hope, which silently says:

This life so free
Is the life for me.

Hardy put those words into the mouth of a convict in hand-cuffs. This small light of hope can flicker on through captivity, adversity or sorrow, and so long as it does survive very much can be endured. The most primitive and precious possession that we have, it is not to be confused with a matured belief in God. It is something older, more instinctive, even than that. It is the will to live, to go on.

Remember that there are those who for the time being at least have felt that light go out, and like Hamlet—'wherefore I know not'—unaccountably have lost all their mirth and cannot by thinking or by willing find it again. Let us remember them. In our great wealth at having that small light, let us spare one thought for those who, lacking that light, however rich in talent or advantage, are most wretched.

It is no good shouting to such people: 'Believe in God!' The best we can do is to reach out a hand, if only in the secret and anonymous guise of praying for them.

At any moment now we may meet such a person, and there will be nothing to tell him or her by. It is a good plan to be always praying, not for goody-goodness but (as is all too likely) in case we shall not notice what needs have brushed close by us and gone.

Bernard Canter

DELIVER CAPTIVES, SET PRISONERS FREE

Christ told us clearly and unmistakably that in any prisoner we visit, we visit Christ himself. There have been times in the history of the Church—sociologically conditioned, no doubt, but they reveal the depth of the Christian attitude—when Christians sold themselves in order to ransom others from slavery. Even physical captivity can be an expression of supreme inner freedom. Christ himself gave his own limited and unsuccessful life, typified by his imprisonment before his death on the cross, an ultimate meaning of inner liberation by accepting it. What took place once and for all in the life of Christ has to be realized daily in our own life: freedom from captivity.

We are all prisoners, each in a different way. Life itself is still

fettered in us. Our pains, obligations, the responsibilities we
have voluntarily undertaken are only a small part of what we
might have been. The inclinations that have gradually taken
shape in us, our friendships and our love, all limit our horizon,
for they only partly fulfil us. Our affections cling to what we
have and what is possible, but that holds us back from other,
perhaps even more wonderful, possibilities. Worry, humiliation, and frustration chain us to the drab cruelty of the daily
round. Our own body is often a prison cell to us. We only
notice this when it begins to threaten us and cramp our minds.
And, deepest of all, we are imprisoned by the strange and
sinister thing we call sin, something essentially alien to us yet
often inescapably close.

A description of the essential features of human captivity, a
study of the symptoms of imprisonment in the human condition, is found in Dante's *Purgatorio*. Exterior visions reveal an
interior landscape of man's soul, the place where man is captive. Man looks upwards and waits in silence for deliverance. 'I
saw that goodly host stand sentinel, / Thereafter, speechless, in
expectant love / Scanning the sky with lowly looks, all pale'
(*Purg.*, VIII, 22–24). Man has to climb seven terraces to reach
final liberation. Each stage represents a stage of existential purification. The transition from one terrace to another costs effort,
but the higher one climbs, the easier the ascent becomes, not
because the path is easier but because the human being is less
burdened. The transformation takes place in this way. First,
pride is atoned for and humility achieved, then envy is overcome and magnanimity attained. Hardness of heart is changed
to meekness. Sloth gives way to joy in action; covetousness is
stripped away and liberality takes its place. Excess is broken
and self-control learned. Lust is burned pure in repentance. To
set captives free, therefore, in another sense means showing
others by living example that it is possible to satisfy our longing
for deliverance even now in our earthly captivity. It means
proving that it is possible even on earth to live in the attitude
that is a condition for entry into the Paradiso. 'No word from
me, no further sign except; / Free, upright, whole, thy will
henceforth lays down / Guidance that it were error to neglect, /
Whence o'er thyself I mitre thee and crown' (*Purg.*, XXVII, 139–

141). By living our hope we should be an 'angel' (God's messenger) for our brother, breaking open the carefully bolted cell of his own self, as an angel once did the door of Peter's dungeon (cf. Acts 12,8–17).

Ladislaus Boros

VERSES FROM 'TO ALTHEA, FROM PRISON'

When (like committed linnets) I
   With shriller throat shall sing
The sweetness, mercy, majesty,
   And glories of my King;
When I shall voice aloud, how good
   He is, how great should be;
Enlarged winds that curl the flood,
   Know no such liberty.

Stone walls do not a prison make
   Nor iron bars a cage;
Minds innocent and quiet take
   That for an hermitage;
If I have freedom in my love,
   And in my soul am free;
Angels alone, that soar above,
   Enjoy such liberty.   *Richard Lovelace*

THE PROPHET

And an orator said. Speak to us of Freedom.
   And he answered:
At the city gate and by your fireside I have seen you prostrate yourself and worship your own freedom,
   Even as slaves humble themselves before a tyrant and praise him though he slays them.
   Ay, in the grove of the temple and in the shadow of the citadel. I have seen the freest among you wear their freedom as a yoke and a handcuff.

And my heart bled within me; for you can only be free when even the desire of seeking freedom becomes harness to you, and when you cease to speak of freedom as a goal and a fulfilment.

You shall be free indeed when your days are not without a care nor your nights without a want and a grief,

But rather when these things girdle your life and yet you rise above them naked and unbound.

And how shall you rise beyond your days and nights unless you break the chains which you at the dawn of your understanding have fastened around your noon hour?

In truth that which you call freedom is the strongest of these chains, though its links glitter in the sun and dazzle your eyes.

Kahlil Gibran

In the prison of his days
teach the free man how to praise.   *W. H. Auden*

NIGHT VOICES IN TEGEL (3)

Twelve cold, thin strokes of the tower clock
Awaken me.
No sound, no warmth in them
To hide and cover me.
Howling, evil dogs at midnight
Frighten me.
The wretched noise
Divides a poor yesterday
From a poor today.
What can it matter to me
Whether one day turns into another,
One that could have nothing new, nothing better
Than to end quickly like this one?
I want to see the turning of the times.

When luminous signs stand in the night sky,
And over the peoples new bells
Ring and ring.

I am waiting for that midnight
In whose fearfully streaming brilliance
The evil perish for anguish
And the good overcome with joy.

The villain
Comes to light
In the judgement.

Deceit and betrayal
Malicious deeds—
Atonement is near.

See, O man,
Holy strength
Is at work, setting right.

Rejoice and proclaim
Faithfulness and right
For a new race!

Heaven, reconcile
The sons of earth
To peace and beauty.

Earth, flourish;
Man, become free,
Be free!   *Dietrich Bonhoeffer*

Extract from N. S. Rubashov's diary, on the twentieth day of imprisonment.

. . . Vladimar Bogrov has fallen out of the swing. A hundred and fifty years ago, the day of the storming of the Bastille, the European swing, after long inaction, again started to move. It had pushed off from tyranny with gusto; with an apparently uncheckable impetus, it had swung up towards the blue sky of freedom. For a hundred years it had risen higher and higher into the sphere of liberalism and democracy. But, see, gradually the pace slowed down, the swing neared the summit and turning-point of its course; then, after a second of immobility, it started the movement backwards, with ever-increasing speed. With the same impetus as on the way up, the swing carried its passengers from freedom to tyranny again. He who had gazed upwards instead of clinging on, became dizzy and fell out.

Whoever wishes to avoid becoming dizzy must try to find out the swing's law of motion. We seem to be faced with a pendulum movement in history, swinging from absolutism to democracy, from democracy back to absolute dictatorship.

The amount of individual freedom which a people may conquer and keep, depends on the degree of its political maturity. The aforementioned pendulum motion seems to indicate that the political maturing of the masses does not follow a continuous rising curve, as does the growing up of an individual, but that it is governed by more complicated laws.

The maturity of the masses lies in the capacity to recognize their own interests. This, however, presupposes a certain understanding of the process of production and distribution of goods. A people's capacity to govern itself democratically is thus proportionate to the degree of its understanding of the structure and functioning of the whole social body.

Arthur Koestler

The two revolutionary concepts that were dearest to him [Beethoven] were freedom and virtue. As a young man in Vienna he had seen Mozart's *Don Giovanni* and had been shocked by its cynicism. He determined to write an opera in which virtuous and unwavering love should be associated with freedom. The subject rumbled about in his mind for years, providing first of all the *Leonora Overtures*, and finally *Fidelio*, where, in addition to the themes of justice and virtuous love, he gives us the greatest of all hymns to liberty, as the victims of injustice struggle up from their dungeons towards the light. 'O happiness to see the light' they say 'to feel the air and be once more alive. Our prison was a tomb. O freedom, freedom come to us again.' This cry, this hope echoed through all the revolutionary movements of the nineteenth century. We tend to forget how many there were—in France, Spain, Italy,

Austria, Greece, Hungary, Poland and always the same pattern: the same idealists, the same professional agitators, the
same barricades, the same soldiers with drawn swords, the same
terrified civilians, the same savage reprisals. In the end one
can't say that we are much further forward. When the Bastille
fell in 1789 it was found to contain only seven old men who
were annoyed at being disturbed. But to have opened the doors
of a political prison in Germany in 1940 or Hungary in 1956—
then one would have known the meaning of that scene in
Fidelio.

Beethoven in spite of his tragic deafness, was an optimist. He
believed that man had within himself a spark of the divine fire
revealed in his love of nature and his need for friendship. He
believed that man was worthy of freedom. The despair that
poisoned the Romantic movement had not yet entered his
veins. Where did this poison come from? Already in the eighteenth century there had been a taste for horror, and even Jane
Austen's heroines had liked to frighten themselves by reading
Gothic novels. But it seemed to be a mere fashion that would
pass. Then in the 1790s the horrors became real, and by about
1810 all the optimistic hopes of the eighteenth century had been
proved false: the Rights of Man, the discoveries of science, the
benefits of industry, all a delusion. The freedoms won by
revolution had been immediately lost either by counter-
revolution or by the revolutionary government falling into the
hands of military dictators. In Goya's picture of a firing squad
(210), called 3 May 1808, the repeated gesture of those who
had raised their arms in heroic affirmation becomes the
repeated line of the soldiers' muskets as they liquidate a small
group of inconvenient citizens. Well, we are used to all this
now. We are almost numbed by repeated disappointments. But
in 1810 it was a new discovery, and all the poets, philosophers
and artists of the Romantic movement were shattered by it.

The spokesman of this pessimism was Byron. He would
probably have been a pessimist anyway—it was part of his
egotism. But appearing when he did, the tide of disillusion
carried him along, so that he became, after Napoleon, the most
famous name in Europe. From great poets like Goethe and
Pushkin, or great men of action like Bismarck, down to the most

brainless school girl his works were read with an almost hysterical enthusiasm which, as we struggle through the rhetorical nonsense of *Lara* or the *Giaour*, we can hardly credit; because it was Byron's bad poetry not *Don Juan* that made him famous. Byron who was very much a man of his time, wrote a poem about the opening of a prison—the dungeon of the Castle of Chillon. He begins with a sonnet in the old revolutionary vein—'Eternal Spirit of the chainless Mind! Brightest in dungeons, Liberty!' But when, after many horrors, the prisoner of Chillon is released, a new note is heard.

> At last men come to set me free;
> I ask'd not why, and reck'd not where;
> It was at length the same to me,
> Fetter'd or fetterless to be,
> I learn'd to love despair.

Since that line was written how many intellectuals down to Beckett and Sartre have echoed its sentiment. This negative conclusion was not the whole of Byron. The prisoner of Chillon had looked from his castle wall onto the mountains and the lake, and felt himself to be part of them. This was the positive side of Byron's genius, a self-identification with the great forces of nature: not Wordsworth's daisies and daffodils, but crags, cataracts and colossal storms: in short, with the sublime.

Kenneth Clark

THE BUNKER OF RAVENSBRÜCK

For Odette what had been designed to be the torture of loneliness became the gift of liberty. She could leave her body in its dark cell and stop her human eardrums to the Rhythm of Ravensbrück. In a dream untroubled by hope, she had the freedom of the universe. In the early days of her imprisonment, when her body was still strong and resentful of her cell walls, fantasy had piled on wilder fantasy. She had looked at her cell door in Fresnes and visualized with all her strength that it was bursting open before her eyes, that she could see a smiling British soldier in battledress on the landing and he would say

'Lady, you're free,' and she would walk out of her cell and along the landing and out into the yard and see khaki everywhere and hear kindly voices and have a cup of tea and be taken to an airfield and ride the clouds back to the England of the hedges and the buttercups and the foaming blossom ... Most inappropriately, Baudelaire was mixed up in this ridiculous dream of England:

> ... Emporte-moi, wagon, enlève-moi, frégate,
> Ici la terre est faite de nos pleurs ...

and the 'wagon' of Baudelaire was the rusty reaper and binder in Mrs Marshall's yard and, in her dream, it was drawn through the corn by a sweating Shire horse, and on its back, laughing, rode Françoise and Lily and Marianne.

She was long past all that beguiling wish-fulfilment now. Escapism, real or imagined, belonged to the days before she limped through the black door of Ravensbrück.

... For fourteen months, she had been the victim of a system designed deliberately to deteriorate her physical and mental condition and consecutive thought was no longer as swift and as agile as it had been before her capture. But it was more detailed and more profound.

... On the 15th of August, a considerable airborne army of British Commandos, French and American troops stormed into the south of France. This military operation was to have a direct repercussion in the Bunker of Ravensbrück in a display of vicarious spite which would have been ludicrous were it not so bestial. The central heating, controlled from outside her cell, was turned on at full strength so that the room, normally cold, became an inferno. In desperation Odette soaked her blankets in cold water and wrapped herself in them, alternately burning and shivering. No food of any sort was brought to the hatch that day, and already weak, she lay on her floorboards, her stomach a twisting lens of pain and her brow an anvil. Four days and nights crawled by before she sank into a sort of dazed coma. Two more days and nights passed ... and she emerged from her black sleep to feel the stab of a hypodermic syringe in her arm and to see bending over her the face of Elisabeth Marschall, Matron of Ravensbrück. There was anxiety in her pale-blue eyes, anxiety not for a woman who was gravely ill, but for a precious prisoner lest she should cheat her future executioners.

This week of starvation was the final blow to Odette's physical health ... Only the brightness of her spirit was undimmed.

Jerrard Tickell

SOLITARY CONFINEMENT

Most people outside the Anglo-Saxon world have political violence in their blood, and with it the necessary antibodies. By political violence I mean everything associated with a mere riot or with foreign occupation, and I am thinking principally of the French because I know them best, though the same can be said with variations of the Italians, Czechs, Poles and even the Germans. Generation by generation they have passed through crisis after crisis, and in the times of peace they do not quite relax, never knowing what upheaval or interference will come tomorrow.

... The Englishman, on the other hand, has for so long been kept at a safe distance from political violence of any consistency that he has lost the character of potential victim and with it his protective colouring. When peace is broken (by foreigners) he goes soberly to war, and if he is taken prisoner he stays in company with his fellows and organizes his existence according to the established rules. He never becomes a foreigner. This is the cohesive strength for which we are so envied abroad and which gives us phlegm, tolerance and our rather priggish conservatism.

In two places in this book I refer to my reluctance to correspond with my neighbour in the cell next door. On the first occasion my reason was a good one, since he might easily have been an informer. But on the second it was pure self-sufficiency. I simply could not be bothered to interrupt my own train of thought. Thinking—musing would be a better word—was by this time my whole life outside my appetite, and I can remember to this day how petulant I became about it. Once I had

embarked on a train of thought I only wanted to stay on it, and
it never occurred to me that my neighbour's desire to talk was
no less legitimate than mine to be silent. If I had, no doubt my
version of legitimacy would have won.

. . . But the greatest achievements of the human being are
only within reach when no more food, no greater warmth or
comfort can be achieved by a man's exertions. We were in that
state in Fresnes, and when we left it we were truly 'poor in
spirit'. Buchenwald put some false notes into the harmony
because it gave opportunities for more or less food, harder or
easier work, and a slower or quicker death. There every crime
was committed and every kindness done, but the essential community, though ragged at the edges, never gave way. For what
breaks community is contempt, and contempt with us was
never a real feeling but only a verbal expletive.

Wariness of the world and acceptance of persons, hard-
headedness and generosity, informal and undisciplined solidarity—these are, I think, the main characteristics of this quality
of the political victim—this rootless familiarity—which is so
different but so difficult to differentiate from simple community
of interest.

. . . Solitude is liberty indeed, bounded only by the obsessive
appetite and the animal lust to roam. But liberty itself is a rare
and refined spirit, so strong that Providence in its wisdom has
arranged that there shall be little of it, making men live in a
society to which solitude is repugnant. Its dilution by the invisible but constant companionship of an active world made these
eighteen months an exercise rather than a transcendance.

. . . Down on the bedrock, life becomes a love affair of the
mind and reality merely the eternally mysterious beloved. Men
are just men like oneself but different, ships plying the same sea
and weathering the same storms, to be fended off only when
they grapple you and otherwise to be saluted, succoured and
respected. All we need is the freedom of this small land-locked
sea and our daily bread, and my appreciation of the latter in its
most rigid sense is not quite equalled by my mistrust of
admirals.

Experiences of such rarity in a lifetime engender some sentiment of privateness which in careless moments can seem par-

adoxically like nostalgia. It is nothing so affectionate, and if the events in this book were repeated I would certainly go quickly out of my mind. But I would not have them undone, for if I did I would lose that strange and faithful fraternity of the windows and those moments when the mind's eye, like a restless prism, could see reality as no more than an outline against the faintly discerned first light of truth.

Christopher Burney

SOLITARY CONFINEMENT (2)

Spring was announced by a blackbird, who chose a platform close outside my window and sang loudly and tempestuously of hope and love and the freedom of the new earth. I told myself stories in the same tenor, in tune with the spirit of the season, so that the blackbird became Sullivan to my Gilbert. But when I remembered, seeing the window and its bars between me and the sun and air, that his world was real and mine a shadow, I wished that he would seek partnership elsewhere. Then, one day, I was let out for exercise.

The prison, as I have told, was composed of three great parallel blocks of cells. The spaces in between seemed like canyons, and it was here that the exercise yards had been built. Along each side of the canyon was a line of little courtyards, each about ten yards square and surrounded by walls of over-grown red brick. They were like miniature Elizabethan gardens, forgotten and nestling together for company under the towering concrete. They were deep in grass and weeds, and the walls were encrusted with little plants and inscribed with salutations, boasts and threats by earlier outlaws whose language, if not Elizabethan, stemmed straight from Rabelais. A brick path, buried in the green undergrowth, was laid in a square following the walls, and along the whole row was a cat-walk from which sentries, dispelling the illusion, could overlook the inmates.

Fifteen of us were let out at one time. As soon as the preceding group was safely back, our doors were opened one by one and, with a good interval between us to keep us from talking, we were driven downstairs with a barrage of shouts.

. . . For all the studied segregation there was a great whistling and chattering all around, to which the sentries on the catwalk paid but fitful and benign attention. It was often a surprise and something of a relief to find that the humbler among our oppressors were prone to embarrassment rather than to bullying and tried, with uniform inaction, to avoid our hatred and their master's fury at the same time. Now gossip bubbled over.

. . . I listened for a while, finding the voices strange and delightful in their way, but having no wish to join them. I wanted to enjoy the newly-discovered things about me and would have preferred to be alone to absorb the sky and grass and air, so that I felt a faint resentment at the noise and a fear that one of my neighbours would waste some precious minutes by talking to me, like those people who insist on whispering in concerts. But my tongue was securely tied, and perhaps it was better that the new world was kept human in its due proportion.

. . . Meanwhile, my feet were recognizing the strange but well-loved feeling of treading on soft turf, and my eyes and nose were engaged in their own rediscoveries of life. Although I was in the canyon, the enormous sweep of the sky was overwhelming, and the light coming from all directions instead of through a window gave everything a startling brilliance. Perhaps best of all was the careless way of the growing grass, short here, long there, facing in all directions, and with dandelions spreading darker patches waywardly where their seed had dropped. An abandoned plot, it would be called; in England someone would be told to plant cabbages in it; but to me it was Arcadia. ('I guess it is the handkerchief of the Lord,' said Walt Whitman.) I walked around it, avoiding the brick path which had no business there, and felt the air, suddenly warm and throbbing, pouring life into me as it did into the grass.

And knowing that the time would be short, I tried to store it all in my mind, to imbue myself with it as a proof against my cell, as I might drink some rum before leaving a sinking ship. But it would not be captured. The clatter and shouting started again and the doors were opened and I wondered whether to take my last look at the sky or at the grass. I picked a small snail off the wall to serve as a companion and as a memorial. Then we resumed our shuffling back to the third floor.

Back in my cell, I put the snail on the table and tried to recall the sensations of outside. But they would not come back, and I spent the rest of the morning frustrated, concentrating on smells and sights and feelings which would not come of their own selves now that the physical forms in which they travelled were excluded.

When the soup came, I gave the snail little pieces of cabbage, but they did not seem to strike its fancy. It stayed for one night but disappeared during the second. When it had gone I told myself that I had been ridiculous in bringing it back with me, but it was company of a sort, and as it were an emissary from the world of real life; and its going reminded me of freedom, even suggesting that what a snail obtained so easily might still be possible for me.

For a few days I waited impatiently to be let out again. My little sky was no longer enough, and when I remembered the warmth of the air I realized that I was still shivering, even though wrapped in a blanket. But although nothing further happened, I could not live through the Spring without gladness: I did not feel in duty bound to be happy, as Wordsworth once did; I could not help it. Now I liked to wake early and listen to the blackbird singing and think about daffodils and budding silver birches and what I was doing last Spring and all the Springs before, *laudator temporis acti se puero*.

Christopher Burney

A little bird I am,
Shut from the fields of air;
And in my cage I sit and sing
To him who placed me there;
Well pleased a prisoner to be,
Because, my *God*, it pleases thee
But though my wing is closely bound,
My heart's at liberty:
My prison walls cannot control
The flight, the freedom of the soul.

Jeanne Guyon

While there is a lower class, I am in it,
While there is a criminal element I am of it;
While there is a soul in prison I am not free.

Eugene Victor Debs

THE FREEDOM OF AUSCHWITZ

The possibility of freedom in slavery is a spiritual act, in
which everything that is done is first received.

Thus the freedom of Auschwitz, too, must be wholly distin-
guished from any system of ethical duties. Its very concreteness
derives from the transcendent freedom of the will without
which liberation on such a scale cannot be initiated.

Similarly our 'What shall we do?' is still-born even as a
question unless it is lifted to the appropriate level of freedom,
which is called faith.

Ulrich Simon

Discipline
If you set out to seek freedom, then learn above all things to
govern your soul and your senses, for fear that your passions
and longing may lead you away from the path you should
follow. Chaste be your mind and your body, and both in sub-
jection, obediently, steadfastly seeking the aim set before them;
only through discipline may a man learn to be free.

Action
Daring to do what is right, not what fancy may tell you,
valiantly grasping occasions, not cravenly doubting—
freedom comes only through deeds, not through thoughts tak-
    ing wing.
Faint not nor fear, but go out to the storm and the action,
trusting in God whose commandment you faithfully follow;
freedom, exultant, will welcome your spirit with joy.

Suffering
A change has come indeed. Your hands so strong and active,
are bound; in helplessness now you see your action
is ended; you sigh in relief, your cause committing
to stronger hands; so now you rest contented.

Only for one blissful moment could you draw near to touch
    freedom;
then, that it might be perfected in glory, you gave it to God.

Death

Come now, thou greatest of feasts on the journey to freedom
    eternal;
death, cast aside all the burdensome chains, and demolish
the walls of our temporal body, the walls of our souls that are
    blinded,
so that at last we may see that which here remains hidden.
Freedom, how long we have sought thee in discipline, action,
    and suffering;
dying, we may now behold thee revealed in the Lord.

Dear Eberhard,

I wrote these lines in a few hours this evening. They are
quite unpolished, but they may perhaps please you and be
something of a birthday present for you. Dietrich.

I can see this morning that I shall again have to revise them
completely. Still I'm sending them to you as they are, in the
rough. I'm certainly no poet!

Dietrich Bonhoeffer

SHEET ANCHOR (1)

O freed of those twin tyrants, time and space,
The soaring spirit, whose unfettered mind
And soul's alacrity shall now embrace
Truth irrevealable to humankind! . . .

That fountain love, incalculably springing
From the profound unmeasured lake of God,
Its clear renewal every morning bringing
A fresh delight in every pathway trod;
The sudden knowledge, the surprise of joy
In the mysterious tidings of a face,
That faith and certainty in the employ
Of love that is not virtue but is grace,
That loss whereon we thrive,
That headlong death of self, by which we come alive.

All of true love, the passion and compassion,
The quenchless pity, the untrammelled pride,
The knowledge whence divided lovers fashion
Their bread of life—the body's bread denied,
The dear affection, the surpassing peace,
The friendship that is daylight in the soul,
The body's ardour, and the mind's release,
Love, that alone makes man entire and whole,
Quiet and intent and gay
The calm celestial dullness of love's day-to-day—

This is the fortress centuries cannot storm,
These are the lifted gates of David's story,
Shut fast against the insurgent minutes swarm,
Flung open to receive the King of Glory;
This is the native element of man,
This climate of content and sudden laughter,
Whilst angry aeons fret their sluggard span,
This was before, this is for ever after—
Though time's malign misprision
Darkens and separates and dulls the mortal vision.

Eve Stuart

IN DEFIANCE

And then at last, I was free to be myself, free to sob and cry
when I wanted, free to sleep when I felt like it, free to dream,
free to sing, free to do, in my limited kingdom, exactly as I
wished, and I celebrated my freedom with a wild dance in the
worst of taste.

Of course I realized that new prisoners were arriving all the
time and that I would probably not enjoy my solitude for long,
and I must make the most of it.

First of all, I needed exercise. Apart from the ten minute
walk round the garden which prisoners were allowed to take in
a long crocodile carefully guarded, I had had no exercise
whatever for the last ten days or so! I pushed the bed, the
chairs and all other obstacles to the middle of the room so that

I had a running track all along the walls. Sixty-five rounds would make a kilometre! It was better than nothing. I stripped and ran—not very fast, not very well—once, twice, sixty-five times round the room. Exhausting, but I felt much better. I did it again the next day and again . . . Once in the middle of the exercise, the spy hole opened and I had a glimpse of the eye of the hated chief warder, a sergeant, and there was a twinkle in his wicked eye. Alas, after a few days I had angry protests from the prisoners below me who couldn't stand the elephant's dance over their heads and I had to give it up.

My thirst for exercise quenched, I spent peaceful hours in my library. With a little guile and a lot of skill, I had obtained three of my favourite books from the prison library. There was Pascal, an invaluable friend when I found myself in a dreamy and philosophical mood, there was *White Fang* and all the skill of Jack London to give me a breath of fresh air and a vision of wide open spaces when I felt frustrated and realized my prison. And best of all perhaps, for the moments when I felt full of heroism and unspent energy, there was the thrilling play by Herman Closson *Le Jeu des Quatre Fils Aymon*. I had watched the Comediens Routiers many times as they took this play all round Belgium. Many times its finale had raised such enthusiasm that we feared the play might be banned by the Germans. And now in my lonely cell, I was all at once the players and the audience and, as I read them aloud, the well-known words acquired a new magic.

Renaud, Robert, Guiscart, Allard,
Renaud le sage, Robert le fort,
Guiscart le fol, Allard l'enfant,
En quatre coeurs une seule pensée
En quatre corps un même élan,
Pays d'Ardenne, voilà ton sang.

*　　*　　*

But there was still plenty of time to dream. I didn't feel sorry for myself; this life was a great improvement on my 'hiding' days but I was worried for Etienne and Toutou of whom I had no news, and for Maman who I realized must miss me very much. And as I got to know my neighbours I became acutely

conscious of their many tragedies—Marilou whose husband
was condemned to death in the adjoining wing, Elizabeth who
had no news of her two babies and who had a miscarriage all
by herself in her cell. There was plenty to think about.

Every Sunday we were taken to Mass in the circular chapel
over the central hub of the prison. Each prisoner sat in her own
cubicle, row upon row of them forming circles around the altar.
Each of us could see nothing of her companions, nothing but
the altar and the priest celebrating Mass (there were also the
German guards perched on wooden towers from which they
could watch the whole place; but we ignored them) so that she
was alone, alone with her Maker in such intimacy that she
could lay bare her soul at His feet—I have never anywhere met
such intensity of emotion. There was nothing to see; you were
alone in your box and yet you could feel them all around you,
five hundred souls steeped in prayer . . .

It was strangely moving.

*   *   *

Our morning 'promenade' round the grounds was far too
short and all too often suspended. It was maddening to see the
blue sky through the window, to read in the papers—when we
got them—that this was the best summer for years. My cell was
facing west and every day about five o'clock the sun on its way
down would allow one timid little ray to settle on my wall for a
few minutes, but so high up that even on tip-toe I couldn't
reach it. Again the bed proved very useful. I pushed it into a
corner, put the chair on it and settled myself on top of it all
sunbathing gratefully. It lasted but a few minutes, but these
were very precious minutes when I was in touch again with
Nature, and with life.

*   *   *

PRISONER

> Four walls and a palliasse
>   My kingdom of solitude.

> Life goes by
>   bitter and biting as an asp.

Beyond my walls I see nothing. I hear nothing.
　　I let go the mire and I laugh.

Outside they kill, they die,
　　They are hungry, wounded, they cry.
　　　I don't remember.

Outside they have to eat and sleep,
　　They have to speak, they have to smile,
　　　I don't remember.

Fight for today,
　　No matter what to-morrow brings.
　　　I don't remember.

Within my cell all that is nothing more
　　But the dim echo of bedlam.

I have
　　the bird on my window,
　　and the sun on my wall at dusk
　　　Crumbs of true happiness
　　　　Which you have lost,
　　　　　beyond my walls.

They've locked me up with my gladness
And I am free, I am free.
　　Within my four walls and my palliasse
　　My kingdom of solitude.

Françoise Rigby

THE IMPRISONED SPLENDOUR

If we look at history we find that 'love of freedom' has played no inconsiderable part. For this men have fought and died. Yet again and again, after fighting to secure some environmental change that they thought would secure them freedom, it has eluded them. This is because the more important causes of bondage are within men's hearts and minds, not outside them. We are prisoners of our habits, of our fears, our desires, our

hopes and our social interests. We are prisoners of our climate
of thought, our prejudices, our background of teaching, our
mental limitations, our accepted political, scientific, religious
and philosophical beliefs. If to be truly free is to live and act in
accordance with our real inner nature (that of the Self as dis-
tinct from the Ego), the fact is that freedom is a very rare
phenomenon. We are all prisoners, some perhaps tethered with
a longer rope than others, but none of us free except within the
little circle determined by the length of rope. For a large part of
humanity this circle is very small indeed, but people do not
know it. They cherish the illusion of choice and freedom of the
will, and would be offended to be told they were well nigh
automatons. The Ego, that centre in the mind with which we
falsely identify ourselves, is the focus of all the patterns of
thought and desire and action we have built up. The real Self
which alone has freedom gets very little chance to exercise it
because of the dominant Ego. At one extreme there is what we
may call 'animal man', completely governed by the Ego. Place
him in a given situation and you might predict how he would
behave. He may imagine he exercises his will to choose. His
will has, in fact, little or nothing to do with it: he is governed by
the strongest desire at the time. At the other end of the scale is
'spirit-man', the sage or saint, the truly enlightened man,
whose Ego only exists as the perfect vehicle of expression of his
Self in the lower worlds. He alone is free. Indian philosophy
uses the term *moksha*, or liberation, to describe his state. In
between these extremes is the mass of humanity. Let us be
clear, then, that inner freedom is something which has to be
earned and won ... The Buddhist says we are bondslaves of
Ignorance. Jesus proclaims the same thing: 'Ye shall know the
Truth—and the Truth shall make you free.'

Raynor C. Johnson

FREEDOM

For every little boy and girl it's always been the thing
To honour all those authors who the praise of
    freedom sing

But don't you be like them, my son, when you to
    school are sent;
Those smug complacent poets never knew what
    freedom meant.

Secure in England's land they sang 'We must be
    free or die'—
They who had never even felt the threat of tyranny.
But if you're seeking praises that are not mere
    fulsome cant,
A victim of the Kempei or Gestapo's what you want.

For when you've had to fawn upon a callous,
    vicious foe
To get a wretched dole of food, or when you've had to go
And labour in a chain-gang with your friends who
    once were free—
Then, and only then, you'll know the worth of liberty.

So when the theme is freedom and the poet free
    and fat,
Just take a prisoner's word for it, he's talking
    through his hat.
And ask yourself this question when you next read
    Burke and Co.
'What can they know of freedom, they who only
    freedom know?'

Robin Fletcher

MAN'S SEARCH FOR MEANING (7)

In attempting this psychological presentation and a psychopathological explanation of the typical characteristics of a concentration camp inmate, I may give the impression that the human being is completely and unavoidably influenced by his surroundings. (In this case the surroundings being the unique structure of camp life, which forced the prisoner to conform his conduct to a certain set pattern.) But what about human liberty? Is there no spiritual freedom in regard to behaviour and reaction to any given surroundings? Is that theory true which would have us believe that man is no more than a product of many conditional and environmental factors—be they of a biological, psychological or sociological nature? Is man but an accidental product of these? Most important, do the prisoners' reactions to the singular world of the concentration camp prove that man cannot escape the influence of his surroundings? Does man have no choice of action in the face of such circumstances?

We can answer these questions from experience as well as on principle. The experiences of camp life show that man does have a choice of action. There were enough examples, often of a heroic nature, which proved beyond doubt that apathy could be overcome, irritability suppressed. Man *can* preserve a vestige of spiritual freedom, of independence of mind, even in such terrible conditions of psychic and physical stress.

We who lived in concentration camps can remember the men who walked through the huts comforting others, giving away their last piece of bread. They may have been few in number, but they offer sufficient proof that everything can be taken from a man but one thing: the last of the human freedoms—to choose one's attitude in any given set of circumstances, to choose one's own way.

And there were always choices to make. Every day, every hour, offered the opportunity to make a decision, a decision which determined whether you would not submit to those powers which threatened to rob you of your very self, your inner freedom; which determined whether or not you would become the plaything of circumstances, renouncing freedom and dignity to become moulded into the form of the typical inmate.

Seen from this point of view, the mental reactions of the inmates of a concentration camp must seem more to us than the mere expression of certain physical and sociological conditions. Even though conditions such as lack of sleep, insufficient food and various mental stresses may suggest that the inmates were bound to react in certain ways, in the final analysis it becomes clear that the sort of person the prisoner became was the result of an inner decision, and not the result of camp influences alone. Fundamentally, therefore, any man can, even

under such circumstances, decide what shall become of him—
mentally and spiritually. He may retain his human dignity
even in a concentration camp. Dostoevski said once, 'There is
only one thing that I dread: not to be worthy of my sufferings.'
These words frequently came to my mind after I became
acquainted with those martyrs whose behaviour in camp,
whose suffering and death, bore witness to the fact that the last
inner freedom cannot be lost. It can be said that they were
worthy of their sufferings; the way they bore their suffering was
a genuine inner achievement. It is this spiritual freedom—
which cannot be taken away—that makes life meaningful and
purposeful.

Viktor Frankl

1. As springs bereft of water
   and clouds that drift and roam
   are those who in their freedom
   are tied to self alone,
   and all they lend to others
   the emptiness that's theirs;
   their hands hold desolation
   that takes but never gives.

2. God's word speaks not of bondage
   but always it unchains,
   and calls to us to dwell in
   His own creative day.
   Of things we are the masters,
   this is our joy and trust;
   oh, hear how they obey us,
   and answer 'we are here'.

3. Our freedom is in Jesus,
   our world has been restored,
   and reconciled for ever
   by His redemptive work.
   And we who by the spirit
   are brought to God's good spring
   shall never Want for water
   or ever thirst again.

4. Our freedom frees all others
   For brotherhood in God,
   it serves and loves the living,
   not dead demands and laws.
   The burden that we bear, then,
   is light, and freely ours,
   like rain that falls on meadows,
   or like the ocean's song.

Anders Frostenson

Henry Nevinson, in his preface to Steinberg's book on Spiridinova, quotes 'the Frenchwoman's reply to the question where, if ever, she had known the liberty she talked so much about'. Her answer was: 'Only in the Bastille.'

. . . Rarely do our Hitlers find their way behind the prison bars. For the most part the political prisoners are of a very different type. Prophets of human liberation, their first great sacrifice to the freedom of their fellow-men has too often been the loss of their personal liberty. But, being prophets, their inspiration is often found at its highest point in the adversity of imprisonment or the supreme moment when they have faced death. Who can read without emotion the final speeches from the dock of Tone and Casement; the last letters of John Brown and Edgar André? To Vanzetti, as to many others, this was a conscious moment—the keystone of a career which might otherwise have missed its significance: 'If it had not been for this, I might have lived out my life talking at street corners to scorning men. I might have died unmarked, unknown, a failure. Now we are not a failure. This is our career and our triumph.' It is neither pride nor morbidity that compels such words as these, but the sudden insight that sent the Nazarene upon his fatal journey to Jerusalem. For the paradox of the crucifixion still contains this psychological truth: 'And I, if I be lifted up, will draw all men unto me.'

It is said that when Thoreau was imprisoned for refusing to pay taxes to a government which returned fugitive slaves to their owners, he was visited by Emerson, who asked: 'What are you doing here?' Thoreau's reply, 'Waldo, what are you doing

out of here?', may almost be posed as an accusatory query to
those writers who are ineligible for inclusion in the select company which we are honoured to present to the public. There
have been few periods in the history of any State which have
not called for vigorous protests against social iniquities: and
sooner or later the circumstances have nearly always arisen in
which such protests have involved the severest punishment of
those who made them.

... In short, to quote Thoreau once more, 'under a government which imprisons any man unjustly the true place for a
just man is also in prison ... the only house in a slave state in
which a free man can abide with honour.'

... This does not mean, of course, that any hard line can be
drawn between political revolt and religious non-conformity.
Among the Abram Lawlinson Barclay MSS. at Friends House,
London, there are some lines of uncertain authorship, possibly
written in prison, which illustrate this point very well. Writing
in 1662 this unknown Quaker said:

> Your gaoles we fear not, no nor Banishm'
> Terrors nor threats can ere make us Lament
> ffor such e are as fear ye liveing God
> Not being vexed by persecutions rod
> away hipocrisie, Adew false fear
> Imortal lifes ye crown wch we doe bear
> W^{ch} can not be remov'd from us away
> that makes us scorn your threatenings every day
> These are our prayers & thus our souls doe cry
> let Justice live & all oppression dy.

... There have been those who have found with Scawen
Blunt, that 'imprisonment is a reality of discipline most useful
to the modern soul, lapped as it is in physical sloth and self-
indulgence ... the soul emerges from it stronger and more self-
contained.' Clearly it depends largely on the individual. Even
savage animals, said Tacitus, if kept in confinement lose their
courage; and probably the more animal a man is, the more
harm prison will do him, while Blunt found his desired discipline and Lovelace 'an hermitage'.

But unless society admits that its prisons are made for poets,

reformers and revolutionaries, The Devil's observations still
hold good:

> As he went through Cold-Bath Fields he saw
>   A solitary cell
> And the Devil was pleased, for it gave him a hint
>   For improving his prisons in Hell.
>
> *A. G. Stock and B. Reynolds*

ON A POLITICAL PRISONER

> She that but little patience knew,
> From childhood on, had now so much
> A grey gull lost its fear and flew
> Down to her cell and there alit,
> And there endured her fingers' touch
> And from her fingers ate its bit.
>
> Did she in touching that lone wing
> Recall the years before her mind
> Became a bitter, an abstract thing,
> Her thought some popular enmity:
> Blind and leader of the blind
> Drinking the foul ditch where they lie?
>
> When long ago I saw her ride
> Under Ben Bulben to the meet,
> The beauty of her country-side
> With all youth's lonely wilderness stirred,
> She seemed to have grown clean and sweet
> Like any rock-bred, sea-borne bird:
>
> Sea-borne, or balanced on the air
> When first it sprang out of the nest
> Upon some lofty rock to stare
> Upon the cloudy canopy,
> While under its storm-beaten breast
> Cried out the hollows of the sea.
>
> *W. B. Yeats*

The following extract is taken from ' My Return'. Levitin possesses an inner freedom which imprisonment could not destroy. Despite his physical isolation behind bars he was able to remain in communion with the Church, the world and all men.

The greatest miracle of all is prayer, I have only to turn my thoughts to God and I suddenly feel a strength which bursts into me from somewhere, bursts into my soul, into my entire being. What is it? Psychotherapy? No, it is not psychotherapy, for where would I, an insignificant old man who is tired of life, get this strength which renews me and saves me, lifting me above the earth. It comes from without, and there is no force on earth that can even understand it.

I am not a mystic by nature, nor am I characterized by susceptibility to supernatural phenomena or special experiences. I am susceptible only to that which is accessible to every man: prayer. Since I grew up in the Orthodox Church and was raised by it, my prayer pours forth in Orthodox forms (I do not, of course, deny any other forms).

The basis of my whole spiritual life is the Orthodox liturgy. Therefore, while in prison I attended the liturgy every day in my imagination. At 8 a.m. I would begin walking round my cell, repeating to myself the words of the liturgy. At that moment I felt myself inseparably linked with the whole Christian world . . . Reaching the central point of the liturgy, I would say to myself the eucharistic canon—and then the words of the transubstantiation, standing before the face of the Lord, sensing almost physically His wounded and bleeding body. I would begin praying in my own words, and I would remember all those near to me, those in prison and those who were free, those who were alive and those who had died. And my memory would keep suggesting more and more names. I remembered the whole of Russian literature . . . and all the Russian theatre . . . and all those who suffered in our land for righteousness' sake . . .

The prison walls moved apart and the whole universe became my residence, visible and invisible, the universe for which that wounded, pierced body offered itself as a sacrifice. Then the Lord's Prayer sounded in my heart especially insistently, as did the prayer before the communion: 'I believe Lord and confess.' All day after the liturgy I felt an unusual élan of spirit, a clarity and spiritual purity. Not only my prayer, but much more the prayer of many faithful Christians helped me. I felt it continually, it worked from a distance, lifting me up as though on wings, giving me living water and the bread of life, peace of soul, rest and love.

*   *   *

I have shared my life's experience with the reader. I have summoned him to courage, to courage, and once more to courage. But you know, I am not merely an elderly man who has come close to the limit of life. I am a Christian. At once there arises the question of how compatible these appeals are with Christianity. According to the general opinion, Christianity is meekness, submissiveness, and absorption in oneself. Courage— that is an external action, it is energy taken to its limit, it is self-assertion. So how far can the present writer be considered a Christian?

. . . The type of the Orthodox Russian man and the type of the Russian revolutionary are poles apart and mutually incompatible. It would be a completely useless waste of time to deny this.

However, Christianity must not be reduced to the Russian Orthodox Church. For the centre of Christianity is Christ. Christ is broader and deeper not only than any national formation of Christianity or individual confession; he is broader than Christianity itself. Christianity is historical, and therefore limited. Christ is outside history, and therefore universal. The purpose of Christianity consists in reflecting the image of Christ over the centuries.

Anatoli Levitin

PLYMOUTH AT WAR

. . . Remember them. Their fighting kept us free
Of hidden murder and hopeless prisonage
Where living men are turned to nothingness
Dragging their bones in hunger and disease
Loathing each painful drawing of their breath.
They gave us time, however we abuse it;

A moment to be free to start anew,
A time for choosing between life and death.

Never diminish the horror they saved us from,
—The dead, the wounded, and the broken in war—
Hate without pity for the immortal spirit,
For the inner land behind the guarded face
The hidden heart where man is torn or whole; . . .
That ultimate of terror and disgrace
And loss of human heart, of human shape;
Battle *à l'outrance* in the lonely cell
Where cruelty exacts its final toll;
That ever-dreaded, screaming, face-to-face,
Where the wild eyeballs roll in search of escape
While torture runs like fire through the soul
And all but the bravest falter to their knees;
Where man is licked by the long tongue of hell—
    Death in the dark of the earth where no man sees.
                                        Priscilla Napier

THE NIGHT OF THE NEW MOON (4)

Soon after dark, some thousands of men and hundreds of
their fellows too weak to walk, many near dying and carried on
stretchers, marched out of the prison for the last time, all of
them on the first stage of their way to liberation and home;
except me myself, who was now faced with another immediate
mission, physically weak as I was, and with several more years
of a new sort of war in South-east Asia ahead of me. But the
feeling of gratitude to life and Providence that all these men
were safe at last overwhelmed everything else in me. . . . It was a
feeling as of music everywhere within and about me.

As I watched the long slow procession of men march into the
night, this feeling of music everywhere rose within my liberated
senses like a chorale at the end of a great symphony, asserting a
triumph of creation over death. All that was good and true in
the dark experience behind me, combined with my memory of
how those thousands of men, who had endured so much, never

once had failed to respond to the worst with what was best in them, and all that had happened to me, in some mysterious fashion seemed to have found again the abiding rhythm of the universe, and to be making such a harmony of the moment as I have never experienced.

All I was feeling then, so utterly beyond words, seemed confirmed when I looked up and saw that the clear receptive air, standing so still and high like the water of a deep well in that raised plain of Bandoeng, was beginning to fill with the light of a rising moon. . . . It seemed suddenly to send, unbidden, another great light over the rim of my war-darkened memory, flooding my heart with a bright feeling of continuity, restoring me to the stream of all the life that had ever been and ever could be. The feeling quickly transformed itself into the most evocative words. The words were not my own but those of a moving D. H. Lawrence poem, a declaration of the rights of life, based on the image of the moon, beginning with the bugle call:

> And who has seen the moon, who has not seen
> Her rise from out the chamber of the deep
> Flushed and grand and naked . . .

The poem ascended from there on in my mind in great chords of music to the final affirmation that when the moon is 'spread out and known at last'

>   . . . We are sure
> That beauty is a thing beyond the grave,
> That perfect, bright experience never falls
> To nothingness, and time will dim the moon
> Sooner than our full consummation here
> In this odd life will tarnish or pass away.

I thought instantly then that the poem had come to me at that moment because alone in a Japanese tramp steamer, barely nineteen and on my way back from Japan to Africa in 1926, I had first read this poem on a moonlit sea off Java, and had been inexpressibly touched by it. I realized however a second later, it had done so even more because it introduces a series of poems that make up one of the greatest and most uncom-

promising manifestos of life written in my generation under the
title: 'Look! We have come through!'

Laurens Van Der Post

ESCAPED!

A man had fled . . .! We clutch the bars and wait;
The corridors are empty, tense and still;
A silver mist has dimmed the distant hill;
The guards have gathered at the prison gate.
Then suddenly the 'wildcat' blares its hate
Like some mad Moloch screaming for the kill,
Shattering the air with terror loud and shrill,
The dim, grey walls become articulate.

Freedom, you say? Behold her altar here!
In those far cities men can only find
A vaster prison and a redder hell,
O'ershadowed by new wings of greater fear.
Brave fool, for such a world to leave behind
The iron sanctuary of a cell!

Ralph Chaplin

'WHO DIES FOR JUSTICE'

I had not long finished translating this paragraph from the
'Polycraticus' when the Governments of England and France
prevailed on Czechoslovakia to surrender her western frontier
to the Third Reich.

The months that followed were not happy, even for those
more rich in hope; it was difficult for anyone to support the
spectacle of the guaranteed frontiers slipping, like the bat-
tlements one makes with spade and bucket, into the incoming
tide. It was an ugly winter in London, full of illness and ill
news. But midway in January came the first pale spring
Sunday of the year; some of us, thirsty for music, drifted into an
afternoon concert. I have forgotten the player's name, and I sat
where I saw nothing but the reflection of his hands in the dark

mirror of the Bechstein at which he played. I had been brood-
ing, not happily, on the power of physical violence to cripple
men's minds, and on this new evil doctrine of enslaving the arts
to the State: and suddenly the free movement of those hands
against darkness became a symbol.

Even as a bird
Out of the Fowler's snare
Escapes away.
So is our soul set free.
Rent is their net,
And thus escaped we.

I saw the shadow of the player's hands
Against all Europe
Against all time
I saw the shadow of the player's hands.

In that moment of liberation a forgotten memory of Alcuin
came to me, the fragment on the Lombard occupation of Rome
that begins:

By these, by these same chains, O Rome . . .
        Thou art more strong,
        Thy faith more absolute
        Against the wrong.
For ever art thou free: what bonds avail
When he hath touched them who absolveth all?
That heart unconquered and these solemn walls
Shall stand, shaken it may be, not destroyed
By any trampling of the hosts of hate.
That road is closed to war, whose gate
Stands open to the stars.

For the poems themselves I make no great claim, even in the
original Latin, still less translation. Their value lies not in the
quality of their poetry, but in their courage and their poignancy; indeed in their bare existence. They are like the inscrip-
tions scratched on dungeon walls or prison windows, the
defiance of the spirit of man against material circumstance.

Alcuin's lament for the sack of Lindisfarne by the Northmen seemed to me when I read it years ago a little trite, and full of ancient platitude; now that the bombers circle over Holy Island, I read it with a kind of contemporary anguish. 'By these, by these same chains' was strong consolation, when the banners of the swastika moved through the streets of Prague.

Boethius' *Consolation of Philosophy*, indeed, is in a different category: in every century men have listened to it, heard in it a kind of Angelus rung in the evening of the ancient world . . . But when the veiled figure stands beside him in the dungeon at Pavia, looking upon him with more than mortal eyes, the moment of recognition is not for him only. Pavia becomes Dachau; the senator's toga a German pastor's dress. 'Whoever he be,' wrote John of Salisbury, 'that is willing to suffer for his faith, whether he be little lad or man grown, Jew or Gentile, Christian or Infidel, man or woman, it matters not at all: who dies for justice dies a martyr, a defender of the cause of Christ.'

Helen Waddell

CAPTIVITY AND FREEDOM

'Prisoner, tell me, who was it that bound you?'

'It was my master,' said the prisoner. 'I thought I could out do everybody in the world in wealth and power, and I amassed in my own treasure house the money due to my King. When sleep over-came me I lay upon the bed that was for my Lord, and on waking up I found I was a prisoner in my own treasure-house.'

'Prisoner, tell me who was it that wrought this unbreakable chain?'

'It was I,' said the prisoner, 'who forged this chain very carefully. I thought my invincible power would hold the world captive, leaving me in a freedom undisturbed. Thus night and day I worked at the chain with huge fires and cruel strokes. When at last the work was done and the links were complete and unbreakable, I found that it held me in its grip.'

Rabindranath Tagore

Self is the only prison that can kill the soul.
                                                        Henry Van Dyke

The need for freedom is an ultimate necessity for living
things, and its withdrawal brings members of the animal world
near to the basic fear of annihilation—as witness the terrified
panting of a bird when caught in the hand. Even more is
freedom essential to the condition of being human, for the need
of it runs from the animal-linked instinct through to consciousness with all its complexity of mind, spirit, emotion and
will. The human therefore fights, like the animal but with
increased power, to overcome a threat to his or her freedom;
and gives it up only with the utmost reluctance. In the relation
to God, the human finds himself willing to yield freedom only
when it is perceived that an extended and enhanced freedom is
held out, and to those who enter into such a relation. This
principle holds good at a purely human level. Men and women
will, to a certain degree, give away their freedom in the interests of love, and may if they are fortunate, find that their
freedom has been not diminished but increased. Love not only
gives away its own freedom but in so doing bestows liberation
on the one who is loved.
                                                    Andrew Elphinstone

THE ABSENCE OF THE SUN

Here I told her I so wished she could have seen the Bushmen
in their hunter's life of constant movement, a flicker of precise
apricot flame in the trembling, burning desert furnace scene.
. . . How this freedom of movement impelled their imagina-
tions and became as necessary as food to them. I told her how for
example I arrived at a desert outpost once to find a Bushman
dying in gaol. He had been caught eating a great bustard he had
killed when starving, and as the bird . . . was protected by law, he
had been sentenced as a result to a month in prison.
Immediately he became ill. A doctor was summoned at once,
. . . his prosecutors were not monsters without compassion but just
ordinary men convinced that they were doing their duty.
The doctor could find nothing wrong with him. All he would

say to the doctor was that he could not bear not seeing the sun set any more because of the prison walls. He died that night. I am certain because his spirit had been starved to death by this absence of his daily view of the sun going down in that infinitely mythological way it has in the western desert of Southern Africa.

Laurens Van Der Post

INTO THE NEW AGE

The two meanings of *zoë aionios*—'the life of the new age' and 'eternal life'—come together to describe that quality of life which the Son of Man sets free in men.

But this resurrection life can only come through death. This new consciousness is a free gift which comes through the death and resurrection of the total reality of myself / the other / God. When someone dies whom we have loved, they are lifted out of the interplay of human fallibilities, and now from beyond death they come to us with an unambiguous freedom which lifts us both into a new dimension of relationship.

We die with the dying:
See, they depart, and we go with them.
We are born with the dead:
See, they return, and bring us with them.

For Christians this human experience is focused in the risen Christ who has passed through the ultimate point where good and evil interlock, and now through the interaction of faith he comes to us with unambiguous forgiveness—setting free in us the courage to know ourselves, to have compassion, and to respond to the divine centre.

This is the contemplative life, to be lived when we have passed through the antechamber of contemplative prayer. I once asked the Mother General of an order of contemplative nuns, 'What is this life which you are leading?' and she replied, 'It is to stand with Christ where good and evil interlock.'

Stephen Verney

SHEET ANCHOR (2)

They who endured this waste and this unreason,
This dull and brutal cancelling of hope,
Behaved with faith through all this fog of treason,
Knew the compelling light for which we grope.
This is unfaith—the penury of spirit,
The ignorance, the Pilatry, the sloth,
The long degrading failure to inherit
Our hard-won throne of century-slow growth,
This freedom, still a crown
Yearly re-won, lest inattention rust it down.

All that they saved is never safe,
The tyrant waves for ever chafe
On freedom's shore; justice and peace
Enjoy no durable release
From the betrayal of sloth and spite:
Virtue has never won outright.

All knowledge, all benignity,
All fiery truths that set men free
Are mortal, and their mortal spans
Depend on us; only in man's
Eternal willingness to die
To save them, does their safety lie.

Fortunate, whose live eyes behold
The evening hills aslope in gold,
Reject no more the sacrifice
That bought man's freedom at such a price;
Love well, yours is the darling kiss
Free men foreswore at Salamis.   *Eve Stuart*

In the civilization of ancient Greece an ambassador was
sancrosanct. He was the means of communication between city
states, and was protected by the laws of men and of the gods. In
one of Euripides' plays an ambassador is accidentally struck,
and a terrible vengeance unfolds upon the perpetrator of this
immoral blasphemy. But within the last decade it has become
common practice to kidnap ambassadors and hold them to

ransom. It has become common practice to beat up, rob and kill harmless men and women walking in the streets of a city—in parts of New York people do not dare to walk alone after dark, or open their windows to let in the fresh air for fear of setting off their burglar alarms. Bombs are exploded in public places to kill innocent victims. Planes are hijacked and the passengers held as hostages and murdered unless demands are met—or these same defenceless planes, as they go about their peaceful business, are blown up in mid-air with a total loss of life.

These things were almost unthinkable a generation ago. They offend against the most profound convictions and customs by which the human race has kept open the possibilities of social life, and of communication between its members.

But this outbreak of violence seen from one point of view as terrorism, can be seen from another as the struggle for freedom and justice. In World War II I served for a time with the Greek Resistance. We were called terrorists by the Germans and heroes by the British. Some of our most devoted supporters were monks, who let us use their monasteries for secret meetings, and kept weapons hidden in holes in the walls and floors. The British were particularly warm in their admiration of churchmen who were ready to stand up and fight for freedom against the oppressor. A few years later another Greek Resistance movement began operating in Cyprus, this time against the British, by whom they were now labelled terrorists. When a bishop's house was searched and a bomb was found hidden in his garden wall, there was an outcry of indignation against the hypocrisy of this spurious church leader whose actions were so contrary to the teaching of his master.

Again, we find that good and evil are interlocked. Even in the disintegration of society and the outbreak of violence there seems to be a creative and hopeful element. At the heart of student unrest there is a vision of a better world, in which professors and students will be colleagues learning together, and the rat race for money and power will have given way to concern that people develop their true selves, and be just and compassionate to one another.

Stephen Verney

THE CAPTIVE CONSCIENCE (1)

Christian concern for prisoners of conscience throughout the
world goes beyond pure humanitarian sentiment. Apart from
anything else, we are conscious not only that *some* fellow-
Christians are suffering for their faith but also that *every*
Christian is potentially a prisoner of conscience. Christians by
definition are a possible danger to any State. Their allegiance
is uncertain, their patriotism qualified and conditional. They
have only one absolute loyalty, stated with classical simplicity
by Peter when hauled before the authorities in Jerusalem, 'We
must obey God rather than men!' That is not a repudiation of
political responsibility nor rejection of the duties of citizenship.
Just fair warning that if the crunch comes, the Christian's conscience is captive to the Word of God, as Martin Luther King
put it, rather than to the *dictat* of the State. So the Christian
with typical perversity stands the obvious question on its head,
and asks himself, when confronted by the issue of prisoners of
conscience, not 'Why do *they* do it?' but 'Why am *I* not doing
it?' . . .

The Christian statement of the theme of human rights is
majestic, even cosmic in scope, for it is concerned with one who
has the stuff of divinity woven into his nature—Man made a
little lower than the angels. But the programme which flows
from that statement is, by contrast, almost prosaic in its practical, down-to-earth nature. For the Christian faced with a
painful truth—and prisoners of conscience do *that* for sure—the
appropriate question is the one wrung from the rich young
ruler when Jesus confronted him with another painful truth. It
is not the question, 'What ought I to think?' or 'How can I
endure?' or even 'Why me?', but 'What must I *do*?'

What, then, must we do; what *can* we do to alleviate the
plight of untold thousands of prisoners of conscience throughout the world suffering unimaginable misery because they will
not bow the knee to Baal? Let me detail some of the essential
elements in a Christian response to the challenge thrust in the
face of all humanity when any part of it is robbed of that
freedom which does not merely dignify Man but defines him.
And we do well to take account of some words of Gerald

Winstanley, leader of the Diggers, a seventeenth-century protest movement of the English peasantry against the worldliness of the Church and the tyranny of the rich. Winstanley and his followers paid a heavy price for their resistance to the State, and from bitter experience, he wrote: 'There are but few who act for freedom, and the actors for freedom are oppressed by the talkers and verbal professors of freedom.'

Colin Morris

WHY THE DIALOGUE ON HUMAN RIGHTS MUST CONTINUE

We argue about human rights. We do battle for them. We uphold and defend the rights of men. And even, from time to time, we put special sections about them into 'agreements on security and cooperation in Europe', as we did in the document signed in Helsinki. And so, consequently, the Soviet Union also puts its name to the observance of 'the rights of man', since this seems to be the way things are done in Europe. 'And besides,' says the Soviet Union with a sweet smile, 'in our country all these "human rights" of yours (God damn them!) were established years ago, even more so than in Europe. So there is really no point in our discussing "human rights" as a separate subject. . . . But under one condition—complete non-interference in our internal affairs which are "the sovereign authority of a sovereign state".'

So everybody is happy. Everything seems to be in order. Everyone is in favour of sovereign rights. And everyone is in favour of human rights.

But suddenly, as soon as one touches the question of these 'rights' with any degree of reality, the cloudless, peace-loving mood suddenly fades away and the faces of the Soviet leaders instantly darken. The Soviet Government turns to the West and announces coldly, 'So, you want another cold war, do you? Or maybe not only a *cold* war? Very well, we're ready! Anytime you like!'

The world does not seem able to get away from these human rights. The explanation is very simple. 'Human rights' do not exist in the Soviet Union, everybody knows this, including the Soviet Government, but they pretend that 'human rights' exist and are observed, so as not to scare away their foreign friends. You see, our men and women ('the people') have entrusted their rights to the State, and the State decides what is useful to them and what is harmful to them. The State knows best.

This subtle political distinction can be illustrated by the recent behaviour of a certain K.G.B. colonel, who was interrogating a 'religionist' (that is to say, someone arrested for believing in God) before sentencing him to ten years in the camps. While arguing with the colonel in defence of 'human rights', the prisoner referred to the paragraph in our Constitution that guarantees 'freedom of conscience'. In other words he pushed the colonel up a logical cul-de-sac. But the colonel kept his head. 'Our Soviet constitution,' he said, 'is enshrined in letters of gold . . .' He thought for a minute and added, 'We write one thing, for abroad . . . (pause) . . . we say another thing . . . and we do . . . (at this point he approached the prisoner and held his fist under his nose) . . . we do as we please! Understand?'

Individual paragraphs of the agreement do provide for renunciation of families, marriages with foreigners and non-destruction of journalists' films. But try to imagine these paragraphs in the context of relations between, say, Britain and France, each sentence individually discussed and repeatedly negotiated. Suppose that there was now an agreement allowing a Luxemburger to visit his Belgian wife. Read carefully the points in the agreement which Western diplomats managed to push through with such labour and cunning. And you will shudder at the monstrosity of these human recommendations, the contents of these paragraphs, where meetings between husband and wife or father and daughter have had to be specially established and proved as part of the process of détente. What sort of 'free exchange of people and ideas' is this? It is laughable.

The only thing the agreement seems to lack is the special chapter banning the slave trade between European nations, or inviting the participating states to abolish forced labour camps and to remove works of literary fiction from the list of especially dangerous crimes. But as for preventing customs men from confiscating manuscripts—this the West was unfortunately unable to obtain. Already the 'human rights' of the agreement begins to look like a parody of the K.G.B. colonel's fist.

The further one goes the harder the road, from Helsinki to Belgrade, the road towards détente and verification of the agreement. And how does the Soviet Union show that its iron rules have been relaxed? In the same way as before, by arresting dissidents, by arresting in particular those who voluntarily worked to *fulfil* the agreement—Alexander Ginsburg, Yuri Orlov, Anatoli Shcharansky and others. Translated into diplomatic language this means, 'Don't stick your nose into our affairs. We've put them inside and we'll keep putting them inside, to maintain human rights and freedom of speech. Understand?'

I am afraid that once again the West will not understand. Because the parties to the agreement not only spoke, but also thought in different languages—one in the language of dialogue, the other that of monologue. In the West everything is built up by dialogue: parliament, politics, press controversy, the development of art or the economy. This is why to differ is not a crime here, because it is a condition of dialogue. The Soviet Union, on the other hand, is exclusively monological. The State delivers its monologue non-stop, while the citizen's duty is to join in like a chorus, accepting what is said and putting it into practice. This is the way of doing things which the Soviet Government would like to teach the West. *We* are the ones who speak, *you* are the ones who say yes. And if you start raising objections, it means you're anti-Soviet. In fact, you belong in Siberia!

It is this system of monologue which creates the paradoxes. For instance, take a Soviet citizen who suddenly announces that there is no freedom of speech at home. He is imprisoned for slander or treason—in order to prove that in fact freedom of speech flourishes. Or on the international level, the Soviet state tells the West it has waged and will continue to wage an 'ideological struggle' against it. But if a European, to say nothing of a Soviet citizen, starts stammering out objections to all this he is immediately listed as a war-monger. These are the objectors we have to fight against, the ones who disagree with us. Our good and honourable ideas have a right to get through to *you*—you do, after all, have freedom of speech—but your bad and bourgeois ideas have no such right because we have achieved the highest form of freedom, freedom for our ideas and ours alone. Is this sophistry? No, it's just monologue, heavy, pompous monologue, boring everyone to death including those who deliver it. But just try and interrupt and see what happens—to you!

But let us try to see the position of the one who delivers the monologue, the dictator. He has to be understood too. It is not the dictator's fault that he is organically incapable of dialogue. That's why he was made a dictator. He doesn't ask and he doesn't listen—he dictates. The dictator cannot do without the monologue system, which explains the monologue nature of Soviet thought. What sort of a dictator will he be if he says his piece and then people start asking embarrassing questions or engaging him in conversations, in dialogue? It's wounding, very wounding. And the dictator feels particularly hurt when amid the calm and peace of today's Europe people ask him about some sort of 'Soviet dissidents'. For him dissidents are no more than common criminals or lunatics. It's humiliating and insulting.

Who are these dissidents, and what is their guilt in the eyes of the State? They are not political opposition. They are not revolutionaries. They are not enemies or opponents of the Soviet regime. They are people who dare to ask the government questions. For instance: 'Do we have freedom of speech, as it says in the Helsinki Agreement?' 'Is a Soviet citizen who is not a Jew allowed to "emigrate"?' 'Can I take out a subscription to the *Daily Telegraph*, or at least to *The Guardian*?' In other words they are shouting for 'human rights', a matter which was supposed to have been decided. There are not very many of these dissidents, but they do exist, some in prison, some out of it. And they keep asking questions, making protests and complaints, and when their complaints aren't answered, they send them secretly to the West, where suddenly our dictator finds himself being asked (in an extremely wounding way), 'Can you tell me, please, who are these dissidents and why do you persecute them?' Ah, the West, the West always asking questions that shouldn't be asked.

Why have the dissidents become such a bone of contention? Only because of these questions, this illicit urge to ask 'Who killed Kirov? Who killed Gorki? Why did our tanks crush Czechoslovakia?' The State pretends not to hear and accuses the imperialists of once again threatening our security. Don't ask questions, don't start a dialogue! The dictator . . . is pronouncing his set speech on the subject of 'human rights'.

I see no way out. The two-language conversation will continue without noticeable success. But the most terrible thing would be to give in to the jargon and monologue of the dictator. And nothing can ensure salvation more than staying oneself and behaving naturally—thinking, asking and answering. The dissidents have found a language in common with the West, not because both groups are dedicated to 'imperialism'. It is simply that both are open to dialogue. In the end dialogue is one of the qualities of human thought and life, and of that part of the world's culture which has not yet been gripped by a vice. Let them shout all they want, but keep asking questions, if not of the Soviet Government, at least of yourself, both about freedom of conscience and about the right to go out and come in. Don't be afraid that the dictator will call you 'an enemy of détente'. Détente is part of dialogue. Be natural and ask the question, 'How many have you now arrested for exercising "human rights" and free dialogue?'

Andrey Sinyavsky

The author is a Russian writer and literary critic. He left the Soviet Union in 1973 having been imprisoned there from 1966 to 1972.

A DAY IN THE LIFE OF IVAN DENISOVICH

It was at the evening recount on their return through the gates that the prisoners, freezing and famished, found the icy wind hardest to bear. A bowl of thin cabbage soup, all scorched up, was as grateful to them as rain to parched earth. They'd swallow it in one gulp. That bowl of soup—it was dearer than freedom, dearer than life itself, past, present, and future.

. . . Shukov took off his hat and laid it on his knees. He tasted one bowl, he tasted the other. Not bad, there was some fish in it. Generally the evening skilly was much thinner than at breakfast: if they're to work, prisoners must be fed in the morning; in the evening they'll go to sleep anyway.

He set to. First he only drank the liquid, drank and drank. As it went down, filling his whole body with warmth, all his guts began to flutter inside him at their meeting with that skilly. Goo-ood! There it comes, that brief moment for which a zek lives.

And now Shukov complained about nothing: neither about the length of his stretch, nor about the length of the day, nor about their filching another Sunday. This was all he thought about now: we'll survive. We'll stick it out, God grant, till it's over.

. . . Shukov shot up to his own bunk like a squirrel. Now he could finish his bread, smoke a second cigarette, go to sleep.

But he'd had such a good day, he felt in such good spirits, that somehow he wasn't in the mood for sleep yet.

He must make his bed now—there wasn't much to it. Strip his mattress of the grubby blanket and lie on it (it must have been '41 when he had slept in sheets—that was at home; it even seemed odd for women to bother about sheets, all that extra laundering). Head on the pillow, stuffed with shavings of wood: feet in jacket sleeve; coat on top of blanket and—Glory be to Thee, O Lord. Another day over. Thank you I'm not spending tonight in the cells. Here it's still bearable.

He lay head to the window, but Alyosha, who slept next to him on the same level, across a low wooden railing, lay the opposite way, to catch the light. He was reading his Bible again.

The electric light was quite near. You could read and even sew by it.

Alyosha heard Shukov's whispered prayer, and turning to him: 'There you are, Ivan Denisovich, your soul is begging to pray. Why, then, don't you give it its freedom?'

Shukov stole a look at him. Alyosha's eyes glowed like two candles. 'Well, Alyosha,' he said with a sigh, 'it's this way. Prayers are like those appeals of ours. Either they don't get through or they're returned with "rejected" scrawled across 'em.'

Outside the staff-hut were four sealed boxes—they were cleared by a security officer once a month. Many were the appeals that were dropped into them. The writers waited, counting the weeks: there'll be a reply in two months, in one month . . . But the reply doesn't come. Or if it does it's only 'rejected'.

'But Ivan Denisovich, it's because you pray too rarely, and badly at that. Without really trying. That's why your prayers stay unanswered. One must never stop praying. If you have real faith you tell a mountain to move and it will move.'

. . .'Well,' he said conclusively, 'however much you pray it doesn't shorten your stretch. You'll sit it out from beginning to end anyhow.'

'Oh, you mustn't pray for that either,' said Alyosha, horrified. 'Why d'you want freedom? In freedom your last grain of faith will be choked with weeds. You should rejoice that you're in prison. Here you have time to think about your soul.'

. . . Shukov gazed at the ceiling in silence. Now he didn't know either whether he wanted freedom or not. At first he'd longed for it. Every night he'd counted the days of his stretch—how many had passed, how many were coming. And then he'd grown bored with counting. And then it became clear that men of his like wouldn't ever be allowed to return home, that they'd be exiled. And whether his life would be any better there than here—who could tell.

Freedom meant one thing to him—home.

But they wouldn't let him go home.

Alyosha was speaking the truth. His voice and his eyes left no doubt that he was happy in prison.

'You see, Alyosha,' Shukov explained to him, 'somehow it works out all right for you: Jesus Christ wanted you to sit in prison and so you are—sitting there for His sake. But for whose sake am *I* here? Because we weren't ready for war in '41? For that? But was that *my* fault?'

. . . Shukov went to sleep fully content. He'd had many strokes of luck that day: they hadn't put him in the cells; they hadn't sent the team to the settlement; he'd pinched a bowl of kasha at dinner; the team-leader had fixed the rates well; he'd built a wall and enjoyed doing it; he'd smuggled that bit of

hack-saw blade through; he'd earned something from Tsezar in
the evening; he'd bought that tobacco. And he hadn't fallen ill.
He'd got over it.
   A day without a dark cloud. Almost a happy day.

Alexander Solzhenitsyn

When Yahweh brought Zion's captives home,
   at first it seemed like a dream;
then our mouths filled with laughter
   and our lips with song.

Even the pagans started talking
   about the marvels Yahweh had done for us!
What marvels indeed he did for us,
   and how overjoyed we were!

Yahweh, bring all our captives back again
   like torrents in the Negeb!
Those who went sowing in tears
   now sing as they reap.

They went away, went away weeping,
   carrying the seed;
They come back, come back singing,
   carrying their sheaves.

Psalm 126 JB

Bring to us, prisoned in time, the timelessness,
The soaring wonder of the angel's song;
Be born in us; and hold us, build us strong
With thine unswerving staunch heart-singleness.

Dorothy Margaret Paulin

PART IV

THE COMPANION

Lo, I am with you alway, even unto the end of the world.

Matthew 28: 20 AV

'Now there are certain Jews to whom you have entrusted the
affairs of the province of Babylon: Shadrach, Meshach and
Abednego; these men have ignored your command, O king;
they do not serve your gods, and refuse to worship the golden
statue you have erected.' Furious with rage, Nebuchadnezzar
sent for Shadrach, Meshach and Abednego. The men were
immediately brought before the king. Nebuchadnezzar addressed them, 'Shadrach, Meshach and Abednego, is it true
that you do not serve my gods, and that you refuse to worship
the golden statue I have erected? When you hear the sound of
horn, pipe, lyre, trigon, harp, bagpipe, or any other
instrument, are you prepared to prostrate yourselves and worship the statue I have made? If you refuse to worship it, you
must be thrown straight away into the burning fiery furnace;
and where is the god who could save you from my power?'
Shadrach, Meshach and Abednego replied to King
Nebuchadnezzar, 'Your question hardly requires an answer: if
our God, the one we serve, is able to save us from the burning
fiery furnace and from your power, O king, he will save us; and
even if he does not, then you must know, O king, that we will
not serve your god or worship the statue you have erected.'
These words infuriated King Nebuchadnezzar; his expression
was very different now as he looked at Shadrach, Meshach and
Abednego. He gave orders for the furnace to be made seven
times hotter than usual, and commanded certain stalwarts from
his army to bind Shadrach, Meshach and Abednego and throw
them into the burning fiery furnace. They were then bound,
fully clothed, cloak, hose and headgear, and thrown into the
burning fiery furnace. The king's command was so urgent and
the heat of the furnace was so fierce, that the men carrying
Shadrach, Meshach and Abednego were burnt to death by the
flames from the fire; the three men, Shadrach, Meshach and
Abednego fell, still bound, into the burning fiery furnace. And
they walked in the heart of the flames, praising God and blessing the Lord. Azariah stood in the heart of the fire and he
began to pray.

All this time the servants of the king who had thrown the
men into the furnace had been stoking it with crude oil, pitch,

tow and brushwood until the flames rose to a height of forty-nine cubits above the furnace and, leaping out, burnt those Chaldaeans to death who were standing round it. But the angel of the Lord came down into the furnace beside Azariah and his companions; he drove the flames of the fire outwards, and fanned in to them, in the heart of the furnace, a coolness such as wind and dew will bring, so that the fire did not even touch them or cause them any pain or distress.

Then King Nebuchadnezzar sprang to his feet in amazement. He said to his advisers, 'Did we not have these three men thrown bound into the fire?' They replied, 'Certainly, O king.' 'But,' he went on, 'I can see four men walking about freely in the heart of the fire without coming to any harm. And the fourth looks like a son of the gods.' Nebuchadnezzar approached the mouth of the burning fiery furnace and shouted, 'Shadrach, Meshach and Abednego, servants of the Most High God, come out, come here!' And from the heart of the fire out came Shadrach, Meshach and Abednego. The satraps, prefects, governors and advisers of the king crowded round the three men to examine them: the fire had had no effect on their bodies: not a hair of their heads had been singed, their cloaks were not scorched, no smell of burning hung about them. Nebuchadnezzar exclaimed, 'Blessed by the God of Shadrach, Meshach and Abednego: he has sent his angel to rescue his servants who, putting their trust in him, defied the order of the king, and preferred to forfeit their bodies rather than serve or worship any god but their own. I therefore decree as follows: Men of all peoples, nations, and languages! Let anyone speak disrespectfully of the God of Shadrach, Meshach and Abednego, and I will have him torn limb from limb and his house razed to the ground, for there is no other god who can save like this.'

Daniel 3:12–23, 46–50, 91–7 JB

COMPANION IN THE FIRE (Daniel 3:25; Isaiah 43:2)

Lord, I do not know
   if three men ever went
   through physical fire
   unscathed.
But the message is clear—
   there is always a fourth
   with men in their fire,
   a man such as us
   but bearing thy nature,
   sharing thy eternity.
Thy promise is clear—
   When thou goest through the waters
     they shall not o'erwhelm thee,
   or through the fire
     it shall not consume or destroy.
To see the fourth
   is safety and salvation
   the containment of pain,
   its cleansing power,
   the calming of fear.
Lord God,
   let me see the fourth,
   let all men become aware
   that he is present
   if unperceived.
And we shall come through
   unscathed
   nay, cleansed and enriched.
The fire is thine
   and that which is eternal
   shall be preserved
   indestructible and refined,
   in its predestined beauty and usefulness.

George Appleton

THE FIERY FURNACE

Peter.   What's coming, Corporal?
Adams. You two, let's know it: we have to meet the fire.
David. Tied hand and foot: not men at all!
Peter.   O how
   Shall we think these moments out
   Before thinking splits to fear. I begin
   To feel the sweat of pain: though the pain
   Hasn't reached us yet.
Adams.   Have your hearts ready:
   It's coming now.
David.   Every damned forest in the world
   Has fallen to make it. The glare's on us.
Peter.   Dead on.
   And here's the reconnoitring heat:
   It tells us what shall come.
Adams.   Now then! Chuck down
   Your wishes for the world: there's nothing here
   to charm us. Ready?
David.   I've been strong.
   The smoke's between us. Where are you, Adams?
Adams. Lost.
Peter.   Where are you, Adams?
                        (Adams *cries out and falls to his knees.*)
David. It's come to him, Peter!
Peter.   We shall know!
David. Scalding God!!
                        (*They, too, have fallen on their knees.*)
Adams. What way have I come down, to find
   I live still, in this round of blaze?
   Here on my knees. And a fire hotter
   Than any fire has ever been
   Plays over me. And I live. I know
   I kneel.
David. Adams.
Adams.   We're not destroyed.
David. Adams.
Peter.   Voices. We're men who speak.

David. We're men who sleep and wake.
  They haven't let us go.
Peter.　　　　My breath
  Parts the fire a little.
Adams.　　　　But the cords
  That were tying us are burnt: drop off
  Like snakes of soot.
Peter.　　　　Can we stand?
David. Even against this coursing fire we can.
Peter. Stand: move: as though we were living,
  In this narrow shaking street
  Under the eaves of seven-storeyed flames
  That lean and rear again, and still
  We stand. Can we be living, or only
  Seem to be?
Adams.　　　　I can think of life.
  We'll make it yet.
David.　　　　That's my devotion.
  Which way now?
Peter.　　　　Wait a minute. Who's that
  Watching us through the flame?
      (Meadows, *a dream figure, is sitting on the side of his bunk.*)
David.　　　　Who's there?
Adams. Keep your heads down. Might be
  Some sniper of the fire.
                              (Meadows *crows like a cock.*)
Peter.　　　　A lunatic.
Adams (*calling to* Meadows). Who are you?
Meadows.　　　　Man.
Adams.　　　　Under what command?
Meadows. God's.
Adams.　　　　May we come through?
Meadows.　　　　If you have
  The patience and the love.
David.　　　　Under this fire?
Meadows. Well, then, the honesty.
Adams.　　　　What honesty?
Meadows. Not to say we do
  A thing for all men's sake when we do it only

    For our own. And quick eyes to see
    Where evil is. While any is our own
    We sound fine words unsoundly.
Adams.   You cock-eyed son
    Of heaven, how did you get here?
Meadows. Under the fence. I think they forgot
    To throw me in. But there's not a skipping soul
    On the loneliest goat-path who is not
    Hugged into this, the human shambles.
    And whatever happens on the farthest pitch,
    To the sand-man in the desert or the island-man in the sea,
    Concerns us very soon. So you'll forgive me
    If I seem to intrude.
Peter.   Do you mean to stay here?
Meadows. I can't get out alone. Neither can you.
    But, on the other hand, single moments
    Gather towards the striking clock.
    Each man is the world.
Peter.   But great events
    Go faster.
David. Who's to lead us out of this?
Meadows. It's hard to see. Who will trust
    What the years have endlessly said?
Adams. There's been a mort of time. You'd think
    Something might have come of it. These men
    Are ready to go, and so am I.
Peter. But there's no God-known government anywhere.
Meadows. Behind us lie
    The thousand and the thousand and the thousand years
    Vexed and terrible. And still we use
    The cures which never cure.
David.   For mortal sake,
    Shall we move? Do we just wait and die?
Meadows. Figures of wisdom back in the old sorrows
    Hold and wait for ever. We see, admire
    But never suffer them: suffer instead
    A stubborn aberration.
    O God, the fabulous wings unused,
    Folded in the heart.

David.   So help me, in
 The stresses of this furnace I can see
 To be strong beyond all action is the strength
 To have, But how do men and forbearance meet?
 A stone forbears when the wheel goes over, but that
 Is death to the flesh.
Adams.   And every standing day
 The claims are deeper, inactivity harder.
 But where, in the maze of right and wrong,
 Are we to do what action?
Peter.   Look, how intense
 The place is now, with swaying and troubled figures.
 The flames are men: all human. There's no fire!
 Breath and blood chokes and burns us. This
 Surely is unquenchable? It can only transform.
 There's no way out. We can only stay and alter.
David. Who says there's nothing here to hate?
Meadows. The deeds, not those who do.
Adams. Strange how we trust the powers that ruin
 And not the powers that bless.
David.   But good's unguarded,
 As defenceless as a naked man.
Meadows. Imperishably. Good has no fear;
 Good is itself, whatever comes.
 It grows, and makes, and bravely
 Persuades, beyond all tilt of wrong:
 Stronger than anger, wiser than strategy,
 Enough to subdue cities and men
 If we believe it with a long courage of truth.
David. Corporal, the crowing son of heaven
 Thinks we can make morning.
Meadows.   Not
 By old measures. Expedience and self-preservation
 Can rot as they will. Lord, where we fail as men
 We fail as deeds of time.
Peter. The blaze of this fire
 Is wider than any man's imagination.
 It goes beyond any stretch of the heart.
Meadows. The human heart can go to the lengths of God.

Dark and cold we may be, but this
Is no winter now. The frozen misery
Of centuries breaks, cracks, begins to move;
The thunder is the thunder of the floes,
The thaw, the flood, the upstart Spring.
Thank God our time is now when wrong
Comes up to face us everywhere,
Never to leave us till we take
The longest stride of soul men ever took.
Affairs are now soul size.
The enterprise
Is exploration into God.
Where are you making for? It takes
So many thousand years to wake,
But will you wake for pity's sake.

Christopher Fry

BONHOEFFER

In recent years the most influential exponent of 'God *versus*
Religion' has been Dietrich Bonhoeffer, the Lutheran theologian
and pastor who was put to death in a Nazi concentration camp
a few weeks before the end of the war in Europe. Bonhoeffer's
Letters from Prison have been widely read, and it will not be
surprising if they take their place among the lasting classics of
Christian spirituality. In loneliness and privation and in suffering made the more acute by his sensitivity of mind, Bonhoeffer
found that God was there; and with the realization of God's
presence he knew an unearthly selflessness and peace.

'Please do not ever get worried or anxious about me, but
don't forget to pray for me. I am so sure of God's guiding hand
that I hope I shall never lose that certainty. You must never
doubt that I am travelling my appointed road with gratitude
and cheerfulness. My past life is replete with God's goodness,
and my sins are covered by the forgiving love of Christ
crucified. I am thankful for all those who have crossed my
path, and all I wish is never to cause them sorrow . . . Please
don't for a moment get upset about all this, but let it rejoice
your heart also.'

God was there, in the midst of suffering and the approach to death. With the growing awareness of God's presence Bonhoeffer found in the two years of his imprisonment a growing vigour of thought. He was allowed to read books and to write; and he wrote much about his prophetic theme that Christianity, man's essential fellowship with God in Christ, will remain but religion will pass away. Religion, pious practice, belongs to man's immaturity. When man comes of age and finds himself, no longer bewildered, childish and dependent upon God in childish ways, the practice of what has hitherto been known as religion will disappear. It is the medium of a relation to God but only for the immature, for children; man coming to be adult and 'finding' himself will know and obey God, but not using the old medium of religion. He will know God in life itself, in the relation of person with person, and in the decisions there of faith and obedience.

A. M. Ramsey

CHRISTIANS AND PAGANS

Men go to God when they are sore bestead,
Pray to him for succour, for his peace, for bread,
For mercy for them sick, sinning, or dead;
All men do so, Christian and unbelieving.

Men go to God when he is sore bestead,
Find him poor and scorned, without shelter or bread,
Whelmed under weight of the wicked, the weak, the dead;
Christians stand by God in his hour of grieving.

God goes to every man when sore bestead,
Feeds body and spirit with his bread;
For Christians, pagans alike he hangs dead,
And both alike forgiving.

Dietrich Bonhoeffer

THE WOMAN WHO COULD NOT DIE (5)

Silence. Profound, dead silence.

Dead? With the syncopated beat of hundreds of agonized hearts weighing down, pressing in on all sides? With hundreds of veiled, attentive eyes peering through eyeholes pierced in the doors of our cells?

It must have lasted hours already, this strangely alert lack of sound. Ever since the glaring naked bulb, hung from the centre of the ceiling on a length of flex, was lit. Before then, during the day-time, my cell was filled with a dim grey-green twilight, as though it were fathoms below the sea, and the silence was blunt, opaque. I had dozed a lot, then. But when velvet dusk crept in over the roofs and down into the streets it vanished from my cell, alas.

First the crude light had been a cause for irritation, annoyance. Now it is quickly becoming a source of sustained, unavoidable pain. Round my eyelids a tingling rim is forming, smarting intolerably. Will my eyelashes come out if this goes on for long?

Long! Should length of time be measured in hours, days, weeks, months, or years here?

Not years, not even months, surely! Women are never kept in solitary confinement for more than two weeks in the Inner Prison of the G.P.U., or so we had always been told. They become hysterical and have to be removed to other cells—not 'solitary' ones—in other, less silent prisons.

Silence ... No, rather a throbbing, living lack of audible sound. And it has become incalculably more acute after a sudden muffled sneeze outside my cell door. Nicolay? Is it, can it be Nicolay?

A whispered admonition out there and seconds of the most intensely alert silence I have ever known. Then the cr-rick of an opening eyehole. My eyes had been closed because of the light and the smarting pain. I lock them, seal them now. I had been lying on the camp-bed limply, on my back. Now I stiffen, longing to sink deeper into the thin straw mattress. They shall not see. They must not know. Oh, men, science, common sense, someone, something, tell me—can a woman recognize the sneeze of the man she has been married to for fifteen years? Can she?

Absurd. Ridiculous. Funny? Am I going to laugh? Is this hysteria already? Can the eye out there see my twitching lips, the knotted lump swelling in my throat? It cannot see, perhaps, but the jailer will surely guess . . . He must not, shall not. I must relax. I will. *I will it.*

I? . . . but who, what am I?

. . . I the schoolgirl who spoke French and English well but Russian rather badly and was much teased about it. At twelve she read the *Fore-runner*, as most Russian children do, and was impressed by Leonardo's capacity for taking note of horror-stricken expressions and repellent detail in monstrosities without having any feeling about it. She had recognized the same capacity in herself and henceforth called it the Leonardo. As she grew the Leonardo developed, becoming more clever, without, however, seeming to affect her own cleverness directly. Still, she would use the fruits of the Leonardo's slightly cynical wisdom as a matter of course when she found it convenient to do so.

. . . Cr-ing, cr-ang. The door is being unlocked. But surely I was taken to the lavatory hours ago, before I undressed. Can it possibly be morning?

'Your name, Citizen?'

'Iulia de Beausobre.'

'You will be taken before the examining officer. Get ready.'

The jailer vanishes. The door is locked.

My hands, suddenly ice-cold and wringing-wet, fumble helplessly putting on stockings, jersey, skirt . . . Those hands of mine, why do they tremble so? My stiff mouth is quite dried up, I could not say a word. I must pour some cold tea out of the copper kettle on my table into the metal mug. I stand with my back to the door so that no eye shall see my shaking hands. God, how they shake and tremble. I am sure the jailers can see, although my back is turned. Jesus-gentle-shepherd-hear-me. In-the-darkness-be-thou-near-me. Please, please be near me.

From this dithering woman the Leonardo detaches himself, so different from her that he is almost a visual reality.

Fool, he says with cynical superiority, your being physically repellent isn't even the worst thing about you, for you are quickly becoming a repulsive imbecile and a revolting moral coward.

The imputation is so true that a lump of bitter humiliation chokes me and tears come to my eyes.

Tender shepherd, please.

. . .

And the cell fills with a whirling light. It dims the electric bulb and dwarfs the Leonardo into insignificance. Out of the infinite expanse of spinning, throbbing clarity there comes to me a serene look of perfect understanding. But there are no eyes; only I am dimensional while this strange thing lasts. An inaudible voice of tragic beauty envelops me with '*Peace. My peace be with you!*'

. . .

The key turns loudly in the lock. I wheel round. The magic is dispelled. But in a dimmed way the essence of it is and will be present in me always.

'Ready?'

'Yes, comrade.'

My voice is low and cool. I feel serenity and compassion stream out of me. I see the jailer, a clean boy of about twenty with flaxen hair and the sad eyes of a Byzantine Madonna, stare at me in awe. I make an effort not to smile reassuringly; that would never do. Unsmiling, but supremely at peace with the world and all that is within it, I step out of my cell into the passage.

. . . Down, down, down.

Not so quick, Alice, says the Leonardo, you should not hurry when a man with a loaded revolver is following just behind you. It isn't done.

. . .

Peace, says the other. Let peace stream out before you. Let peace stream to the left of you. Let peace stream to the right of you. Let peace remain awhile wherever you may tread. May it spread even to the furthest boundaries of the universe . . . Peace.

                                          Iulia de Beausobre

IT IS FINISHED

Sometimes I wondered where God was.
Now I know.
Sometimes I wandered my own way,
Deliberately choosing, in the midst of what I called life,
The business,
The goodness,
The work,
Which satisfied my present wants—
And left me barren.
Sometimes I gave love, or so I thought,
When all I did was minister to self.
Now I see,
And see,
   not through a glass darkly—
The agony of Calvary,
   its sweat and blood and tears.
See them all in the thorns of life
Made piercing sharp in the wounds,
Christ's wounds, still bleeding in a human heart.
Now I *know* where God is.
He lives, he breathes, he suffers
In my brother's pain, and
In that pain draws near to me.
In my response he speaks to us,
And calls us out beyond ourselves.

He calls us out beyond ourselves, but
Where?
   It is finished—it is finished!
Finished? How?
   The wounds are fresh; the scars unhealed—the
Ones my brother wears; the ones I share
And yet;
   if things and people long ago
Have touched my life—
And touch it still—
   for good or ill,

That lonely victory in our flesh,
Can reach us yet, and find in us
Victory made real, made true
    made here and now.
Your victory, Lord, the victory of love
Which takes away the guilt and pain
And makes the wounds and scars
Signs of triumph; set for all to see;
And gives to me an inward look
Which in my brother's need
Perceives that Calvary is here and now;
And Easter ever fresh.

'God is a new language;
The clasp of your brother's hand
Made articulate.'
    And I have touched that hand
And found you, Lord and Christ.
In the recapturing of the past—its death,
In the facing of it—destruction of its mastery.
In acceptance—discovery of self.
In the very dying
A risen body comes to life—
Your life in him, in me, in us, in all.
It IS finished!—
And it all begins;
For what we have we cannot keep.
We meet in him, to find
There is no staying still.
But there,
Beyond ourselves,
Our brothers wait, to hear that
    it is finished.   *Brother Charles*

THE REAL ENEMY (7)

I awoke calm. Slowly my mind brought me back to my bed
in the hospital. Stretched out on the next bed was my warder,

reading. When he got up and began to dress, I recognized the uniform as that of a corporal of the German army. His new, shining boots were hard to pull on. Then came one of those unexpected moments of grace and charity. He came over to my bed and asked in clumsy French whether I was a Roman Catholic. When I nodded he took from his pocket a rosary of black beads, a dozen of which were missing. He laid it on my bed and, as he turned to leave the room, he waved his hand.

The rosary had a considerable effect upon me. Until then I had hardly thought of God or of asking His help. That morning during my session with the Gestapo man I had asked to be allowed to see a priest, but I had done so without much religious concern, merely out of a conventional reaction to my belief that my death was only an hour or two away. I had been cheered when he had said that I was in no immediate danger of death. Now, with the rosary, and even more because of the way it had reached me, my heart lifted a little and in the movement my mind turned to the feeling of God. Lonely, forsaken and broken, I looked on the little cross as the symbol of hope, or reintegration, of the way back to parents, friends, colleagues, and the normal lasting life of which this state of pain and doubt and fear was merely an interruption. I held the cross and prayed, and in the next few lonely hours was comforted more, looking back on them, than I would have thought possible.

Pierre d'Harcourt

As a wellspring in the night
We have heard His voice in the words he spoke to us,
By word of mouth pass'd on.

As I walk all by myself
On a dark'ning path, by the shore or in the street,
I know He walks by me.

Kindly words that are a friend's
Set my heart ablaze as I listen and I know
The voice I hear is His.

O'er the rim of dawn, the bread,
And the chalice shed, all the world by Him is fed,
Reposing in God's hand.

Anders Frostenson

If I know little of the theology of Christ, what then do I
know of Him as life? I have come to see Him as the WAY of
life. To me He is the precept and example of all that can be
known here concerning Reality. As the example He is the
Divine Love working through the love of law. As the precept
He is the Law of Love made manifest.

I see Christ as the Saviour of mankind, individually and
collectively, for except by the Law of Love, I can conceive no
genuine salvation. Nor can I perceive salvation present in the
man while the love of law is absent. I see everything, therefore,
which is less than Christ, or less than the precept and example
for which He stands, as a compromise with destiny: a way, but
not the WAY of life.

Likewise I perceive Christianity as man's noblest hope for
the ultimate establishment of a workable social science on
earth. I perceive this because I see in Christianity the noblest
possibility for the competitive nature of man and the co-
operative nature of woman to come together in Christ and live
for the good of all. I perceive in Christianity the noblest hope
for a workable natural science. One of America's most distin-
guished scientists recently remarked to a friend of mine that
except for the spiritual application being made of scientific
discoveries those discoveries were worse than useless. A broad
statement, a sweeping indictment, a powerful challenge; but a
little thought will justify it. Science without Christ is insufficient. It cannot time its discoveries, nor can it control them. In
the absence of a redeemed humanity and an adequate social
science what it uncovers as a blessing becomes likewise a curse.
Finally I perceive in Christianity the noblest of all experience,
direct and conscious contact with God through the ever present
medium of Christ and the action of the Holy Spirit.

In this I am not unmindful of other religions. ('In my

Father's house are many mansions.') All are of the same blood, and all are children of the same God. While there are other folds, I only repeat that no religion can aim higher than the Law of Love, nor inspire any loftier sentiment than the love of Law. So far as I know Christ alone of all the great religious leaders advocated an uncompromising 'Give yourself'. While the others focused attention upon the *self*, as a method for self-improvement and final self-conquest, He focused attention on the Kingdom, and on the forgetting of *self* in the loving service of the neighbour.

Perhaps a secondary difference between the religion of Christ and that of other great religious leaders is to be found in the factor of Grace, which is essentially a Christian tenet, and which belongs to the Christian by virtue of the fact that he recognizes and accepts it as an authoritative gift from the founder of Christianity Himself.

My knowledge of other religious forms precludes the gift of Grace, as I conceive Grace to be. In these other religions there is justice (Karma) and help for those who help themselves. You must reap what you sow. But Christ is not limited to this concept. He breaks through it at will and by special acts of Grace saves those who will not and cannot help themselves. In Him is the hard justice of the righteous man plus the tender love of the merciful man. I shall point out many examples, my own included, in this volume, of men who were saved by Grace in spite of themselves—all testimonies of seemingly unmerited divine mercy. The case of the Apostle Paul is an outstanding historical example of a man who, from a relative point of view, did not merit the Master's mercy, but who received it nevertheless, and with it an unblemished passport to Glory.

If this Grace were not possible I should in all probability be somewhere today festering in a prison cell, instead of sitting here in my study, a comparatively free man, in a position to go and to come at the Master's beck and call.

To me, then, Christ becomes in practice the love of law: in essence the Law of Love. Not *a* way, but *the* WAY! Full of Grace and Mercy and Authority! A Friend and an Intercessor! A warm colourful personal Friend upon whom we can call! An Advocate who prompts us to act and then responds to our action! A Companion of the road, a Comrade of the quest! One to whom we belong!

I know that so long as I belong to Christ all good belongs to me. I can rest in Him, forcing no issue, allowing what belongs to me to happen at the right time and in the right place. When I belong to Him the next thing that happens in my life has got to be the best thing and the right thing.

As the love of law Christ can with ease obey even the narrow and unreasonable laws of men. He can show His followers how to do likewise, how to render unto Caesar what belongs to Caesar, while in nowise sacrificing the Higher Law in the lesser obedience.   *Starr Daily*

'YOU THAT ARE STRONG'

On Sunday, September 23rd, Leonard Wilson preached at the official thanksgiving service in St Andrew's Cathedral, and some extracts from this show his thoughts at the time. He said:

'Our thanksgiving is first for the cessation of hostilities. There is a deliverance from battle, murder and from sudden death. Looked at from God's point of view this was a civil war between his children, though so few acknowledge Him. A sound cause for thankfulness is that we were found worthy of victory. But to pour out thanks for a favourable verdict runs the risk of seeming to betray a bad conscience and to have a poor idea of the judge's office. Yet we must use our judgement and without priding ourselves too much on the height of our ideals, we have good reason to say that the war was between humanity and inhumanity, and we thank God humanity won.'

Then turning to the other aspect of his theme, service, he went on:

'For the most part I am talking to those who are strong. Strong not only as a conquering force but strong in the power you can exercise. Most of you, whatever your rank or station, are by your victories equipped with tremendous power. What are you going to do with it? Upon all of us there still lies a great and heavy responsibility for which we need not only the physical and mental strength, which, in large measure, are already assured, but a spiritual strength for which we are dependent upon God Himself by prayer, recollection and sacraments. This is of vital importance. Many victories have been won without any recourse to spiritual power and there is a great danger that we fall back upon that agelong fallacy that education, discipline, government or scientific machinery will give us all the strength we need to solve the problems of the world. It is a vain thing fondly imagined and may God save us from those years of futile disillusionment that so many experienced between two wars ... Many of the weapons which have been most useful in winning the war must be discarded if we are to win the peace ... Our greatest need at the moment I think is to take upon ourselves the burden of the infirmities of the weak. In war it is impossible to tolerate the timidity, the conventionality, the feebleness and the prejudice of the weak. Patience with such weakness and futility is impossible in wartime and many of us have lost the art. But now St Paul's injunction is relevant. You that are strong must bear the infirmities of those who are weak. This patience is needed now, and something more than patience, an understanding sympathy. If we are going to help people we must for their sakes forgo something of our own strength and share the fear, the dimness, the anxiety, and the heart-sinking through which they have to work their way. We will have to forgo the privilege of strength in order to understand the weak and backward, to be with them, to enter into their thoughts, to advance at their pace ... If we are to serve aright God and our fellow-men we ought not to try and prove to ourselves or to others that we are strong. Self-assertion, wilfulness or even standing aloof in critical reserve is not the Christian way of proving our greatness. The kings of the earth exercise dominion and power, but said Jesus, "The greatest among you is he that serveth." '

Soon after Leonard got back to the hospital in Sime Road, after his seven and a half months in the military police headquarters, Sorby Adams, who was working in the hospital, asked him what he had learnt from his long ordeal. He answered, 'I have learnt that the purgatory of joy is greater than the purgatory of suffering, because it does not destroy.' He referred to this again in his broadcast sermon in 1946, when he said, 'For

months afterwards I felt at peace with the universe although I
was still interned and I had to learn the lesson or the discipline
of joy. How easy it is to forget God and all his benefits. I had
known Him in a deeper way than I could have imagined, but
God is to be found in the Resurrection, as well as in the Cross,
and it is the Resurrection that has the final word.'

In March 1969, Leonard went back to Singapore to take
part in a B.B.C. film. The programme was called *Mission to
Hell*. Jean-Paul Sartre has said that, 'Hell is other people'.
Possibly the converse is also true, and if this is so, this programme might have been more properly called *Return to Heaven*.
For it was then that Leonard felt most certain of his faith, and
the living presence of Christ both in his ordeal and after it. He
felt accepted and upheld by his fellow prisoners, and knew that
he also gave strength to them. This was in complete contrast to
the torture of his school days. The feeling of fellowship that he
came to know in those years at Singapore was a unique experience which remained with him all his life. He knew that the
grace of God had transformed hell into something like heaven.

Roy McKay

But with unhurrying chase,
and unperturbèd pace . . .
Halts by me that footfall:
Is my gloom, after all
Shade of His hand, outstretched caressingly?
'Ah fondest, blindest, weakest,
I am He Whom thou seekest!
Thou dravest love from thee, who dravest Me.'

Francis Thompson

ALYOSHA'S VISION

Something glowed in Alyosha's heart, something filled it
suddenly till it ached, tears of ecstasy were welling up from his
soul . . . He stretched out his hands, uttered a cry and woke up . . .
Suddenly turning away abruptly he went out of the cell . . .
He did not stop on the steps, but went down rapidly. His soul,

overflowing with rapture, was craving for freedom and unlimited space. The vault of heaven, studded with softly shining stars, stretched wide and vast over him. From the zenith to the horizon the Milky Way stretched its two arms dimly across the sky. The fresh, motionless, still night enfolded the earth. The white towers and golden domes of the cathedral gleamed against the sapphire sky. The gorgeous autumn flowers in the beds near the house went to sleep till morning. The silence of the earth seemed to merge into the silence of the heavens, the mystery of the earth came in contact with the mystery of the stars . . . Alyosha stood, gazed, and suddenly he threw himself down flat upon the earth.

He did not know why he was embracing it. He could not have explained to himself why he longed so irresistibly to kiss it, to kiss it all, but he kissed it weeping, sobbing and drenching it with his tears, and vowed frenziedly to love it, to love it for ever and ever. 'Water the earth with the tears of your gladness and love those tears', it rang in his soul. What was he weeping over? Oh, he was weeping in his rapture even over those stars which were shining for him from the abyss of space and 'he was not ashamed of that ecstasy'. It was as though the threads from all those innumerable worlds of God met all at once in his soul, and it was trembling all over 'as it came in contact with other worlds'. He wanted to forgive everyone for everything, and to beg forgiveness—oh! not for himself, but for all men, for all and for everything, 'and others are begging for me', it echoed in his soul again. But with every moment he felt clearly and almost palpably that something firm and immovable, like the firmament itself, was entering his soul. A sort of idea was gaining an ascendency over his mind—and that for the rest of his life, for ever and ever. He had fallen upon the earth a weak youth, but he rose from it a resolute fighter for the rest of his life, and he realized and felt it suddenly, at the very moment of his rapture. And never, never for the rest of his life could Alyosha forget that moment. 'Someone visited my soul at that hour!' he used to say afterwards with firm faith in his words . . .

Three days later he left the monastery in accordance with the words of his late elder, who had bidden him 'sojourn in the world'.   *Dostoyevsky*

A LETTER TO HIS WIFE

Here, in the heart and love and life of Nature, and with Christ by my side, I cannot bring myself to go to Church, when the whole creation calls me to worship God in such infinitely more beautiful and inspiring light and colour and form and sound. Not a single thing out here but suggests love and peace and joy and gratitude . . .

If I didn't feel and know that He was there with me always, natural things—trees, skies, flowers and animals—would have no fascination for me whatever. But I know that every joy I feel in a wood is understood and felt more perfectly by Christ at my side: I feel always as though he were leading me about and showing me things and for everything I thank Him.

Edward Wilson

O Lord, we lift our hearts to Thee this day in great thankfulness, humbly acknowledging Thy mercy and Thy Truth. Thy large and tender providence. Thy nearness at all times. Grant us Thy Spirit of Wisdom and Might and Peace, that all we say and do and think may be to Thy greater glory.

Anonymous

My Brothers and my Sister: I am so alone in my world. There is a room in which I am; in it I am completely alone, as in a grave. The icy breath of a hand forces me from afar into helplessness, into staring wordlessly at the prison walls that hold me fast. There is nothing here that brings joy or warmth. I only know that you are here, my God, you whom I have made God in my temple of suffering, companion of my solitude, my confidant in all my thoughts and desires. Thoughts and desires! Here in your creation stands a portion of your omnipotence, given me by you as part of my life, which I am to bring with me on my journey to you—man. You inhabit his spirit; you look at me through his eyes; he stands on every road I take— your creation, man. In my pastoral life you have given him to me that I should utterly immerse myself in him, feeling with him, living with him, and bleeding with him, as a redeemer jointly with you.

. . . For in order to come to you completely, one must always first traverse a zone of silence and weeping, for you are to be found only on the paths of compassion and charity. Then all at once you are the Father who walks among his children, who rejoices and weeps with them, and who has understanding even for their slightest trouble.

. . . There is always a stretch of the road that each must go alone, and that is precisely the most difficult and the darkest part of the road, on which lies the peak of the mount of suffering. Thither each must let the other go—all alone, and that is the personal Golgotha of the individual brother or sister.

Joseph Müller

Child of my love, fear not the unknown morrow,
Dread not the new demand life makes of thee,
Thy ignorance doth hold no cause for sorrow,

*   *   *

For what thou knowest not is known to me.
Thou canst not see today the hidden meaning
Of my command, but there no light shalt gain.
Walk on in faith, upon my promise leaning,
And as thou goest, all shall be made plain.
One step thou seest, then go forward boldly,
One step is far enough for faith to see.
Take that, and thy next duty shall be told thee,
For step by step thy Lord is leading thee.

Sue Ryder

MOUNT KENYA

It was already very cold and the prospect was not welcome. But later breaks began to appear in the mist, the moon came out and there was enough light to enable us to climb on down slowly. I felt very tired and the phantom moonlight, the shadowy forms of ridge and pinnacle, the wisps of silvery mist, the radiant expanse of the Lewis glacier plunging into soundless depths below induced a sense of exquisite fantasy.

I experienced that curious feeling not uncommon in such
circumstances that there was an additional member of the
party—three of us instead of two.

Eric Shipton

THE GLISSADE

Down below us was an almost precipitous slope, the nature
of which we could not gauge in the darkness and the lower
part of which was shrouded in impenetrable gloom. The situation looked grim enough. Fog cut off our retreat, darkness
covered our advance.

After a moment or two Shackleton said, 'We've got to take a
risk. Are you game?'

Crean and I declared that anything was better than delay.

'Right,' said Shackleton; 'we'll try it.'

We resumed our advance by slowly and painfully cutting
steps in the ice in a downward direction, but since it took us
half an hour to get down a hundred yards, we saw that it was
useless to continue in this fashion.

Shackleton then cut out a large step and sat on it. For a few
moments he pondered, then he said:

'I've got an idea. We must go on, no matter what is below.
To try to do it this way is hopeless. We can't cut steps down
thousands of feet.'

He paused, and Crean and I both agreed with him. Then he
spoke again.

'It's a devil of a risk, but we've got to take it. We'll slide.'

Slide down what was practically a precipice, in the darkness,
to meet—what?

'All right,' I said aloud, perhaps not very cheerfully, and
Crean echoed my words.

It seemed to me a most impossible project. The slope was
well-nigh precipitous, and a rock in our path—we could never
have seen it in the darkness in time to avoid it—would mean
certain disaster. Still, it was the only way. We had explored all
the passes: to go back was useless: moreover such a proceeding
would sign and seal the death warrant not only of ourselves but
of the whole of the expedition. To stay on the ridge longer

meant certain death by freezing. It was useless therefore to think about personal risk. If we were killed, at least we had done everything in our power to bring help to our shipmates. Shackleton was right. Our chance was a very small one indeed, but it was up to us to take it.

We each coiled our share of the rope until it made a pad on which we could sit to make our *glissade* from the mountain top. We hurried as much as possible, being anxious to get through the ordeal. Shackleton sat on the large step he had carved, and I sat behind him, straddled my legs round him and clasped him round the neck. Crean did the same with me, so that we were locked together as one man. Then Shackleton kicked off.

We seemed to shoot into space. For a moment my hair fairly stood on end. Then quite suddenly I felt a glow, and knew I was grinning! I was actually enjoying it. It was most exhilarating. We were shooting down the side of an almost precipitous mountain at nearly a mile a minute. I yelled with excitement, and found that Shackleton and Crean were yelling too. It seemed ridiculously safe. To hell with the rocks!

The sharp slope eased out slightly toward the level below, and then we knew for certain that we were safe. Little by little our speed slackened, and we finished up at the bottom in a bank of snow. We picked ourselves up and solemnly shook hands all round.

'It's not good to do that kind of thing too often,' said Shackleton, slowly. 'Thanks be that the risk was justified this time.'

We turned and looked up at the mountain down which we had just sped. I judged that we had travelled down about three thousand feet, and it was difficult to realize that we had reached the bottom in less than three minutes after we had left the top. This of course included the slowing down at the bottom.

. . . That night, I started out on a Whaler to bring in the three men whom we had left under the upturned boat at King Haakon Sound. I was content to leave the navigation to the Norwegian Captain, and the last sound that I heard as I fell asleep while we were steaming out of the harbour was the scream of a blizzard blowing down from the mountain range

we had just crossed. It could blow as hard as it liked up there—
now. Incidentally I learnt afterwards that we had crossed the
island during the only interval of fine weather that occurred
that winter. There was no doubt that Providence had been
with us. There was indeed one curious thing about our crossing
of South Georgia, a thing that has given me much food for
thought, and which I have never been able to explain. Whenever I reviewed the incidents of that march I had the subconscious feeling that there were four of us, instead of three. Moreover, this impression was shared by both Shackleton and
Crean.

Frank Worsley

Tired
And lonely,
So tired
The heart aches.
Meltwater trickles
Down the rocks,
The fingers are numb,
The knees tremble.
It is now,
Now, that you must not give in.

On the path of the others
Are resting places,
Places in the sun
Where they can meet.
But this
Is your path,
And it is now,
Now, that you must not fail.

Weep
If you can,
Weep,
But do not complain.
The way chose you—
And you must be thankful.

Dag Hammarskjöld

Farewell letter from Helmuth von Moltke to his wife.

Tegel, January 10th, 1945

My dear,

I must first say quite decidedly, that the closing hours of a man's life are no different from any others. I had always imagined that one would have no feeling beyond shock, and that one would keep saying to oneself, 'This is the last time you'll see the sun go down, this is the last time you'll go to bed, you've only twice more to hear the clock strike twelve.' But there is no question of any of that. Perhaps I'm a little above myself, I don't know, but I cannot deny that I feel in the best of spirits at the moment. I can only pray to our Heavenly Father that he will keep me thus, since to die so is obviously easier for the flesh. How good God has been to me! I must risk sounding hysterical, but I'm so filled with gratitude that there's really room for nothing else. His guidance of me was so sure and clear during those two days. Had the whole court been in uproar, had Herr Freisler and the surrounding walls tottered before my eyes, it would have made no difference to me. I felt exactly as it says in Isaiah, chapter 43, verse 2: 'When thou passest through the waters, I will be with thee; and through the rivers, they shall not overflow thee: when thou walkest through the fire, thou shalt not be burned; neither shall the flame kindle upon thee' . . . that is to say upon thy soul. When I was called upon to make my final statement, I was in such a spirit that I almost said, 'Slay my body, destroy my property, wreak you will on my wife and child, do your worst, you still have not the victory, the city of God remaineth' (Luther).

But that would only have made things worse for the others. So I merely said, 'I have nothing further I wish to say, Herr Präsident.'

Now there remains but a short, hard way before me, and I can only pray that God will continue as good to me as He has been hitherto. Eugen had written out for us for this evening, Luke, chapter 5, verses 1–11. He meant it differently, but it is true all the same, that today has been a day of great fishing for me, and that tonight I can say with all my heart, 'Depart from me; for I am a sinful man, O Lord.' And yesterday, my dear, we read this beautiful passage. 'But we have this treasure in earthen vessels, that the excellency of the power may be of God, and not of us. We are troubled on every side, yet not distressed; we are perplexed but not in despair; persecuted, but not forsaken; cast down, but not destroyed; always bearing about in the body the dying of the Lord Jesus, that the life also of Jesus might be made manifest in our body.' Thanks be, my dear, before all things to God. Thanks also to your dear self, for your intercessions, and thanks to all those who have prayed for us and for me. That I, your husband, weak, cowardly, 'complicated', very ordinary though I be, should have been allowed to experience this! Were I now to be reprieved—which I swear is no more and no less likely than it was a week ago—I must admit that I should have my way to find all over again, so tremendous has been the demonstration of God's presence and mighty power. He shows us these and shows them quite unmistakably, precisely when he deals with us as we ourselves should not choose. All other theories are nonsense.

There is only one thing, my dear, that I can say: May God be as good to you as he has been to me, then even the death of your husband will not count. God can show himself all-powerful at any time, whether you are making pancakes for the boys or whether you are looking after their little insides. I ought to say Good-bye to you—but I cannot; I ought to deplore and lament all your hum-drum daily toil: I cannot; I ought to think of all the burdens which now fall on your shoulders, but I cannot. There is only one thing which I can say: if you keep the consciousness of absolute security when the Lord gives it to you—a security which you would never have known if it had not been for this time and its issue—then I shall leave behind me as my legacy a treasure which none can confiscate, against which even my life cannot weigh in the balance . . .

I will write again tomorrow, but since one cannot tell what will happen I want to have touched on all subjects in my letter. Of course I do not know whether I shall be put to death tomorrow. It may be, that there will be a further hearing, perhaps I shall be beaten or put in store. Try to get in touch with me for that may perhaps preserve me from too fierce a beating. Although I know after to-day's experience that God can turn to naught this beating too—even if I have no whole bone in my

body before I am hanged—although therefore at the moment I
do not fear it, yet I should prefer to avoid it. So Goodnight, be
strong and of a good courage.

Helmuth von Moltke

HOUR OF GLORY (John 17:1)

Lord, you were not only tempted
for forty days down by Jordan
but constantly all through
    your ministry

Not to obvious blatant sins
but to subtler defections
from the Father's will;
to cunning compromises
which would defeat
    the Father's purpose.

And as the last days drew near
the evil efforts were redoubled,
for the spirit of evil knew
that the last and fiercest strife
    was close at hand.

The Greeks who wanted to greet you—
did their coming suggest
a wider mission
where men would listen
    and welcome you?

You saw the evasion of the cross
in their innocent request
and knew that without the death of the seed
    there would be no harvest in nature.

So without your sacrifice
there would be no harvest of souls.
Only uttermost love
loving in death
    could avail

In the garden of Olives
across the valley
you wrestled with the doubt
that death could be
    the Father's will.

Agony of soul and sweat of blood
before the issue was decided;
then stepping forth
calm and unafraid
you offered your hands
    for the handcuffs.

Before Pilate you could have
pleaded your case
against your accusers—
your only appeal
to the kingdom of truth.

In the fiercest moments of pain
with piercing nails
and the dragging body
and the mocking cry:
    *Come down from the cross
    and we will believe.*

George Appleton

My beloved darling,
    . . . My thoughts and prayers concern you before all else and
encompass in the greatest love your entire life for the future.
My very dearest one, in all sorrow you must perceive constantly that you are not facing life alone! He is with you every
moment, and he may even be mindful of my entreaties on your

behalf when he helps you—just as your prayers and Mama's smoothed the way for me. Then besides, there is the firm assurance that some day, together before his throne, we shall give thanks and praise for all undeserved mercies, of which the greatest is that he at one time brought us together—the greatest at least of the earthly gifts.

You must know with absolute certainty that my whole heart belongs to you only, by virtue of bonds that can be conferred only once in life, because they reach beyond life into eternity. And next to the thanks I render to the Lord, my most ardent, never-ending thanks go to you, dear heart, and will be yours to my last heart-beat. Thank you for the inexpressible love that you have unceasingly spread about me like a mantle of gold.

And now our two beloved children whom by the will of God, I must leave bereft of me, but whom I know to be sheltered in his love and your care. Tell them that the ardent last prayers of their father and his great love accompany them through life, and tell them to give all their love to you and always whenever they think of me, to do something especially nice for you as a greeting from me. What they will be and what they will do at some future day is of no importance. It is *how* they do it—that is, whether they do it under God's guidance—that counts. Their father has often failed in this respect, yet the hand of the Lord never let him go; it needs only to be sought with fervour.

Give my thanks likewise to all others whom I love—to Mama, my brothers and sisters, your parents. All of them, but especially my beloved Mama, have given me much, much more love than they have received, and thereby have brought much more sunshine into my life, which has been such a full and happy one, than they have ever realized. To them likewise I dedicate the wish, 'One day above in the light!'

Alexis, Baron von Roenne

WHO AM I?

Who am I? They often tell me
I stepped from my cell's confinement
Calmly, cheerfully, firmly
Like a squire from his country-house.

Who am I? They often tell me
I used to talk to my warders
freely and friendly and clearly,
as though it were mine to command.

Who am I? They also tell me
I would bear the days of misfortune
equably, smilingly, proudly,
like one accustomed to win.

Am I then really all that which other men tell of?
Or am I only what I knew of myself,
restless and longing and sick, like a bird in a cage,
struggling for breath, as though hands were compressing my
      throat,
yearning for colours, for flowers, for the voices of birds,
thirsting for words of kindness, for neighbourliness,
trembling with anger at despotisms and petty humiliation,
tossing in expectation of great events,
powerlessly trembling for friends at an infinite distance,
weary and empty at praying, at thinking, at making,
faint, and ready to say farewell to it all?

Who am I? This or the other?
Am I one person today and tomorrow another?
Am I both at once? A hypocrite before others,
and before myself a contemptibly woebegone weakling?
Or is something within me still like a beaten army,
fleeing in disorder from victory already achieved?

Who am I? They mock me, these lonely questions of mine,
Whoever I am, Thou knowest, O God, I am Thine!
                                        Dietrich Bonhoeffer

SAFER THAN A KNOWN WAY (1)

General Wingate's first expedition, Burma 1943, 250 miles from railhead
... Those first six months of 1943 brought us all the most fantastic adventures of our lives. ... Some men suffered the experience of being wounded and taken prisoner; some of being wounded and left to die; some of being wounded and befriended by gallant Kachin tribesmen (I picked up two of these the following year); some of wandering about the jungle, not only starving but delirious; some, while so lost, of bumping unexpectedly into other formed parties of our own; some of being fired on and sunk in that most vulnerable of situations—in a boat crossing one of these wide rivers. The extraordinary thing about MacHorton's story is that he underwent not one of these special experiences, but each and all of them; and survived to tell the tale.

Here that tale begins. I vouch for its truth. Although I had not met, or hardly met, MacHorton in those days, his story was widely known to us, and there were plenty of surviving witnesses of his wounds, his appearances and disappearances.

... Even his account of what went through his mind at different moments rings true to me; and although I did not undergo a tithe of the ordeal which was his, I am enough of an initiate to recognize the authentic. I, too, was once separated from my friends without map, compass, or food; and I, too, stumbling vaguely northward through Burma, almost without purpose, met them again. I wrote afterwards, and I still aver, that I have never been more aware of God's mercy.

Bernard Fergusson

Voice piercing iron and stone,
Borne on the dark to me,
Whose is this voice I hear?
Don't be afraid, it is me!

Voice before night and day,
Questions and answers, He
Bears up the whole wide world.
Don't be afraid, it's me!

With me where'er I go,
Closest when least I see;
Downcast in darkness' hour.
Don't be afraid, it is me!

When you have gone again
I fear no emptiness,
In me I hear this voice,
Peace you have given to me.

Anders Frostenson

SAFER THAN A KNOWN WAY (2)

When I awoke the bright moonlight was streaming through
the open doorway, silvering the prostrate forms of my two
guards, for both the sentry and the truck driver lay across the
threshold. Everywhere was pervaded by an uncanny almost
phosphorescent silver glow, and the whole world seemed poised
in utter stillness. I had the curious feeling that I was not of this
world, but was part of that glow. If I could merge with it, and
rise in a silver mist to escape up a moonbeam, I would be clean
again and safe for ever. Then my spirit seemed to rise to the
moon's soft beckoning. My imagination took over completely,
and in my imagination I stood up. With a lithe strength with
which I was suddenly imbued I noiselessly and easily jumped
over the bodies of both the Japs. I found myself standing in the
doorway wondering at the magnificence of the dappled blue-
and-silver night.

I gripped my water-bottle tightly and turned to look once
more at the two soundly-sleeping Japs over whom I had passed
with such light-footed ease. It gave me a flippant pleasure to
note that their rifles were both loaded and cocked, and that the
slings were wrapped tightly round their wrists, so that they
would awake fully prepared to kill on the instant of alarm.
They had not even bothered to take turns at sentry-go.
Obviously they did not fear me in any way for they knew that
at my slightest movement towards them they would wake.
Jungle-sharp, they would respond to the slightest sound, and to

fire would be instinctive. Perhaps, maybe, they thought to themselves that even if I were to escape I would soon die in the mountainous jungle which bulked huge, black and ominous. Emaciated and weakened by wounds and privations as I was, the Japs knew that I was no longer a force to reckon with.

I have heard it said that people who have nearly died, but have recovered, sometimes tell of strange near-psychic experiences while deeply unconscious. Whether I was near death at this time I do not know, but I do know that in this strange experience I felt as though my spirit had completely left my body. I saw myself lying down there asleep in the corner. I saw myself there with all hope abandoned but, in that abandonment, resigned completely to the will of God.

From outside in the cool cleanness of the moonlight, where my spirit stood, I looked in to where a slanting moonbeam fell upon my recumbent form, crumpled and pathetic. If only I could depart now, leaving this torn, blood-stained bundle behind me, a voice whispered to me. Without that useless, battered body I could soar like a mountain spirit and cross the looming jungle and span the mountain effortlessly. And thus, light and free and splendid, untroubled by heavy pack or equipment, I could swoop down from the skies and land among my joyous and welcoming comrades in safety the other side of the Chindwin.

Out there in the moonlight I was not hungry any more. I felt young and strong in body and soul. I felt sorry for that pain-racked creature that I knew was me back there in the hut. Then abruptly, I was back in that body. And my body opened its eyes and a flood of determination and strength welled up within me: 'I am not dead. I will live,' I said: 'I will cross the Chindwin. Nothing to stop me now!'

I must have said it aloud, for the Japanese sentry stirred. He opened his eyes and looked at me, and then shut them and continued his sleep. He saw only my shrunken, battered body. He knew I did not even require guarding. I slept.

Ian MacHorton

THE DREAMER

No one can follow the dreamer;
He goes alone, out of his walled body and room
On pilgrimage which takes him instantly beyond
A year's trudging to any Saint's, Prophet's or God's tomb.

No one can follow the dreamer through dreams;
Even his own numberless selves of Sleep
Can never clearly conceive
The relic of Understanding whose shrine is sought.
Is it a past life, jewel, Beauty or heart's peace?
Mountain, valley, Knowledge or legend of love?
Fruit of a tree, triumph, or joining in one for vision
Lying beyond the power of divided self to achieve?

No one can answer the dreamer searching through dreams;
There he may find
The dead walking alive, like-wandering friend:
There meet the beloved stranger who will kiss, lips hard,
Bliss to the touching sense, deprived in a dream-world;
May see black suns flying like swans
Outstretched behind the flash of long, gold rain
Or find a dark boat with oars on a dark sand
Verged on a sea that runs to horizons never found.

But nothing's found in dreams that's ever held.
Neither the kiss, nor suns, nor boat nor sea's end;
Empty handed the dreamer returns to his room
Where his body refills with himself and wakes
To find no splinter of Cross, no shred of a Saint's dress
As witness of pilgrimage in the finger's grasp—
All it knows its own, easy content.
Nor can the mind, though struggling, ever recall
What kiss, sun, boat or any symbol meant.

                                                    Dorothea Eastwood

SAFER THAN A KNOWN WAY (3)

That the Japs had gone well away from me was very certain. Not even the faintest sound of them could be heard in the overall murmur of the jungle. God, I felt, must have decreed that they would pass me by. It must be a sign that I would live. With this assurance growing in my mind, again the will to live, the insistent hope against hope welled up inside me.

. . . If I could manage only one mile each day I had a chance of getting through to China.

. . . I was ready to go. All I had to do was to walk.

I rolled on to my right side, lifting my body up so that I took all the weight on my arms, and twisting so that at the same time I could draw up my right leg underneath me. I pressed upwards with the right leg and started to turn my body more fully. I could not restrain a cry of agony, despite my gritted teeth, as a vicious stab of pain shot through the gashed and torn muscle I was twisting. The wounded hip joint, also beginning to take some of the strain, was suddenly hot with a searing agony.

I slumped back to the ground, soaked with sweat and sick with pain. My agony of soul was even greater. It could not be done after all. Without someone to help me I could never stand up. Just for that very reason, just because I could not raise myself from the horizontal to the perpendicular to lever myself on to the crutch, my body could not set out on the journey my ambitious mind had planned for it.

Tears of pain, and of rage and desperation, sprang to my eyes. I ground the heel of my good foot into the dry soil in a fury that was also an agony of despair. I slumped back, my body clammy with cold sweat and hot blood pounding at my temples. Now I had toppled down the yawning chasm of despair and was stretched at the bottom, fingers clawing the earth around me.

I lay there for a long while, until the pains which had tortured my body subsided, and the pain in my mind gave way to a dull emptiness. Then I felt for my pipe once more and lit it, and lay back puffing at it steadily. Slowly my hopelessness drained out of me.

My pipe went out and I felt in my jacket pocket for my matches to light it again. As I did so my fingers came in contact with a folded piece of paper which I could not remember putting there. . . . I drew it out. I opened it to find, not a map, but a printed text that my mother had sent to me in the last letter I had received from her. Against the day when I 'might need some extra help', she explained, she had sent me that quotation from M. Louise Haskins which was made famous by King George VI in his memorable broadcast to the Nation during Britain's first wartime Christmas of the Second World War.

'I said to the man who stood at the gate of the year: "Give me a light that I may tread safely into the unknown." And he replied: "Go out into the darkness and put your hand into the hand of God." That shall be to you better than a light and safer than a known way!'

I read it. I read it again. Then, as I carefully folded it and returned it to my pocket, something of its message seemed to infuse itself into me. I felt a new courage and determination well up inside me. What if there was no known way for a wounded soldier, abandoned by his comrades as incapable of walking, to escape through hornets' nests of Japanese aroused by the Chindits in the hell of this Burmese jungle? Never in all my life had I been so alone and so friendless. Yet suddenly I was fully prepared to do just what the text said. I would put my hand into the hand of God—of whom I knew no more than an average schoolboy would—and set out into the darkness of the jungle believing that my faith in His love and protecting guidance would be better than any known way. It made up my mind for me. I would try again to walk.

. . . Aloud I said: 'China, here I come.'

I was all too conscious, as I staggered up the slope, that I was going out into the darkness. It was the darkness of an ominous, dangerous jungle. I was alone as few men can have been alone. My enemies were many and cruel and they were everywhere—the Japs, possibly treacherous and murderous tribesmen, hungry carnivorous beasts, and venomous snakes. Even the very jungle itself was against me. And I was not only alone, but I was distressingly crippled.

The track ahead was a twilight trail into a gloomy and

sinister cavern. My mode of progress was quaint and laughable, had it not been so painful and pathetic. I could not march face forwards, striding out boldly into the unknown up the steep slope of the track. Instead, like a skier walking up a snowy ski-run, I had to take shuffling side-steps all the time.

Ian MacHorton

IN THE HEART OF THE FOREST

In the heart of the forest,
The shuddering forest,
The moaning and sobbing
Sad shuddering forest—
The dark and the dismal
Persistent sad sobbing
Throughout the weird forest.

Ah! God! they are voices—
Dim ghosts of the forest
Unrestfully sobbing
Through wistful pale voices,
Whose breath is the wind and whose
    lips the sad trees;

Whose yearning great eyes
Death haunted for ever
Look from the dark waters,
And pale spirit faces
Wrought from the white lilies.

Isaac Rosenberg

SAFER THAN A KNOWN WAY (4)

I struggled on. The haunted trees and moribund clumps of vegetation trapped like me in this swamp, seemed to rear up in the mist as gigantic things. My world was now a blue-grey haze, scattered with dancing pinpoints of light and with anything that stood up in it and from it elongated and drawn up in jagged black verticals to disappear through the roof of mist above.

Then I collapsed unconscious on a mudbank. When I recovered consciousness again it was to find myself completely clear-headed and without any fear. I felt very confident that I was going to win through. I was hardly aware of my gaunt and shrunken body with all its marks of pain and suffering. I felt clear and spiritual and capable of travelling vast distances unhindered by my body. And miraculously, the mist had lifted from the swamp.

Without moving, I turned my eyes to the left. At once I came face to face with a pale-green lizard. The lizard rolled one eye to study me critically while the other looked back the other way, apparently seeking the safest line of retreat. My mind appreciated that it was food. I drew my knife. At its glint the lizard scampered away along the mudbank, stumbling in its haste as it went into a depression. But it recovered and continued. I did not see it disappear, because my eyes had left the lizard and were riveted in absolute amazement upon the depression that had caused it to stumble. Slowly I rose to my feet and, with my eyes still fixed upon that depression, I stumbled as fast as I could towards it. When I reached it I went down on my hands and knees and stared at it unbelievingly. My fingers traced its outline. It was something the presence of which in this place, completely astounded me. But I did not attempt to reason how or why it got there. There, before me, was the undeniable imprint of a British Army boot.

From tracing my finger around its outline, I pushed it into each of the stud marks across the sole. Yes, there were thirteen studs in that boot. Without the faintest shadow of doubt, it was the footprint left by a British Army standard issue ammunition boot. As the joy of my discovery welled up within me I looked up and onwards in the direction towards which the toe of the boot was pointing. Yes. There, clearly discernible as they stretched away before me, were more boot-prints. They led away from where I knelt in a direction cutting diagonally across the wide mudbank. As straight as a ruled line they went, but becoming almost invisible after the first few. I blessed that lizard which had led me to them. Quite unquestioning, I set out to follow the boot-prints.

On and on they led me. Unhesitatingly, and filled with the

confidence that at last I was being led back to safety, I followed them. I did not look to left or right, neither did I fear that if I followed this clearly marked track I might step on to treacherous ground that would suck me down to die in the black and stinking mud. In complete and utter faith, I followed the bootprints onwards, and always they led me across the swamp on ground which bore my weight and took me from one firm mudbank to another. The mud was hardening beneath my feet: before long I was on firm dry earth. I was through the swamp. Those blessed prints made by a British soldier's boots had led me safely through.

I could see that the trail continued straight and true across the dry earth from where I now stood; on to where the forest towered up again and a track was discernible disappearing into it. I had to rest for a short while, for I was very weak, so I slumped down on the earth where I was. Again I examined closely the nearest boot-mark. The British soldier, whoever he was, could not be very far in advance of me. The prints were undeniably recent. Minute piles of earth stood behind each of the marks made by each one of the regulation thirteen studs. The hot sun had not yet crumbled and broken them down. The man I was following must be very close. I stood up and I called after the British soldier, hoping to attract his attention. I shouted for him. I shouted again. A lonely man calling for the companionship he knew to be only a few minutes in front of him. But I called in vain. I sank to the ground again, then leaned back wearily against a tree trunk and took a long drink from my water bottle.

Revived somewhat, I corked the bottle and put it down beside the nearest boot-print. I looked back at the trail that had been my salvation and as I did so I was overwhelmed with a sense of the unearthly. My scalp crawled and my heart palpitated with a great fear of the unknown. Behind me, and back into the swamp as far as I could see, were only the prints of my own naked feet. There were absolutely no trace at all of any booted feet having come that way!

Unbelievably, I got to my feet and slowly walked back along the trail left by my own bare feet. But although I retraced my steps for more than a hundred yards, and well back into the swamp, I could not find even the slightest trace of the booted feet of a British soldier having passed that way. There was only the imprint of my own naked feet. My spine prickled at the uncanniness of it all. I turned and stumbled back to where I had left my water bottle. Would I find the boot-marks still where I had seen them before, leading off towards the jungle track? Yes, they were there, those prints I had yet to follow. At regular intervals, firmly pressed into the ground, were the boot-marks, each with its thirteen stud holes. I made no attempt to solve the mystery, if indeed I could ever have found an explanation for it. I was quite content to follow my guide who had brought me thus far, as far as he chose to lead me. Wherever those boot-marks went, I would go unquestionably. I was too weak and too tired to want to try to find any reason why I should do otherwise.

In any case, now I had recovered from the shock of their mysterious appearance and disappearance behind me, I found the presence of those boot-marks always ahead of me strangely comforting. The aching gap of loneliness was filled and I had a companion again. I had nothing to fear.

Westwards those boot-marks led me. Up hills they went and down into rocky chaungs; through jungle and out again; across dusty paddy-fields. On and on we went, my mysterious foot-print guide and I. As we marched we discussed the relative beauties of the gentle jungle orchids and the gaudy flame of the forest. We kept no secrets from one another. Those boot-marks understood my innermost fears and we were content in each other's company. In my delicious light-headedness, as I lurched and struggled on, I was conscious that I was talking and singing and shouting—talking garrulously and happily to my companion who left only boot-marks but wasn't there, and whose boot-prints themselves vanished once they were behind me.

Abruptly, at the edge of a stream, the footprints ceased. I was alone. For a few moments I stood there in utter bewilderment. What did I do now? Which way did I go? Before the despair which had begun to mount within me could develop I heard the unmistakable clamour of a large river through the forest just ahead of me. The swish of its waters drew me

inevitably, and I surged forward in a new wave of eagerness . . .
I knew that this must be the Yu. Unless the Japanese surrender
notices were true, the British base of Tamu could not be many
days away upstream.

Ian MacHorton

The tension increased.
In the noonday heat
Their wills began to waver.

Night flared.
Phosphorescent,
The jungle wailed in the fierce grip of the storm.

They paid
The full price of love
That others might enjoy a victory.

Morning mist,
Chirping of early birds.
Who recalled the night's sacrifice?

Dag Hammarskjöld

LOOK UPON ZION

I know beyond all shadow of doubt that we live always
under guidance and that this small life is but the 'lowest room'
in our Father's Many Mansions, so why would I mind which
one I dwell in. No-one likes pain of course, but then that can be
minimized these days and even that brings a 'something' which
anyone wanting to experience life to the full would not really
do without. Oh no—all things work together for our good, and
I will never be persuaded otherwise.

Sylvia Pedder

From a letter written when she knew she was dying of cancer.

Now we turn to the region of Arctic Snows. At one place a number of Christian Eskimos have asked the missionary to celebrate the Eucharist; when he arrived they had made ready for him in the only possible place—one of their snow huts. He gives a vivid description of the service in its Eskimo setting. 'First they cleared the place of all rotten meat, etc., and then fresh snow, white and clean, was brought in. A tent was arranged (under the snow roof) to catch any drops that might fall when the hut was crowded during the service. The floor was then covered with caribou skins, so that the worshippers might kneel with less discomfort. A sledge box was placed in a central position on the sleeping platform and acted as the Holy Table, and when carefully covered with new towels of spotless white the sacramental linen and vessels were arranged upon it. Two flickering stone lamps shed a subdued light hardly sufficient for reading, but not unsuitable for the service. The communicants were ten in number, four women and six men . . .

'It is no exaggeration to say that in an almost literal manner the experience of the disciples who walked to Emmaus was repeated at this time, and the Lord was made known to His disciples in the breaking of bread . . .

'After the service the people did not go away. For nearly ten minutes no words were spoken. It was as if we all with one accord felt in our souls that it was "good for us to be here", for we had seen the Lord.'

*   *   *

Thus all over the world, under all kinds of conditions, in exile, prison, concentration camp, on the brink of death as well as in the midst of daily life and at times of festival and rejoicing, the Eucharist is the Feast of the whole Christian Family: 'in heaven and on earth'. And wherever it is celebrated we are 'at home' for here is the foretaste of the Father's House which is for all nations.

Olive Wyon

That same day two of them were on their way to a village called Emmaus, which lay about seven miles from Jerusalem, and they were talking together about all these happenings. As they talked and discussed it with one another, Jesus himself came up and walked along with them; but something held their eyes from seeing who it was. He asked them, 'What is it you are debating as you walk?' They halted, their faces full of gloom, and one, called Cleopas, answered, 'Are you the only person staying in Jerusalem not to know what has happened there in the last few days?' 'What do you mean?' he said. 'All this about Jesus of Nazareth,' they replied, 'a prophet powerful in speech and action before God and the whole people; how our chief priests and rulers handed him over to be sentenced to death, and crucified him. But we had been hoping that he was the man to liberate Israel. What is more, this is the third day since it happened, and now some women of our company have astounded us: they went early to the tomb, but failed to find his body, and returned with a story that they had seen a vision of angels who told them he was alive. So some of our people went to the tomb and found things just as the women had said; but him they did not see.'

'How dull you are!' he answered. 'How slow to believe all that the prophets said! Was the Messiah not bound to suffer thus before entering upon his glory?' Then he began with Moses and all the prophets, and explained to them the passages which referred to himself in every part of the Scriptures.

By this time they had reached the village to which they were going, and he made as if to continue his journey, but they pressed him: 'Stay with us, for evening draws on, and the day is almost over.' So he went in to stay with them. And when he had sat down with them at table, he took bread and said the blessing; he broke the bread, and offered it to them. Then their eyes were opened, and they recognized him; and he vanished from their sight. They said to one another, 'Did we not feel our hearts on fire as he talked with us on the road and explained the Scriptures to us?'

Luke 24:13–32 NEB

UXBRIDGE ROAD

The Western Road goes streaming out to seek the cleanly
   wild
It pours the city's dim desires towards the undefiled,
It sweeps betwixt the huddled homes about its eddies grown
To smear the little space between the city and the sown:
The torments of that seething tide who is there that can see?
There's one who walked with starry feet the western road by
   me!

He is the Drover of the soul; he leads the flock of men
All wistful on that weary track, and brings them back again.
The dreaming few, the slaving crew, the motley cast of life—
The wastrel and artificer, the harlot and the wife—
They may not rest, for ever pressed by one they cannot see:
The one who walked with starry feet the western road by me.

He drives them east, he drives them west, between the dark
   and light;
He pastures them in city pens, he leads them home at night,
The towery trams, the threaded trains, like shuttles to and
   fro
To weave the web of working days in ceaseless travel go.
How harsh the woof, how long the weft! who shall the fabric
   see?
The one who walked with starry feet the western road by me.

Throughout the living joyful year at lifeless tasks to strive,
And scarcely at the end to save gentility alive;
The villa plot to sow and reap, to act the villa lie,
Beset by villa fears to live, midst villa dreams to die;
Ah, who can know the dreary woe? and who the splendour
   see?
The one who walked with starry feet the western road by me.

Behold! He lent me as we went the vision of the seer;
Behold! I saw the life of men, the life of God shine clear.

I saw the Spirit's hidden thrust, I saw the race fulfil
The spiral of its steep ascent, predestined of the Will.
Yet not unled, but shepherded by one they may not see—
The one who walked with starry feet the western road by me!

Evelyn Underhill

I began to look for a meaning in life other than what I could find through purposefulness. Studying and making oneself useful for life didn't convince me at all. All my life up to now had been concentrated on immediate goals, and suddenly these became empty. I felt something immensely dramatic inside myself, and everything around me seemed small and meaningless.

Months passed and no meaning appeared on the horizon. One day—it was during Lent, and I was then a member of one of the Russian youth organizations in Paris—one of the leaders came up to me and said, 'We have invited a priest to talk to you; come.' I answered with violent indignation that I would not. I had no use for the Church. I did not believe in God. I did not want to waste any of my time. The leader was subtle— he explained that everyone who belonged to my group had reacted in exactly the same way, and if no one came we would all be put to shame because the priest had come and we would be disgraced if no one attended his talk. 'Don't listen,' the leader said, 'I don't care, but just sit and be a physical presence.' That much loyalty I was prepared to give to my youth organization, so I sat through the lecture. I didn't intend to listen. But my ears pricked up. I became more and more indignant. I saw a vision of Christ and Christianity that was profoundly repulsive to me. When the lecture was over I hurried home in order to check the truth of what he had been saying. I asked my mother whether she had a book of the Gospel, because I wanted to know whether the Gospel would support the monstrous impression I had derived from his talk. I expected nothing good from my reading, so I counted the chapters of the four Gospels to be sure I read the shortest, not to waste time unnecessarily. I started to read St Mark's Gospel.

While I was reading the beginning of St Mark's Gospel,

before I reached the third chapter, I suddenly became aware
that on the other side of my desk there was a presence. And the
certainty was so strong that it was Christ standing there that it
has never left me. This was the real turning-point. Because
Christ was alive and I had been in his presence I could say with
certainty that what the Gospel said about the crucifixion of the
prophet of Galilee was true, and the centurion was right when
he said 'Truly he is the son of God'. It was in the light of the
Resurrection that I could read with certainty the story of the
Gospel, knowing that everything was true in it because the
impossible event of the Resurrection was to me more certain
than any event in history. History I had to believe, the
Resurrection I knew for a fact. I did not discover, as you see,
the Gospel beginning with its first message of the Annunciation
and it did not unfold for me as a story which one can believe or
disbelieve. It began as an event that left all problems of dis-
belief behind because it was a direct and personal experience.
   . . . I became absolutely certain within myself that Christ is
alive and that certain things existed. I didn't have all the answers, but having touched that experience, I was certain that
ahead of me there were answers, visions, possibilities. This is
what I mean by faith—not doubting in the sense of being in
confusion and perplexity, but doubting in order to discover the
reality of the life, the kind of doubt that makes you want to
question and discover more, that makes you want to explore.

                                                    Anthony Bloom

You must picture me alone in that room in Magdalen, night
after night, feeling, whenever my mind lifted even for a second
from my work, the steady, unrelenting approach of Him whom
I so earnestly desired not to meet. That which I greatly feared
had at last come upon me. In the Trinity Term of 1929 I gave
in and admitted that God was God, and knelt and prayed:
perhaps, that night, the most dejected and reluctant convert in
all England, I did not then see what is now the most shining
and obvious thing; the Divine humility which will accept a
convert even on such terms . . . The hardness of God is kinder
than the softness of men, and His compulsion is our liberation.

                                                    C. S. Lewis

THE EUCHARIST IN THE WORLD CHURCH

All over Europe, during the war years, in circumstances of extreme difficulty and danger, the Eucharist was often celebrated by priests in hiding or in disguise: sometimes in frozen dug-outs in the depths of the forest, close to the Red Army sentries, patrolling near at hand: sometimes in prison cells or sick rooms, or in poor lodging houses, and often at 1 a.m. as the safest hour.

Bishop Sloskans, a Latvian by birth, who had entered Russia secretly, in order to help maintain the life of his Church there during an era of severe persecution, was captured by the Russian Secret Police, and tortured so severely that when he was only in his thirties he looked like an aged broken man.

He spent seven years in imprisonment in Siberia and on the shores of the White Sea. In some way or another it became known that the prisoner was a Bishop, and one political prisoner after another managed to provide grapes and bread for the Sacrament.

Secretly and at night he celebrated the Eucharist and gave Communion to over one thousand Catholics in the Siberian Camp till he was most marvellously set free.

In Russia during a period of persecution there were many 'secret priests'—men who wore ordinary clothes, did ordinary work, and yet managed to carry on the worship of the Church 'underground'. Under such conditions the central act of Christian worship becomes a capital crime against the State. Yet so deep is the desire for the Sacrament that men and women will risk their lives to take Communion.

These instances come from Eastern Europe and from the Roman Catholic and Eastern Orthodox Churches. Now let us turn to the West, and to the Protestant Churches. Bishop Lilje's experience in prison on Christmas Eve, 1944, ranks high among these great Sacramental occasions. Dr Lilje had been in prison since August of the previous year, and his fate was still uncertain; he never knew whether at any moment he would be wakened in the middle of the night to be taken away and shot. On this Christmas Eve he was alone in his cell, thinking of his family and his congregation, and longing to be allowed to exercise his ministry when his number was called; a guard came to the door and told him to follow—wondering what was about to happen Lilje obeyed. He was taken to the Commandant, who led the way silently to another cell. At the door of the cell the Commandant stood still, and said to the guard: 'Bring No. 212 here too!' Then he went into the cell, taking the Bishop with him.

As they entered, a man rose to his feet whom Dr Lilje at once recognized as a certain Count X. He greeted him with eager friendliness, but the Commandant broke in roughly upon their conversation: 'I did not bring you two gentlemen together for social purposes.' Turning to the Count he said, 'You asked for a pastoral visit from a Chaplain who is your friend; unfortunately this was not possible, but here is Dr Lilje who will speak to you.' Dr Lilje then asked the Count what he would like him to do. He replied: 'I would like to make my confession and receive the Sacrament.' A cup was provided, a small amount of wine, and some white bread. Meanwhile No. 212 was brought in; he was an accomplished violinist. The service began with a beautiful Christmas chorale played by the musician. Then Bishop Lilje proceeded to celebrate the Eucharist according to the Lutheran custom; as the Count knelt on the stone floor to receive absolution and Communion the tears ran down his face, but it was a peaceful hour, full of the Presence of Christ; the Commandant himself was deeply moved; when the service was over he shook the Bishop's hand with great warmth, saying: 'I thank you. You do not know what you have done for me this evening in the midst of my difficult heart-breaking work!' With joy and praise in his heart the Bishop was taken back to his cell. Later he heard that Count X was removed to a concentration camp; the violinist was murdered by the Gestapo; and the Commandant was relieved of his post because he was too humane. But the memory of that Christmas celebration in 1944 has remained a precious memory with Bishop Lilje ever since.

Olive Wyon

The centre of me is always and eternally a terrible pain. A curious wild pain—a searching for something beyond what the world contains, something transfigured and infinite—the beautiful vision—God. I do not find it, I do not think it is to be found—but the love of it is my life—it's the passionate love for a ghost.

Bertrand Russell

PARACELSUS

Truth is within ourselves; it takes no rise
From outward things, whate'er you may believe.
There is an inmost centre in us all,
Where truth abides in fulness; and around,
Wall upon wall, the gross flesh hems it in,
This perfect, clear perception—which is truth.

A baffling and perverting carnal mesh
Binds it, and masks all error: and to *know*,
Rather consists in opening out a way
Whence the imprisoned splendour may escape,
Than in effecting entry for a light
Supposed to be without.

Robert Browning

Discovery of the deep centre is not confined to the mystics. Nor is it necessary to use the constructive technique to come upon it. Wherever men live life responsibly, the deep centre may be to some extent experienced. Especially is this true in times of danger or of great emotional stress, when, almost without knowing it, a man seeks strength beyond his own. In the searing years of this present century, under bombing and shell fire, in prison compounds and concentration camps, in long agonized waiting, in fear and suffering and the presence of death, some such encounter as the following may well have come to many, whether or not at the time they had the means to hold it.

'In the summer of 1916, I was moving up with my battalion to the line. We were eager and rather nervous. It was our first active experience of war. The last march before the trenches had to be made in the late afternoon and at night. We started, heavily laden, stumbling over the cobbled roads. The rain pelted down, soaking us. We went on till midnight, and came, in the black, to a half-ruined village. Everything was quiet, almost peaceful. We quartered in such barns and farm build-ings as still had roof and walls; struggled out of our equipment and were asleep at once, as our bodies touched the ground.

'I awoke with a start; a shrieking in my ears and a crash like the sound of falling fragments. Again the ghastly drawn-out shriek and another, more shattering explosion. As I lay there on the floor, torn from the depths of sleep, I felt such extremity of fear as I had never known. From the waist downwards I shook in an uncontrollable trembling, horrible to experience. In the same fraction of time the upper part of me reached out instinctively, with a deep gasping breath, to something beyond my knowledge.

'I had the experience of being caught, as neatly and cleanly as a good fielder catches a ball. A sense of indescribable relief flowed through my whole being. I knew with a certainty, such as no other certainty could be, that I was secure. There was no assurance that I would not be blown to pieces in the next instant. I expected to be. But I knew that, though such might be my fate, it was not of great account. There was something in me that was indestructible. The trembling ceased and I was completely collected and calm. Another shell came and burst, but it had lost its terror.

'Some weeks later, in taking over a new position in the line, I again had occasion to be terribly afraid. I remembered how I had felt under the baptism of fire and tried to recapture the contact with what it was I had then reached. I found myself breathing deeply and with this "drawing-in", as I phrased it to myself, came the same feeling of assurance. Whereas a moment before I had been shaking with fear, it became as if I had down the centre of my body a cylinder of steel.

'After that I often had recourse to this means of reaching out for help. Sometimes it was difficult to break through, but if I persisted the contact was always made, and the indestructible something was there. Sometimes for whole weeks or months, I forgot about it. But, at whatever long intervals, always I came back to it as the supreme value, as that one thing on which I could depend.'

The finding of the deep centre does not necessarily come about in some sudden burst of insight such as this. More usually it is a gradual development, so gradual that with most people it is unperceived, unrealized, in the main unused. In effect, it is the crucial point of the individuation process, the means of differentiation and of integration alike.

... And as when a man, caught in the insoluble problem of the opposites, seeks not a way out but a way through, it is the deep centre, variously expressed in the transforming symbols coming to him, that enables the way through to be found.

... The deep centre is not only the something indestructible in the depths, the certitude, the rock. It is experienced as the 'strait gate' by which a man finds his way to God, or however else he may name the creative principle.

P. W. Martin

Yahweh went before them, by day in the form of a pillar of cloud to show them the way, and by night in the form of a pillar of fire to give them light: thus they could continue their march by day and by night. The pillar of cloud never failed to go before the people during the day, nor the pillar of fire during the night.

*   *   *

The cloud covered the Tent of Meeting and the glory of Yahweh filled the tabernacle. Moses could not enter the Tent of Meeting because of the cloud that rested on it and because of the glory of Yahweh that filled the tabernacle.

*   *   *

At every stage of their journey, whenever the cloud rose from the tabernacle the sons of Israel would resume their march. If the cloud did not rise, they waited and would not march until it did. For the cloud of Yahweh rested on the tabernacle by day, and a fire shone within the cloud by night, for all the House of Israel to see. And so it was for every stage of their journey.

Exodus 13 : 21–2; 40 : 34–8 JB

Moses used to take the Tent and pitch it outside the camp; at some distance from the camp. He called it the Tent of Meeting. Anyone who had to consult Yahweh would go out to the Tent of Meeting, outside the camp. Whenever Moses went out to the Tent, all the people would rise. Every man would stand at the door of his tent and watch Moses until he reached the Tent; the pillar of cloud would come down and station itself at the entrance to the Tent, and Yahweh would speak with Moses. When they saw the pillar of cloud stationed at the entrance to the Tent, all the people would rise and bow low, each at the door of his tent. Yahweh would speak with Moses face to face, as a man speaks with his friend.

*   *   *

Moses said to Yahweh, 'See, you yourself say to me, "Make the people go on," but you do not let me know who it is you will send with me. Yet you yourself have said, "I know you by name and you have won my favour." If indeed I have won your favour, please show me your ways, so that I can under-stand you and win your favour. Remember, too, that this nation is your own people.' Yahweh replied, 'I myself will go with you, and I will give you rest.' Moses said, 'If you are not going with us yourself, do not make us leave this place. By what means can it be known that I, I and my people, have won your favour, if not by your going with us? By this we shall be marked out, I and my people, from all the peoples on the face of the earth.' Yahweh said to Moses, 'Again I will do what you have asked, because you have won my favour and because I know you by name.'

Moses said, 'Show me your glory, I beg you.' And he said, 'I will let all my splendour pass in front of you, and I will pron-ounce before you the name Yahweh. I have compassion on whom I will, and I show pity to whom I please. You cannot see my face,' he said, 'for a man cannot see me and live.' And Yahweh said, 'Here is a place beside me. You must stand on the rock, and when my glory passes by, I will put you in a cleft of the rock and shield you with my hand while I pass by. Then I will take my hand away and you shall see the back of me; but my face is not to be seen.'

Exodus 33 : 7–23 JB

LORD HALIFAX'S GHOST BOOKS (I)

I do not know if you have ever heard of our dear Bishop King of Lincoln's experience. He told it to Canon Perry, when my sister was staying with him and the Bishop came to tea, as at that time he often did in order to consult him on Canon Law, when those creatures were prosecuting him. (The famous trial of Bishop King before Archbishop Benson in 1890.) When the Bishop was a young man, he was curate in a village. One wet cold night he had come home very tired and had just got his boots off, when his landlady came in and said that a farmer, living three miles off across the fields, had met with a serious accident and wanted King to come at once. She did not know the messenger, and he refused to come in because he was so wet. King put his boots on again and started off; but it was very dark and he missed the man who had brought the message. When he reached the house to which he had been summoned, the door was opened to his knock by the farmer himself, hale, hearty and much surprised to see his visitor. No message had been sent, and, greatly mystified, King went home. The man who had summoned him had gone, and the matter remained unexplained.

Some years afterwards, in another county, King was ministering to a dying man in hospital, and the man said: 'Don't you remember me, Sir?' The Bishop could not recall him until he gave his name, which was that of a very bad character who had lived years ago in that village where King was a curate. The man went on: 'It was lucky for you that you brought a friend with you that night when you thought you had a call to the

farm. I meant to murder you, only I couldn't, as there were
two of you.' The Bishop had seen and heard nothing, but the
man was certain that he had been accompanied by a second
great-coated figure walking beside him.

A similar occurrence was told me by a young priest who was
working in a mining district in Canada. He had to go a long
ride through thickly wooded country. He did not relish the job,
as there were plenty of undesirable characters about: but duty
called and he went, returning in perfect safety. Some little
while afterwards he was called to see a dying man in hospital
who told him that he and a 'pal' had been so furious with him
for his interference with their doings that they had determined
to kill him. Knowing of his journey, they lad lain in wait for
him in the loneliest part of the way, but, to their great annoyance, two other men were riding, one on each side of their
proposed victim, so that they could not get a shot at him. Like
Bishop King, the priest thought that he was alone.

Charles Lindley Wood, Viscount Halifax

THE FRIEND

Not from the heavy soil,
where blood and sex and oath
rule in their hallowed might,
where earth itself,
guarding the primal consecrated order,
avenges wantonness and madness—
not from the heavy soil of earth,
but from the spirit's choice and free desire,
needing no oath or legal bond,
is friend bestowed on friend.

Beside the cornfield that sustains us,
tilled and cared for reverently by men
sweating as they labour at their task,
and, if need be, giving their life's blood—
beside the field that gives their daily bread
men also let the lovely cornflower thrive.
No one has planted, no one watered it;

it grows, defenceless and in freedom,
and in glad confidence of life untroubled
under the open sky.
Beside the staff of life,
taken and fashioned from the heavy earth,
beside our marriage, work, and war,
the free man, too, will live and grow towards the sun.
Not the ripe fruit alone—
blossom is lovely, too.
Does blossom only serve the fruit,
or does fruit only serve the blossom—
who knows?
But both are given to us.
Finest and rarest blossom,
at a happy moment springing
from the freedom of a lightsome, daring, trusting spirit,
is a friend to a friend.

Playmates at first
on the spirit's long journeys
to distant and wonderful realms
that, veiled by the morning sunlight,
glitter like gold;
when, in the midday heat
the gossamer clouds in the deep blue sky
drift slowly towards them—
realms that, when night stores the senses,
lit by the lamps in the darkness
like treasure prudently hidden
beckon the seeker.

When the spirit touches
man's heart and brow
with thoughts that are lofty, bold, serene,
so that with clear eyes he will face the world
as a free man may;
when then the spirit gives birth to action
by which alone we stand or fall;
when from the sane and resolute action
rises the work that gives a man's life

content and meaning—
then would that man,
lonely and actively working,
know of the spirit that grasps and befriends him,
like waters clear and refreshing
where the spirit is cleansed from the dust
and cooled from the heat that oppressed him,
steeling himself in the hour of fatigue—
like a fortress to which, from confusion and danger,
the spirit returns,
wherein he finds refuge and comfort and strengthening,
is a friend to a friend.

And the spirit will trust,
trust without limit.
Sickened by vermin
that feed, in the shade of the good,
on envy, greed, and suspicion,
by the snake-like hissing
of venomous tongues
that fear and hate and revile
the mystery of free thought
and upright heart,
the spirit would cast aside all deceit,
open his heart to the spirit he trusts,
and unite with him freely as one.
Ungrudging, he will support,
will thank and acknowledge him,
and from him draw happiness and strength.

But always to rigorous
judgement and censure
freely assenting,
man seeks, in his manhood,
not orders, not laws and peremptory dogmas,
but counsel from one who is earnest in goodness
and faithful in friendship,
making man free.

Distant or near,
in joy or in sorrow,
each in the other
sees his true helper
to brotherly freedom.

At midnight came the air-raid siren's song;
I thought of you in silence and for long—
how you are faring, how our lives once were,
and how I wish you home this coming year.

We wait till half past one, and hear at last
the signal that the danger now is past
so danger—if the omen does not lie—
of every kind shall gently pass you by.

Dietrich Bonhoeffer

LORD HALIFAX'S GHOST BOOKS (2)

One stormy night a man, known to be of great help to those
who were distressed in body or mind, was startled by a loud
ring at his bell. Going to the door, he found a messenger from
an invalid living some miles off who was in grave trouble and
begged for this man to go and see him. (I have forgotten the
invalid's name and am not sure whether or not he was a relation.)

The first man dismissed the messenger, saying he would go as
soon as he could. As he was starting off, he hesitated and even
thought of giving up the journey. It was a terrible night, and
the storm had increased to such a pitch that there was a risk of
his lantern light being blown out. However, he went. What
with the intense darkness and the wind and rain, he had some
difficulty in walking along; but presently he had a curious
feeling as of someone by his side. He could neither see nor hear
anyone, but the sensation that he had a companion was extremely strong and continued until he arrived at his destina-
tion, where he stayed for some time.

On his way home the storm was as bad as ever, but he again
had the feeling of being accompanied. Yet, mysterious and
unaccountable as it was, he was not in the least afraid.

Many years afterwards, he had a request one day to visit a
prison where a man was condemned to be hanged. He was not
surprised at receiving such a message, as he often called at that
particular prison to bring comfort and help to its inmates. He
found the man who had sent for him, and the prisoner said that
he did not wish to die with any crime unconfessed, whether or
not it had been actually carried out. 'Do you remember,' he
asked, 'walking along a dark lonely road in a storm several
years ago?' The visitor replied that he did. 'I knew you had
been sent for to a dying person,' the prisoner went on, 'and that
you always wore a valuable watch and might have money on
you. I lurked under a hedge prepared to attack and rob you,
but as you walked along, someone else was walking with you,
so I waited for your return. But when you came back, the
person was still there, walking by your side, and I did not dare
attack two people.'

Charles Lindley Wood, Viscount Halifax

I lift my eyes to the mountains:
    where is help to come from?
Help comes to me from Yahweh,
    who made heaven and earth.

No letting our footsteps slip!
    This guard of yours, he does not doze!
The guardian of Israel
    Does not doze or sleep.

Yahweh guards you, shades you.
    With Yahweh at your right hand
sun cannot strike you down by day,
    nor moon at night.

Yahweh guards you from harm,
    he guards your lives,
he guards you leaving, coming back,
    now and for always.

Psalm 121 JB

MAN'S SEARCH FOR MEANING (8)

One day, a few days after the liberation, I walked through the country past flowering meadows, for miles and miles, toward the market town near the camp. Larks rose to the sky and I could hear their joyous song. There was no one to be seen for miles around: there was nothing but the wide earth and sky and the larks' jubilation and the freedom of space. I stopped, looked around, and up to the sky—and then I went down on my knees. At that moment there was very little I knew of myself or of the world—I had but one sentence in mind—always the same: 'I called to the Lord from my narrow prison and He answered me in the freedom of space.'

How long I knelt there and repeated this sentence memory can no longer recall. But I know that on that day, in that hour, my new life started. Step for step I progressed, until I again became a human being.

Viktor Frankl

THE CAPTIVE CONSCIENCE (2)

The Christian contention is that every evidence of evil is an act of cosmic defiance, a violation of the moral structure of the universe. We stand, however shakily, for the good, not in a morally neutral world—which would leave all the key questions unanswered, nor in an evil world which must eventually render void our hopes and ideals. We stand for the right in a good world, marred, scarred and warped, but still a good world. According to the Book of Deuteronomy, God put before people just like us, weary in well-doing, the same choice which we face—'I have set before you this day, life and good, death and evil; therefore choose life!' And with breath-taking aplomb, given the kind of world we have inherited and the enormity of the evils with which we must do battle, the Gospel claims that we can choose life and good in the confidence that the universe stands behind us when we do well and resists us when we do ill. 'Why do you kick against the pricks', God asks a demon-driven Paul, implying that there is a cosmic pulse beneath the drift of things as inexorable though apparently insignificant as that which impels a tiny seedling to force its way up to the light through layers of concrete.

This affirmation that the universe is friendly—biased towards our good intentions—is no cause for superficial optimism. In the short run, evil can and does frustrate our noblest endeavours and brings undeserved suffering upon our fellow men. But it does make a difference to both the quality and persistence of our struggle for justice to be able to believe that there is no dark, sinister force at the heart of the universe which laughs at our heroism, nor a gaping void into which all the love and compassion of which we are capable are poured and lost for ever.

I cannot end without recording my conviction that there is a force at work in human affairs which is not the product of our natural aptitudes nor corporate strategies—a creative factor which I can only describe as the grace of God. It unsnarls log-jams, spans unbridgeable gulfs and resolves apparent dead-locks. I have seen this happen too frequently in concrete political situations to write off talk of God's grace as pious cant. It operates through men of affairs who make surprising renun-ciations and undreamed-of sacrifices, who have unaccountable changes of mind and heart, and as a consequence, against all odds, tiny but significant victories of love are achieved. This power, opaque to human reason, we can neither command nor demand; merely accept with gratitude when we sense its presence.

That 'harvest-time' which Jesus promised, might just arrive during Prisoners of Conscience Year, overtaking our well-meaning but pathetic efforts on their behalf. But it would be foolish to bank on the possibility. Meanwhile we must press on, trying to smash rocks with our feather dusters, realistic in our expectations but undiscouraged in our persistence. For when every vestige of human achievement or tyranny has been wiped off the face of the earth, creative acts of compassion will remain and have eternal significance as the effectual signs of the presence of the Kingdom of Heaven.

Colin Morris

DUNAMIS

The silent activity
of yeast
in dough;
doubling, trebling its size,
transforming
its substance.

The delicate searching thrust
of blades of grass
through the dark soil;
invisibly
clothing
the bare earth
in green.

The persistent pressure
of brittle roots
against stone,
until the crack is seen.

A man,
vulnerable,
crucified,
imprisoned in a tomb,
yet breaking through
the stubborn rock
which cannot hold
God's love.

G. Betty Hares

Every day it becomes clearer to me that we human beings—
especially we people of the white race, we Europeans—put false
valuations on everything because we have become estranged
from God. The world of today no longer has a true scale of
values. Men chase after fleeting goals and no longer know what
happiness is, nor where it lies; they really no longer even know

what they should be thankful for. But precious beyond all else
are the love and mercy of God, who will save everyone who
believes in him from all distress and all pain, and who even in
this earthly life gives help through his Spirit. God has revealed
to us everything that we need for living and for dying. I have
actually experienced it: 'Nevertheless I am continually with
thee: thou hast holden me by my right hand, Thou shalt guide
me with thy counsel, and afterwards receive me in glory . . .
And there is none . . . that I desire besides thee.' I have experienced it with an indescribably blissful certainty. I have
learned to thank God, and learned what is meant by the
precept, 'And thou shalt love the Lord thy God with all thine
heart.' He has never let me fall by the way. In his loving
kindness he has always drawn me to himself again.

And where the wisdom of the wise man fails
The childlike heart's simplicity prevails.

. . . Man should turn with all his troubles and joys to God,
lest he lose the loving contact with him. It should be done with
concentrated, earnest absorption; it should be an opening of
oneself to God. In praying one should hear and be willing to
hear; God does not remain silent. This I know.
. . . I should like to have a great many people hear and
understand that happiness lies within one and not in outward
things—solely in the living union with God.
. . . The worth of a nation is determined only by the extent to
which it is directed to God. A non-Christian people may be
much closer to God than a Christian people. The Christian
peoples of today are very far from God.

Ewald von Kleist-Schmenzin

*Imprisoned by the Gestapo, he died on April 15, 1945, in Plötzensee, at
the hands of the hangman.*

DEAR LORD,
You fill my dark with light,
With shade my road's fierce glare;
My desert you make green and bright,
My garden fair.

Your star-hung skies' infinity
   Lends rose and rock their part.
And time from your eternity
   To read my heart.

The silent cell of sorrow's core
   Your small clear voice does fill.
And waters loud that round me roar
   Bids 'Peace, be still.'

In loneliness confined, I see
   Your saints' brave multitude;
In thronging crowds you comfort me
   With solitude.

And when we weep you crucified,
   Reborn you heal our pain.
Triumphant in your Eastertide
   You rise again.

Geoffrey Jackson

THE MYSTIC'S VICTORY

Edith Stein typified in her frail person the Jewish and Christian reply to Auschwitz, because it was given to her by God to implant the Cross in this complete desert of hatred.

As one who awaited beatific perfection in profound peace she was completely prepared for the meaningless hell of perpetual destruction. The works that have been done in her name since 1945—and, of course, in the names of others like her—are evidence not only for spiritual achievement but also for immortality and consummation.

The mystics' victory and intercessory power are seen to have surmounted wires, gassings, and burnings, in the aureole of eternal glory.

Ulrich Simon

A CONCENTRATION CAMP SOMEWHERE IN POLAND

Five o'clock was reveille. It was pitch dark except for dimly lit camp lights, and every now and then the searchlight would glide through from the watch-towers. It was freezing cold outside and the frost lay thick on the window panes.

Magda, aged nineteen, could not get up. Feverish, she lay on her bunk, with pains all over her body. She was shivering with cold all through the night. If she reported sick, she thought, she might be put to work in the camp, perhaps digging ditches, emptying the latrines and other endless camp duties, under the eyes of the 'Aufseherinnen'—female overseers. You might end up standing on a slope in the coldest and windiest spot in the camp for a couple of hours as punishment because they didn't like the way you walked, or looked, or because your nose was running and you didn't have a nice clean handkerchief, or your dress was tattered and torn, or you wore rags round your feet in sandals. When you dared to say that everything had been removed from you down to the very last garment, your head was shaved. You were given only one dress and a pair of sandals, no underwear, because it was summertime when you entered the camp. You had to sleep in the dress. The one blanket that you were given wasn't enough to keep you warm at night. The Aufseherin would squeak like a rat; 'You pig Jew, You pig Jew', whilst whipping you.

Magda still lying on the bunk felt that every limb in her body was out of joint. Suddenly the bunk began to sway and shake as the other occupants hurriedly got up, which meant that the 'Blockälteste'—the head prisoner—was nearing. If you were not fully dressed, your bed with the bug ridden straw mattress not tidy, you were in for trouble. As soon as she passed each hut everybody headed for the door to stand outside for 'Appell'— roll call. . . .

It was still dark though the sky was beginning to lighten. They stood there five in a row, huddled together for warmth. They stood there in the dark, in the cold, hungry and in silence, stamping up and down, up and down to keep warm. Magda grew stiff with cold, she couldn't find the strength even to stand. The can of the bitter ersatz coffee was already waiting to be distributed. If only the guards would hurry up and count the inmates—but they never do when it is very cold—an additional way of tormenting them. At last three of the guards arrived. You couldn't recognize one from the other, wrapped all over except for the eyes; one with a whip in his hand. It was much too cold even for them in their thick boots and fur-lined coats, to linger on and find ways of further humiliation, as was their daily custom. The counting was soon over.

As they strode back, the coffee was being handed out. Magda couldn't keep the mug in her frozen hands, her neighbour had to help her to steady it.

Back in the hut the bread was being rationed out. Magda, timid by nature, couldn't stand up for her rights and ended up always with the thinnest slice. This time she didn't even glance at it. What bliss, what happiness to be back in the hut. Soon enough the guards shouted 'out'! Everybody wrapped themselves in every rag and paper they possessed. At the gates they were frisked. The guards never knew what to look for.

Five in a row, hands behind their backs, escort guards in front, to the right, left and at the back of the column, rifles at the ready. The wind was slashing their faces as they moved on in silence. Their working place was a deserted area, on one side, and overlooking the area was a hut for the guards. They were divided into teams; half of them dug pits, the other half filled them in—useless, pointless labour.

The wind was cruel—not a bit of shelter; nowhere to warm up. Magda ached all over. How should she work—her hands were numb and her toes stung. God—to be near a stove, to warm oneself a little, her whole body craved for a little warmth. The only way to warm up was with work. To add to the misery they sadistically let one team work whilst the other had to wait and watch and freeze.

The cold grew keener, the icy wind was the hardest to bear. Freezing and famished they somehow managed to survive the day. Their faces were quite grey as the sun was beginning to set. Magda's face looked as if all life had drained out of her. A spasm of pain seized her heart—she could hardly breathe.

The escorts came on shouting 'form five', and soon started counting again. Whilst marching back to the camp they had to

sing. Between the camp's inner and outer gates they had to stop
and wait for the guards to let them in. After a whole day in the
freezing cold, chilled to the marrow, they were kept waiting
another hour.

Magda ached and throbbed all over. At that moment she
only craved to be back in the hut. A bowl of warm watery soup
mattered more to her than freedom itself. As she passed the
inner gates a hand pointed towards her and a few others to step
aside. They were ordered to follow one of the commanders to
the residential block, where in front of the house the ice melted,
forming a slushy pool. Magda and the others were ordered to
lie down in the pool and roll over a few times until the path
was dry. A door opened and the High Commander stepped out
smiling and congratulated his junior on the excellent idea,
other officers joined in the laughing.

Magda, lifting herself dirty and wet, her face black, stood
erect and determined. She will survive; she will not give in; she
will go on living. As they marched back her aches and pains
left her, her face became alive; she didn't feel the hunger and
the cold so strongly any more. The only way of fighting these
miserable little men is by staying alive. She felt strong—she felt
ten feet tall.

                                                      Naomi Blake

THE HOSTAGES

On the night of December 6, 1975, Mr Matthews, aged 56, a
Post-Office supervisor, and his wife, Sheila, aged 53, decided to
spend a quiet evening at home watching the television. He said:

Suddenly there was a terrific commotion outside and I
opened the balcony door. I saw police cars up and down the
street and some officers were hiding behind their vehicles. One
of them shouted to me to go back inside as there were armed
men about.

I did not hang about, and went inside. There was a ring at
the door and I thought it was the police. I opened it. Instead it
was these four young Irishmen, all carrying hand guns and one
also had a machine gun.

For the next six days and five nights I was forced to lie on the settee while my wife was across the room curled up on an armchair.

From the moment they burst in until the second we were freed we could never be sure we would come out alive. It is still a nightmare.

Relaxing, ironically on the same leather settee, Mr Matthews added:

I can say it now, I feel sorry for those four young men. I cannot say the same for the thugs who sent them to Britain. They are the ones who should be in the dock.

We tried to talk to the gunmen and discover why they were treating us in such a way. That was almost fatal, because they became very angry and began blaming us, the British, for just about everything that had gone wrong in the world since time began. We did not dare to try to reason with them after that, just speaking when we were spoken to. They did not ill treat us in any physical way, in fact most of the time they behaved as if we were not there.

Sheila developed chronic back trouble while she was trussed up in the armchair and after the field telephone was lowered by the police from the upstairs flat some pain-killing drugs were passed in to help her. But they did no good because she was getting hardly any food. Whenever any food was lowered to us the four men forced us to eat half of it first in case the police had drugged or poisoned it. They were not taking any chances.

A strange thing happened while we were kept prisoner in our own flat; my wife and I found we could communicate without actually speaking to each other. We found that we were passing messages to each other with the merest flicker of an eyelid, or an unnoticed movement of the body, which, of course, meant nothing to the others in the room.

At one stage I was planning to have a go by diving over the settee but a signal from Sheila warned me against such a move. She was also working on a plan to crash out of the balcony window and attempt an escape, and I knew it, but I managed to signal to her not to do it.

I cannot claim this was some sort of telepathy; we just seemed to be beamed into the same wave-length and instinc-

tively knew what each other was thinking at any time of the
day or night.

This room was a hell-hole then but it is still our home and
neither of us can see any good reason why we should move to a
new address.

The Times

*The title 'Hard Labour in a Foreign Land' is given by Bishop
Dionysius to the entries in his diary which cover the months from June
1944 to April 1945.*

*In the concentration camp the prisoners were ill-clad and cold. No one
ever had enough to eat and all lost weight. They were forced to work
extremely hard, often beyond their strength and powers of endurance.
There was much illness and many cases of frost-bite; some sank into the
depths of despair and one young Greek committed suicide.*

Saturday July 29th:
I had dropped out of the line and was taking the stones out
of my clogs. The guard pretends not to see, and now here come
two together in the line of march. One is a German Catholic
priest. Educated and devout. He has been sanctified too by
privation and suffering. With some difficulty he talks to me
about the persecution of faithful Christians by the Nazis.

'They have slaughtered many of the faithful,' he says—and,
so that I can understand it properly, he draws his wax-pale
hand across his thin throat.

'Because they did not fall down in reverence to pay their
respects to the image of the Führer and did not give him divine
honours. And many of those who survived they threw alive into
the lions' dens, into concentration camps and to the guards.
But,' he continued, 'don't lose hope. The hope we have is in the
Lord.'

At this point the light of triumph shone in the
German priest's eyes. Confined in Dachau alone can be found
more than 20 thousand priests. There to begin with they shut
away the friend I was talking to also. DACHAU—the word
which in our time has taken the place of the word HELL.

And such a Hell that even Dante's imagination could

scarcely have given anything but a pale, long-distance view of it.

At this point in the conversation, the tone of his voice changed. I turned and looked at him. He was choking with sobs.

Deep joy and pride filled my soul. I said to myself, 'Since even today the Church of Christ can muster such faithful, valiant soldiers to oppose her enemies, she has no fear. The Church will win, as she also overcame her first powerful enemies long ago. She will conquer, because she has Christ in her midst.'

'Lo I am with you always, to the close of the age.'

* * *

I went to bed completely exhausted. In an hour a violent pain in my right knee woke me up. I don't know what caused it. The wooden clogs had opened two sores on my heels. But does it come from these? Or is it caused by something else? There are some cases of arthritis in the camp . . . could I be one too?

It is very painful and I cry like a small child. I wrap my jacket round my leg. I get up. I lie down. I put it here; I put it there, but nowhere do I find any relief.

Never before at any time have I felt the extent of our misfortune to be so immense and so tragic. You can feel pain; you can endure unimaginable suffering, and you won't find any help from anybody. Once your cell has been locked, it does not open any more until early morning. Anything you like can happen to you inside it. There's no doctor—unless you really are at death's door.

There is only One who does not remain unmoved by our suffering. He alone watches over us here. In Him we take refuge at such moments. He stretches His divine hand over us in love. He takes us in His arms. He wipes away our tears. He soothes our pain, and many times takes it away completely. Today I saw this happen quite clearly. When the guard came at dawn to take me out to work, I was quite well.

Bishop Dionysius Charalambos

Monday December 25th:

The hands are not working in the factory. Yet the brain is still working in the cell. Poor ill-fated brothers of mine! (I think to myself.) How did you spend these days years ago? And now—in a foreign land, without any preparations for the great feast. No bells, no church, no confession, no Holy Communion. No parties, no visits, no good wishes, no prayers. Not even a little bit of warmth. Not that you have had either a scrap of freedom. Fancy, a little bit of that—for galley slaves! So what can I do to give you a bit of encouragement? How else but tell you something of the love of God for his children in distress? For here it is only His love that accompanies us and remains faithfully by our side.

I have saved a few scraps of paper, perhaps about forty. I write some words of love. I tell them of the love of Christ. Of the great event of the Incarnation. I try to give courage, some hope, to brace the souls who had come close to despair in the perpetual martyrdom of the Hitler hell.

Through the system of communication which we have organized, these bits of paper are distributed to the cells where there are Greeks.

I beseech the Lord to bless this effort.

*   *   *

Friday May 4th:

. . . The torment of the barn still kept its stranglehold on us. Why, even the food remained about the same. Only the guards were changed beyond recognition. The cap-badge (and it was an eagle) flew away and took with it in its talons the coloured epaulettes with the gold stars. Then too the swords which were so highly ornate came to be souvenirs for the victors. And with all this they lost their ferocity. They were 'clothed and in their right mind'. It was now that we began to experience kind treatment too. They took us out into the sunshine. And the day was an absolute delight.

Our wasted lungs filled out now with the pure air. Our ailing bodies revived in the pleasant warmth of the sun. Our whole being, Soul and body, soaked up greedily what they had denied it for so long.

What a wonderful spot we found ourselves in! What a pleasing combination of green and blue! What an enchanting view! In front of us, to the West, stretched a ridge of low hills, thickly covered with vegetation. Not an inch of land bare. To the South and East, not very far away, the Bavarian Alps. Lace made by the hands of God. Here the range was adorned with lofty fir trees. There in the clearings were some little houses, like nests, with strange Gothic roofs.

On our right rolled a boundless plain with a delightful lake like a sea. In the middle of this lake was a small fairy-tale island: I go up to a bit of high ground, my soul is overflowing with gratitude to the Lord. My whole existence, my whole spirit has become a hymn of thanksgiving to our Saviour.

'My soul doth magnify the Lord.'

*   *   *

Sunday May 6th:
CHRIST IS RISEN.

All Christian people rejoice on this holy day of our Lord's life-giving Resurrection. But we are rejoicing three, four, or even five times more than the rest. Because with our joy comes the inestimable benefit that we can add to it the joy which we could not taste for the two miserable Easters in the German labour camps.

In the open air behind the barn the Orthodox are gathering, Greeks and Serbs. In their midst their two priests—one Serb, one Greek. They are not wearing golden vestments. They don't even have cassocks. They are without candles or church service books to hold. But this time they do not need outward material lights in order to celebrate the joy. The souls of every one there are glowing with light—with an inner light.

'God be praised'—my tiny booklet of the New Testament exists for His glory. Over and over again we chant 'Christ is risen', and the echoes reverberate and hallow these days. Finally I remind my comrades in prison of the martyrdoms, the anguish, the dangers which threatened us daily, and of the loving protection of the Risen Lord who has brought us to the great joy of the present day. And I beg them never, never to forget His great loving-kindness. 'We went through fire and water and He brought us out to a place of rest and refreshment.'

The Germany of Hitler, tragic symbol of the world without Christ, no longer existed. And from all hearts went up the hymn of the life of faith. Of the life which makes its way gladly to the Crucified on the green hill of Stein.

Bishop Dionysius Charalambos

THE DREAM OF JACOB

Some instinctive sense perhaps made me turn to the first dream recorded in the Bible, the dream of Jacob and the ladder. This was to me, the greatest of all dreams, the progenitor of all the visionary material and mythological and allegorical activities that were to follow until the traffic and travail of the human spirit hesitate, fearful, on the lip of an immense apocalyptic vista where Alpha and Omega, first and last, speak as one in the Book of Revelations. This dream seemed to me, in a sense, an 'absolute', existing outside space and time, for it had lost none of its freshness and excitement. Even now I have only to close my senses to see in the darkness within a ladder pitched on the stony ground of a great wasteland and reaching to a star-packed heaven, with the urgent traffic of angels phosphorescent upon it.

I was not in the least surprised that this dream should have obsessed the imagination of artists and poets as no other dreams have ever done. I cannot pretend to understand all that the dream is meant to convey. The dreaming process and the symbols through which it seeks to communicate with life still seem to me always more than I for one can say about them . . .

Only the dreaming process itself can know fully what it is, and what its purpose with us can be. So this dream, with a fateful grasp of what is appropriate, begins by defining, in unmistakable imagery, what the dreaming process within itself is. Moreover it does so without any of the oracular ambivalence of so many of its successors, declaring simply that it is the way between life and its ultimate meaning. For that, I believe, is what the image of the ladder and its positioning between Heaven and earth is intended to convey. It asserts that through it men and the source of all their meaning will, forever, be in communication. That is what I suspect the traffic of angels on the ladder represents since angels (as the Greek derivation of the word so clearly denotes) are messengers and visualizations of the means by which the dreamer and cause of dream can speak to each other. No matter how abandoned and without help either in themselves or the world about them, the dream, using Jacob's state and the great and perilous wasteland through which he is fleeting in fear of his life as imagery of man at the end of his resources, affirms that man is never alone. Acknowledged or unacknowledged, that which dreams through him is always there to support him from within. And Jacob had not even had to ask for help. The necessities of his being had spoken so eloquently for him that the dream brought him instant promise of help from the source of creation itself. All this made the coming of the dream appear to me as fateful for life within as had the coming of fire for life on earth without.

. . . The traffic of the spirit which had been so uncompromisingly from above to below, now, was suddenly transformed into a two-way affair also possible from below to above. This would seem to be the meaning of the fact that in Jacob's dream the angels are both descending *and* ascending the ladder. The created is told . . . that he has an inbuilt system of communication for transmitting his needs to the creator and so receiving help in proportion to the will and purpose of creation inflicted on him. . . . Speaking only for myself, all that has come out of the impact of the dream in my early imagination shows that my feelings about it, and its importance have not changed. They still come straight out of feelings belonging to that remote African day when I first heard the dream. So much so that I understood, even as a boy, and without surprise, how the tortured soul of Francis Thompson could write:

Cry; and upon thy so sore loss
Shall shine the traffic of Jacob's ladder
Pitched betwixt Heaven and Charing Cross.

. . . Many years later, I was greatly moved when one of the
first men of Africa, a Stone-Age hunter in a wasteland greater I
believe than even the wasteland in which Jacob dreamt his
dream, informed me 'You know, there is a dream dreaming us.'
To this day I do not know anything to equal this feeling for
what the dreaming process is to life and the implication that it
is enough for creation to appear to us as the dreaming of a
great dream and the un-ravelling and living of its meaning.

Laurens Van Der Post

THE DREAM OF GERONTIUS

I went to sleep; and now I am refreshed.
A strange refreshment: for I feel in me
An inexpressive lightness and a sense
Of freedom, as I were at length myself,
And ne'er had been before. How still it is!
I hear no more the busy beat of time,
No, nor my fluttering breath, nor struggling pulse;
Nor does one moment differ from the next.

*   *   *

This silence pours a solitariness
Into the very essence of my soul;
And the deep rest, so soothing and so sweet,
Hath something too of sternness and of pain.

*   *   *

Another marvel: someone has me fast
Within his ample palm. . . . A uniform
And gentle pressure tells me I am not
Self-moving, but borne forward on my way.
And hark! I hear a singing: yet in sooth
I cannot of that music rightly say
Whether I hear, or touch, or taste the tones.
Oh, what a heart-subduing melody!

Angel
My work is done,
    My task is o'er,
        And so I come,
        Taking it home,
For the crown is won.
      Alleluia,
    For evermore.
My Father gave
    In charge to me
        This child of earth
        E'en from its birth,
To serve and save,
      Alleluia,
    And saved is he.
This child of clay
    To me was given,
        To rear and train
        By sorrow and pain
In the narrow way,
      Alleluia,
    From earth to heaven.

*   *   *

Take me away, and in the lowest deep
  There let me be,
And there in hope the lone night-watches keep,
  Told out for me.
There, motionless and happy in my pain,
  Lone, not forlorn,—
There will I sing my sad perpetual strain,
  Until the morn,
There will I sing, and soothe my stricken breast,
  Which ne'er can cease

To throb, and pine, and languish, till possess't
    Of its Sole Peace.
There will I sing my absent Lord and Love:—
    Take me away,
That sooner I may rise, and go above,
And see Him in the truth of everlasting day.

*   *   *

Lord, Thou hast been our refuge; in every generation;
Before the hills were born, and the world was,
from the age to age Thou art God . . .
Bring us not, O Lord, very low: for Thou hast said,
    Come back again, ye sons of Adam.
Come back, O Lord! how long: and be entreated
    for Thy servants.

*   *   *

Softly and gently, dearly-ransomed soul,
    In my most loving arms I now enfold thee,
And o'er the penal waters, as they roll,
    I poise thee, and lower thee, and hold thee.
And carefully I dip thee in the lake,
    And thou, without a sob or a resistance,
Dost through the flood thy rapid passage take,
    Sinking deep, deeper, into the dim distance.
Angels to whom the willing task is given,
    Shall tend, and nurse, and lull thee, as thou liest;
And Masses on the earth, and prayers in heaven,
    Shall aid thee at the Throne of the Most Highest,
Farewell, but not for ever! brother dear,
    Be brave and patient on thy bed of sorrow;
Swiftly shall pass thy night of trial here,
    And I will come and wake thee on the morrow.

*   *   *

Praise to the Holiest in the height,
    And in the depth be praise:
In all his words most wonderful
    Most sure in all his ways.

                                        Cardinal Newman

Do not be afraid, for I have redeemed you;
I have called you by your name, you are mine.
Should you pass through the sea, I will be with you;
or through rivers, they will not swallow you up.
Should you walk through fire, you will not be scorched
and the flames will not burn you.
For I am Yahweh, your God,
the Holy One of Israel, your saviour.
Do not be afraid, for I am with you.

Isaiah 43 : 1–3, 5 JB

But whatever you have ever read or heard, concerning which there has been that inner flash, that sudden certainty, then in God's name heed it, for it is the truth.

Leslie Weatherhead

Index of Sources
and Acknowledgements

Thanks are due to all those mentioned in the Index who have given permission to reproduce material of which they are the publishers, authors, or copyright owners.

While every effort has been made to trace copyright owners, this has not been possible in a few cases. We apologise most sincerely for any infringement of copyright or failure to acknowledge original sources and shall be glad to include any necessary corrections in reprints of this book.

Sources are given in alphabetical order of author, or of title where no author exists. Page numbers appear in **bold** type.

Allport, Gordon. **4** From Introduction to *Man's Search for Meaning* by Viktor Frankl (q.v.).

Andrew, Father. **72** From *A Gift of Light: A Collection of Thoughts from Father Andrew*, sel. and ed. Harry C. Griffith. A. R. Mowbray 1968.

Anonymous. **vi** From *God of a Hundred Names*, Edited by Victor Gollancz and Barbara Greene. Victor Gollancz 1962. **13** Source unknown. **171** From *And the Morrow is Theirs*. See under Ryder, Sue. **201** Source unknown. **272** From *A Chain of Prayer across the Ages*, ed. S. F. Fox. John Murray 1956.

Appleton, George. **29**, **164**, **171**, **253**, **279** From *The Word is the Seed*. SPCK 1976.

Ascher, Mary. **11** From *Word Alive*, ed. Edmund Banyard. Belton Books 1969.

Auden, W. H. **205** From 'In Memory of W. B. Yeats' in *Collected Poems*. Faber 1976.

Augustine, Saint. **33**

Authorized Version of the Holy Bible, The. **v, 249** The Authorized Version is
     Crown copyright; extracts used herein are by permission.

Beausobre, Iulia de. **65, 67, 153, 156, 260** From *The Woman Who Could Not
     Die: Reminiscences of Imprisonment in Russia*. Chatto & Windus 1938.
     Reprinted by permission of Victor Gollancz Ltd.

Betjeman, John. **132** From *John Betjeman's Collected Poems*, comp. by the Earl
     of Birkenhead. John Murray 1958.

Bible Reading Fellowship, The. **148** Prayer.

Blake, Naomi. **316** From 'A Concentration Camp Somewhere in Poland',
     published privately 1944.

Blake, William. **156** From *The Vision of Judgement*.

Bloom, Anthony. **166** From *Courage to Pray*. Darton, Longman & Todd 1973.
     297 From *School for Prayer*. Darton, Longman & Todd 1957.

Bolt, Robert. **192** From *A Man for All Seasons: A Play in Two Acts*. Heinemann
     1961.

Bonhoeffer, Dietrich. **38, 45, 106, 175, 205, 216, 259, 281, 306** From *Letters
     and Papers from Prison*, ed. Eberhard Bethge, tr. Reginald H. Fuller.
     SCM Press 1953.

Boom, Corrie ten. **149** Source unknown. **169, 173** From *The Hiding Place: The
     Triumphant True Story of Corrie ten Boom*. Hodder & Stoughton 1971.
     Also by permission of Chosen Books Inc.

Booth, William. **12** Source unknown.

Boros, Ladislaus. **151, 202** From *We Are Future*. Search Press 1971. © 1970 by
     Herder & Herder Inc.

Bourdeaux, Michael and Howard-Johnston, Xenia. **99** From *Aida of
     Leningrad*. A. R. Mowbray 1976.

Browning, Robert. **301** From *Paracelsus*. Effingham Wilson 1835.

Bukovsky, Vladimir. **103** Article from *The Times*, 10 May 1977, tr. Lord
     Nicholas Bethell.

Burney, Christopher. **211, 213** From *Solitary Confinement*, 2nd edn. Macmillan
     1961. Reprinted by permission of Macmillan London and Basingstoke.

Byron, Lord. **145** From *The Prisoner of Chillon*. John Murray 1816.

Canter, Bernard. **201** Article 'A Testament of Love' from *The Friend*, 3
     August 1962.

Carroll, O. **201** Source unknown.

Carter, George. **187** From *The Ballad of Misery and Iron*. Found in *A Prison
     Anthology*, ed. A. G. Stock and B. Reynolds (q.v.).

Carter, Sidney. **19** From *Green Songs*. Chapman & Hall 1949.

Chaplin, Ralph. **233** From *Bars and Shadows: The Prison Poems of Ralph Chaplin*.
     Allen & Unwin 1922.

Charalambos, Bishop Dionysius. **30**, **90**, **151**, **320**, **322** From *Faithful Witnesses*, ed. and tr. Margaret I. Lisney. Tr. unpublished.

Charles, Brother. **263** From *One Man's Journey*. A. R. Mowbray 1972.

Chavchavadze, Paul. **72** From *Marie Avinov: Her Amazing Life*. Michael Joseph 1969.

Chenier, André. **161** Found in *A Prison Anthology*, ed. A. G. Stock and B. Reynolds (q.v.).

Churchill, Winston. **48** From *A Thread in the Tapestry* by Sarah Churchill. André Deutsch 1967.

Clark, Glenn. **122** From Foreword to *Release* by Starr Daily (q.v.).

Clark, Kenneth. **207** From *Civilisation*. John Murray 1969.

Daily, Starr. **123**, **266** From *Release*. Arthur James 1945. By permission also of Harper & Row Inc.

Davies-Scourfield, Grismond. **113** From *Détour: The Story of Oflag IVC*, ed. J. E. R. Wood. Falcon Press 1946.

Debs, Eugene V. **216** Found in *A Prison Anthology*, ed. A. G. Stock and B. Reynolds (q.v.).

Dostoyevsky, Fyodor. **270** From *The Brothers Karamazov*, vol. 2, pp. 426–7, tr. David Magarshak. © David Magarshak 1958. Reprinted bypermission of Penguin Books Ltd.

Dreyfus, Alfred. **191** Found in *A Prison Anthology*, ed. A. G. Stock and B. Reynolds (q.v.).

Dyke, Henry Van. **236** From *The Prisoner and the Angel*.

Eastwood, Dorothea. **26**, **31**, **39**, **78**, **286** By permission of Hugo Eastwood.

Ecclestone, Alan. **81**, **196** From *A Staircase of Silence*. Darton, Longman & Todd 1977. The lines by Edwin Muir on p. **81** are from 'The Refugees' in Muir's *Collected Poems*. Faber 1964. Used by permission.

Eliot, T. S. The quotation on p. **iii**, from which the title comes, is from *The Waste Land*. Faber 1909.

Elphinstone, Andrew. **195**, **236** From *Freedom, Suffering and Love*. SCM Press 1976.

Fergusson, Bernard. **282** From Introduction to *Safer Than a Known Way* by Ian MacHorton and Henry Maule (q.v.).

Fletcher, Robin. **222** Privately printed. Used by permission of Margaret Nelson.

Frank, Anne. **21** From *Anne Frank: The Diary of a Young Girl*, tr. B. M. Mooyaart-Doubleday. Constellation Books 1952. Copyright 1952 by Otto H. Frank. Reprinted by permission of Vallentine, Mitchell & Co. Ltd.

Frankl, Victor. **5**, **9**, **12**, **109**, **167**, **201**, **223**, **311** From *Man's Search for Meaning: An Introduction to Logotherapy*, tr. Ilse Lasch,rev. and enlarged edn. Hodder & Stoughton 1964. Copyright © 1959 by Viktor Frankl, rev. edn copyright © 1962 by Viktor Frankl. Reprinted by permission also of Breacon Press.

Frostenson, Anders. **52, 225, 265, 283** From *A Selection of Psalms, Hymns and Songs Translated from the Swedish*. Stockholm, Ab Ansgar, d.u. By permission of the author.

Fry, Christopher. **138, 254** From *A Sleep of Prisoners: A Play*. Oxford University Press 1951. Reprinted by permission of the Oxford University Press.

Gelasian Sacramentary, The. **24.**

Gibran, Kahlil. **204** From *The Prophet*. Heinemann 1926. By permission of the publisher, Alfred A. Knopf Inc. Copyright 1923 by Kahlil Gibran; renewal copyright 1951 by Administrators C.T.A. of Kahlil Gibran Estate and Mary G. Gibran.

Gilmore, Maeve. **146** From *A World Away: A Memoir of Mervyn Peake*. Victor Gollancz 1970.

Giovanitti, Arturo. **128** From *The Walker and the Cage*. Found in *A Prison Anthology*, ed. A. G. Stock and B. Reynolds (q.v.).

Guyon, Jeanne. **215** Source unknown.

Hackel, Sergei. **27** Article in *Christian*, vol. 3 no. 2, 1975/6.

Hacoben, Simon. **116** From *Détour: The Story of Oflag IVC*. See under Davies-Scourfield, Grismond.

Hammarskjöld, Dag. **8, 16, 42, 89, 153, 162, 276, 293** From *Markings*, tr. W. H. Auden and Leif Sjöberg. Faber 1964.

Harcourt, Pierre d'. **14, 16, 26, 40, 111, 117, 264** From *The Real Enemy*. Longmans 1967.

Hares, G. Betty. **313** From the Prayer Sheet of the Guild of St Francis, Wormwood Scrubs.

Herbert, George. **201** Source unknown.

Huddleston, Trevor. **3** From Foreword to *Dying We Live: The Final Messages and Records of Some Germans Who Defied Hitler*, ed. Helmut Gollwitzer, Käthe Kuhn, and Reinhold Schneider, tr. Reinhard C. Kuhn. Copyright © 1956 by Pantheon Books Inc. Harvill Press 1956. Used by permission of Collins Publishers and Pantheon Books Inc., a Division of Random House Inc.

Hutchinson, R. C. **192** From *A Child Possessed*. Garnstone Press 1964.

Jackson, Geoffrey. **113, 119** From *People's Prison*. Faber 1973. **120** From 'Oliver Plunkett's Other Island', art. in *Catholic Herald*, 10 October 1975. **314** From *Telegraph Magazine*, Easter 1976.

Jameson, Storm. **17** From Foreword to *Anne Frank: The Diary of a Young Girl*. See under Frank, Anne.

Jennings, Elizabeth. **166** From an art. by N. Zernov in *Sobornost*, series 6, no. 8, Winter 1973.

Jerusalem Bible. **30, 248, 251, 303, 304, 310, 329** Extracts from the Jerusalem Bible, published and © 1966, 1967, and 1968 by Darton, Longman & Todd Ltd and Doubleday & Co. Inc., are used by permission of the publishers.

Johnson, Raynor C. **221** From *The Imprisoned Splendour: An Approach to Reality*. Hodder & Stoughton 1953.

Johnston, Charles Hepburn. **57** From *Towards Mozambique and Other Poems*. Cresset Press 1947.

Kipling, Rudyard. **83** From *A History of England*. UP 1911. **97** From *Limits and Renewals*. Macmillan 1932. **144** From *A Diversity of Creatures*. Macmillan 1917. By permission of the National Trust and the Macmillan Co. of London and Basingstoke.

Kleist-Schmenzin, Ewald von. **313** From *Dying We Live*. See under Huddleston, Trevor.

Koestler, Arthur. **206** From *Darkness at Noon*, tr. Daphne Hardy. Jonathan Cape 1940.

Kretzmer, Herbert. **86** Article in the *Daily Express*, 6 June 1977.

Levitin, Anatoli. **229** Article in *Religion in Communist Lands*, vol. 2, no. 2, 1974.

Lewis, C. S. **194** From 'Spirits in Bondage' in *A Mind Awake: An Anthology of C. S. Lewis*, ed. Clyde S. Kilby. Geoffrey Bles 1968. By permission of Collins Publishers. **298** From 'Surprised by Joy' in *A Mind Awake*.

Lovelace, Richard. **204** 'To Althea, from Prison'.

MacHorton, Ian and Maule, Henry. **284, 287, 289** *Safer Than a Known Way: One Man's Epic Struggles Against Japanese and Jungle*. Odhams Press 1958.

McKay, Roy. **59, 184, 188, 268** From *John Leonard Wilson: Confessor for the Faith*. Hodder & Stoughton 1973.

Marc, Franz. **1** From *Dying We Live*. See under Huddleston, Trevor.

Martin, P. W. **301** From *Experiment in Depth: A Study of the Work of Jung, Eliot and Toynbee*. Routledge & Kegan Paul 1955.

Moltke, Helmuth James von. **35, 277** From *A German of the Resistance: The Last Letters of Count Helmuth James von Moltke*. Oxford University Press 1946, 2nd edn 1947. Reprinted by permission of the Oxford University Press.

Morris, Colin. **240, 311** From *The Captive Conscience*. Amnesty International 1977.

Mühsam, Erich. **67** Found in *A Prison Anthology*, ed. A. G. Stock and B. Reynolds (q.v.).

Müller, Joseph. **272** From *Dying We Live*. See under Huddleston, Trevor.

Napier, Priscilla. **230** From *Plymouth in War*. Unpublished.

Nehru, Jawaharlal. **63** From *India and the World: Essays*. Allen & Unwin 1936.

New English Bible. **295** Extracts from the New English Bible, 2nd edn © 1970, are used by permission of Oxford and Cambridge University Presses.

Newman, Cardinal. **326** From *The Dream of Gerontius*. 1866.

Odette. **20** From Foreword to *Odette* by Jerrard Tickell (q.v.).

Owen, Wilfred. **169** From 'Agnus Dei' in *War Requiem* by Benjamin Britten. Chatto & Windus 1972. Copyright Chatto & Windus 1946, © 1963. Reprinted by permission also of New Directions Publishing Corporation.

Paulin, Dorothy Margaret. **136, 248** From *Springtime by Loch Ken, and Other Poems*. J. H. Maxwell 1962.

Pedder, Sylvia. **293** From *Word Alive*. See under Ascher, Mary.

Platt, Ellison. **116** From *Détour: The Story of Oflag IVC*. See under Davies-Scourfield, Grismond.

Post, Laurens Van Der. **46, 176, 179, 231** From *The Night of the New Moon*. Hogarth Press 1970. **324** From *Jung and the Story of Our Times*. Hogarth Press 1976. **49, 53** From *A Bar of Shadow*. Hogarth Press 1954. **236** From *A Mantis Carol*. Hogarth Press 1975.

Qedrwl (pseudonym). **182** From *And the Morrow is Theirs*. See under Ryder, Sue.

Ramsey, A. M. **258** From *Sacred and Secular*. Longmans 1965.

Religion in Communist Lands. **85** From vol. 2, no. 2, 1974. **98** From Editorial, vol. 2, no. 1, 1974.

Renvall, Viola. **8** From *A Selection of Psalms, Hymns and Songs Translated from the Swedish*. See under Frostenson, Anders.

Revised Standard Version. **148, 201** Biblical quotations from the Revised Standard Version of the Bible, copyrighted 1946, 1952, © 1971, 1973 by the Division of Christian Education of the National Council of the Churches of Christ in the U.S.A., are used by permission.

Rigby, Françoise. **218, 220** From *In Defiance*. Elek Books 1960.

Rilke, Rainer Maria. **120** From *Twentieth-Century German Verse*, intro. and ed. Patrick Bridgwater. Penguin Poets 1968. © Patrick Bridgwater 1968.

Roenne, Alexis Baron von. **43, 280** From *Dying We Live*. See under Huddleston, Trevor.

Rosenberg, Isaac. **110, 158, 289** From *The Collected Works of Isaac Rosenberg*. Chatto & Windus 1937. Reprinted by permission of the Author's Literary Estate and Chatto & Windus Ltd.

Russell, Bertrand. **301** From *Autobiography*. Allen & Unwin 1967.

Ryder, Sue. **31**, **34**, **273** From *And the Morrow is Theirs*. Burleigh Press 1975.

Saint-Exupéry, Antoine de. **21** From *The Wisdom of the Sands*. Hollis & Carter 1952.

Saint Matthew Passion. **33** From the Elgar/Atkins edition. Novello & Co. Ltd 1911.

Schiller, Friedrich von. **199** Source unknown.

Schwanenfeld, Count Schwerin von. **42** From *Dying We Live*. See under Huddleston, Trevor.

Schwartz, Kurt. **127** Found in *A Prison Anthology*, ed. A. G. Stock and B. Reynolds (q.v.).

Seitz, Paul L. **61** Unpublished.

Shelley, P. B. **179** From *Prometheus Unbound*. C. & J. Ollier 1820.

Shimanov, G. N. **93** From *Notes from the Red House*. Montreal, The Russian Orthodox Church Outside Russia, 1949.

Shipton, Eric. **273** From *Upon That Mountain*. Hodder & Stoughton 1943. By permission of the Executors of the late Eric Shipton.

Simon, Ulrich. **25**, **88**, **216**, **315** From *A Theology of Auschwitz*. Victor Gollancz 1967.

Sinyavsky, Andrey. **241** Article in *The Times*, 17 June 1977. Tr. Lord Nicholas Bethell.

Soelle, Dorothee. **158**, **162**, **182** *Suffering*, tr. Everett R. Kalin. Darton, Longman & Todd and Fortress Press 1975. The letter by Kim Malthe-Brown quoted on p. **158** is taken from *Dying We Live* (see under Huddleston, Trevor). The quotations on p. **162–3** come from *And There Was Light* by Jacques Lusseyran, Heinemann 1963, reprinted by permission of A. D. Peters & Co. Ltd. The letter by Simone Weil on p. **182–4** comes from *Waiting for God*, tr. Emma Crauford, Collins Fontana 1951, reprinted by permission of Routledge & Kegan Paul Ltd.

Solzhenitsyn, Alexander. **75**, **84** From *The Gulag Archipelago*. Collins 1974. Also by permission of Harper & Row Inc. **245** From *One Day in the Life of Ivan Denisovich*, tr. Ralph Parker. Victor Gollancz 1963. **79** From *One Word of Truth: The Nobel Speech on Literature*. The Bodley Head 1972.

Stock, A. G. and Reynolds, B. **226** From Introduction to *A Prison Anthology*. Jarrolds 1938.

Stuart, Eve. **217**, **238** From *Sheet-Anchor*. Sidgwick & Jackson 1944.

Tagore, Rabindranath. **119** From *Fruit-Gathering* in *Collected Poems and Plays*. By permission of the Trustees of the Tagore Estate and Macmillan London and Basingstoke and of Macmillan Publishing Co. Inc. Copyright 1916 by Macmillan Publishing Co. Inc., renewed 1944 by Rabindranath Tagore. **235** From *Gitanjali: Song Offerings*. By permission of the Trustees of the Tagore Estate and Macmillan London and Basingstoke. Published in Canada by Macmillan Publishing Co. Inc. 1913.

Thompson, Francis. **270** From *The Hound of Heaven*. A. R. Mowbray 1947.

Tickell, Jerrard. **21**, **209** From *Odette: The Book of the Film*. Chapman & Hall 1950. By permission of the Estate of the late Jerrard Tickell.

Times, The. **182** From *The Times*, August 1976. Reprinted by permission of Reuters Ltd. **318** From *The Times*, December 1975. Reprinted by permission of Times Newspapers Ltd.

Toller, Ernst. **125** From *Letters from Prison*, tr. R. Ellis Roberts. John Lane 1936.

Underhill, Evelyn. **296** From *Immanence: A Book of Verses*. J. M. Dent 1913.

Verney, Stephen. **104**, **237**, **238** From *Into the New Age*. Collins Fontana 1976.

Vien. **63** From *Suffering* by Dorothee Soelle (q.v.).

Villon, François. **190** Translation by A. C. Swinburne in *Swinburne's Collected Poetical Works*. Heinemann 1924.

Vins, Georgi. **102** From *Religion in Communist Lands*, vol. 2, no. 6, 1974. **165** From *Three Generations of Suffering*. Hodder 1976.

Waddell, Helen. **102** From *Medieval Latin Lyrics*. Constable 1933. By permission of Constable & Co. Ltd. **233** From *The Mark of the Maker: A Portrait of Helen Waddell*, by Monica Blackett. Constable 1973.

Ward, J. Neville. **196** From *Friday Afternoon*. Epworth Press 1976.

Ward, Zoric. **75** Extract from a letter to the publishers by Mrs Ward.

Weatherhead, Leslie. **7** Source unknown. **329** Source unknown.

Webster, Douglas. **121** From *Unchanging Mission: Biblical and Contemporary*. Hodder & Stoughton 1965. The prayer-poem is from an article by Fr Martin Jarrett-Kerr in *Prism*, January 1965.

Whistler, Laurence. **38** From *To Celebrate Her Living*. Rupert Hart-Davis 1967.

Wilde, Oscar. **133**, **134** From *De Profundis*. Methuen 1905. **135** From 'The Ballad of Reading Gaol'. 1903.

Wilson, Edward. **272** From *The Faith of Edward Wilson* by George Seaver. John Murray 1948.

Wilson, Kark. **15** Found in *A Prison Anthology*, ed. A. G. Stock and B. Reynolds (q.v.).

Winton, Peter. **112** From *Détour: The Story of Oflag IVC*. See under Davies-Scourfield, Grismond.

Wood, Charles Lindley Viscount Halifax. **305**, **309** From *Lord Halifax's Ghost Books*. Geoffrey Bles 1936. By permission of Collins Publishers.

Worsley, Frank. **274** From *Endurance*. Geoffrey Bles 1931. By permission of Garnstone Press.

Wotton, Henry. **115** From *Sacred and Secular*, ed. A. Fox and G. & G. Keene. John Murray 1975.

Wyon, Olive. **294**, **299** From *The Altar Fire*. SCM Press 1954. Part of these passages are based on H. P. Thompson's *Worship of the Lord in Other Lands*. S.P.G. 1933.

Yeats, W. B. **228** From *The Collected Poems of W. B. Yeats*. Macmillan 1933. By permission of M. B. Yeats, Miss Anne Yeats, and the Macmillan Co. of London and Basingstoke.